Questioning Belief

QUESTIONING BELIEF

The Right Reverend
Richard Harries DD, FKC
Bishop of Oxford

First published in Great Britain 1995
Society for Promoting Christian Knowledge
Holy Trinity Church
Marylebone Road
London NW1 4DU

Acknowledgements
The text of the Authorized Version of the Bible is the property of
the Crown in perpetuity.

The Revised Standard Version of the Bible is © 1971 and 1952.

Extracts from the Book of Common Prayer of 1662, the rights of
which are vested in the Crown in perpetuity within the United
Kingdom, are reproduced by permission of Cambridge University
Press, Her Majesty's Printers.

British Library Cataloguing-in-Publication Data
A catalogue record for this book is available from the British
Library

ISBN 0-281-04885-1

Typeset by Deltatype Ltd, Ellesmere Port, Cheshire
Printed in Great Britain by The Cromwell Press, Melksham,
Wiltshire

Contents

Preface *vii*

Part One: QUESTIONS OF FAITH AND HOPE

1 True unbelief *3*

2 Ivan Karamazov's argument *12*

3 Evidence for God's love *20*

4 Attitudes to death in the twentieth century *32*

5 'Astride of a grave'—Samuel Beckett and Christian hope *47*

6 'Away grief's gasping'—The note of hope in Hopkins' anguish *59*

7 The resurrection in some modern novels *74*

Part Two: QUESTIONS OF PEACE AND JUSTICE

8 The Christian concept of peace *91*

9 Reinhold Niebuhr and his pacifist critics *105*

10 Power, coercion and morality *116*

11 Human rights in theological perspective *135*

12 World population and birth control *148*

13 Is there a role for charity in a modern state? *161*

14 The morality of good business *174*

Epilogue: Has religion a future? *187*

Notes *201*

Preface

Three convictions underlie the essays on the theme of faith and hope in this book. First, the objections to religious belief are to be taken with the utmost seriousness. They are to be entered into and felt; and this not as a matter of courtesy or duty but simply because they *are* serious. Some pictures of God are deeply flawed and deserve a moral protest. Especially the extent of human anguish and suffering in creation inevitably puts a huge question mark against the possibility of a wise and loving power behind it all.

Second, faced with the tragedy and misery of so much life and the strong case this puts against the idea of a loving God, the whole panoply of Christian truth is needed. It is the Cross of Christ, his Resurrection and the hope of eternal life that enables us to go on living in faith and hope. The fullness of Christian truth is needed if we are to go on believing at all.

Third, it is in literature, novels, plays and poetry, as much as theology, that the profoundest exploration of these issues has been carried on. In European literature over the last 150 years the struggle to believe and the protest against belief have been major themes. Because they have been set in life or set forth in poetry, the language in which they have been expressed gives us a better feel for the real texture and mystery of life than the technical language of theology.

The essays in the last half of the book on issues of peace and justice similarly have a number of unifying concerns. One is both the importance and the difficulty of relating Christian truth to the economic and political order. That it must be done I have no doubt. But it is not easy to do in a way which will persuade all followers of Jesus Christ that certain political conclusions follow logically from certain Christian assumptions.

A second overwhelming concern is the necessity of taking power seriously. It is this which would label the approach taken here as one of Christian realism. In the world of power politics the way we achieve some kind of rough and ready justice is by ensuring that there is an equality of power between the contending parties. In South Africa during the days of Apartheid, this meant using economic power in the form of sanctions to strengthen the struggle by those who had so little at their disposal, except their indomitable courage, humour, patience and faith. In the dark days of the Cold War, it turned out that for the first time in human history it could never conceivably be in the interest of one of the superpowers to launch a nuclear attack on the other, because in all possible circumstances the indescribable loss would outweigh any gain. But the theme of power is no less relevant to the establishment of democracy, the maintenance of an international order, the preservation of human rights in a brutal world and the millions and millions of poor who lose out in an economic order that mainly benefits the powerful at the moment.

Inevitably, a limited selection of essays and articles like this can give only a partial view of the subjects covered and a good number of vitally important themes are not considered at all. But I am grateful to SPCK for wanting to publish such a collection and I offer it in the hope that some will find it helpful in their own pilgrimage of faith and their discipleship for peace and justice.

Part One

QUESTIONS OF FAITH AND HOPE

ONE

True unbelief *

In the small hours of a morning in 1961 Samuel Beckett was sitting over a drink in a Paris café with Harold Pinter. Pinter suggested that Beckett's work was an attempt to impose order and form on the wretched mess mankind had made of the world, but Beckett disagreed. 'If you insist on finding form,' he said, 'I'll describe it for you. I was in hospital once. There was a man in another ward, dying of throat cancer. In the silence I could hear the screams continually. That's the only kind of form my work has.'[1] What happens if we listen to those like Beckett, who hear the screams continually?

Any true sharing of minds involves listening to the other person's point of view and taking it seriously. To take it seriously means being open to the possibility of having one's own outlook modified or even radically changed by what one hears. This sets up a tension for the Christian. As 'stewards of the mysteries' we are aware of the obligation to be faithful, loyal to what God has revealed of himself. How is it possible to be loyal to what one has come to believe and at the same time genuinely open to views that contradict those beliefs?

The concept of being a steward tends to work against openness to the views of others. At the extreme, it makes people dismiss alternative views out of hand. Even in a weaker form it encourages people to listen to others without taking them seriously. This is not because of any deliberate discourtesy. It's just that the whole thrust of loyalty to revealed truth reinforces the tendency of sinful human beings not to take others into account, not to let the outlook of others seriously disturb one's own. Thus, taken in isolation, the notion of stewardship may be harmful. It needs to be balanced by two other values equally important to the Christian faith, love and humility. Loving someone means paying attention to what he feels and says. As Simone Weil put it:

> Not only does the love of God have attention for its substance; the love of our neighbour, which we know to be the same love, is made of this same substance . . . The soul empties itself of all its own contents in order to receive into itself the being it is looking at, just as he is, in all his truth.[2]

* From *Stewards of the Mysteries*, edited by Eric James (Darton, Longman & Todd 1979)

Loving someone means paying attention to what the other person is feeling and saying, and humility leads to a willingness to learn from him. It carries with it a sense that the other person may have something valuable to give, something as precious to him as our own beliefs are to us. Obviously if love and humility were present with no sense of a revealed truth to which one wanted to be faithful, there would be no tension. But in that case there would be no Christian faith either. The conclusion is that we cannot eliminate the tension between being a steward of the mysteries and being open to the truth in views opposed to one's own; we have to live with it. We could only eliminate the tension either by acting towards people of different outlook without love and humility or by having no convictions ourselves. A person will therefore be a person of the borderlands, to use a word of Professor Donald MacKinnon. The Christian will belong to one country rather than another (he is not a stateless person), he has definite beliefs and a specific commitment; but the love and humility which grow from those beliefs lead him to live on the border. He looks across at other landscapes, feeling, on occasions, their truth as his own. What Professor MacKinnon wrote of philosophers is applicable to all Christians: 'Because the philosopher must always be a man of the borderlands, he may perhaps feel a peculiar kinship with those who, from similarly situated territory, make protesting raids upon the theologians' cherished homeland.'[3]

In recent years many Christians have shown a more open attitude to the possibility of truth in the other religions of the world; the concept and practice of dialogue have become familiar. But exciting as it may be to discover a 'converging spirit', the more crucial and testing task of Christians is still in relation to unbelief. There is little sign in most clergy and laity of openness to unbelief, no sense that it is being listened to and taken seriously. This may be one of the main reasons that sermons are so trivial and that Christian utterances come across to the general public at no higher level than that of a party political broadcast—just something we expect people belonging to a particular group to say but with no serious relationship to the way things really are.

People give a variety of reasons for not believing in God. In the 1950s and 1960s some, influenced by linguistic philosophy, held that religious language was meaningless, or at any rate that it did not make factual assertions. Since then the careful work done by a number of Christian philosophers makes this reason for unbelief much less compelling. Indeed *The Coherence of Theism*[4] is positively combative in its thesis that religious language is meaningful or, as

Professor Swinburne prefers to put it, coherent. Then there have always been people who have argued that God's existence cannot be proved. Many Christian philosophers today would agree with this, but would add that his existence cannot be disproved either, and go on to say that the whole attempt to prove the existence of God is, from a religious point of view, inappropriate. All arguments for the existence or non-existence of God leave the matter open, and belief in God is a matter of interpreting experience one way rather than another. How one interprets experience depends upon a number of factors, including the quality of religious life that one has encountered in others, the kind of experiences one has had and one's willingness or reluctance to believe. Rational reflection and argument are only part of this process of interpretation, not the decisive factor.

Finally, there is the extent and intensity of human suffering. This has always been a difficulty for the religious mind, but there are reasons to think that the problem is more acute today than ever before. Anaesthetics and drugs spare those of us who live in the developed Western world from much of the pain that previous generations could not escape. This perhaps makes us more sensitive to the suffering, particularly in others, that has not yet been eliminated. These same drugs, plus improved social conditions, enable a greater number of people to live to an old age. But this in turn makes us more aware of the indignities of old age— senility, incontinence and the sense of being useless. It might be argued that modern urban life with all its stresses causes greater mental suffering than the rooted, settled village life of 100 years ago, even taking into account the terrible rural poverty. Then there are the reasons connected with the decline in religious belief. Even 100 years ago the concept of heaven was very real to most people in England. This life was seen as a preparation for a better one and much suffering—including that which is, by our standards, almost unendurable, such as the loss of all the children in a family in a few weeks from typhoid—was nobly borne in the light of this belief. Now, not only has the belief in heaven faded, even for people who go to church, but progressive social policies continue to shape the climate of opinion, so that, perhaps for the first time in human history, people really believe that they can and ought to be happy. This might be a good thing (I personally believe it is), but it does mean that when people are not happy, as is so often the case, their high expectation of happiness intensifies their misery. Finally, many of the reasons that people in the past gave as a way of coming to terms with suffering, such as the existence of the devil, God's just punishment of sinners, even God's testing of potential saints, are no longer acceptable to the majority.

We are face to face with suffering. It cannot be thought away.

Faced with suffering the 'true believer' is likely to exhibit three characteristics: first, a sense of anger. The classic expression of this is by Ivan in Dostoevsky's *The Brothers Karamazov*. Under no circumstances, he argues, would it be right for a mother to forgive someone who has ordered his dogs to tear her child to pieces: 'I do not want a mother to embrace the torturer who had her child torn to pieces by his dogs! She has no right to forgive him! . . . I don't want harmony. I don't want it, out of the love I bear to mankind. I want to remain with my suffering unavenged.'[5] A future state of total harmony would be morally unacceptable because it could only be brought about by a forgiveness we could not morally offer. Furthermore, no future state, however blissful, could justify the fact of children having been tortured: 'It's not God that I do not accept, Alyosha. I merely most respectfully return him the ticket.' Alyosha replies, 'This is rebellion',[6] and in his study of rebellion Camus comments that here for the first time moral truth is given priority over everything else: 'Ivan does not say that there is no truth. He says that if truth does exist it can only be unacceptable. Why? Because it is unjust. The struggle between truth and justice is brought into the open for the first time.'[7]

This sense of anger is not empty posturing for the purpose of literature. Samuel Beckett's mother was an emotional tyrant, and a large part of him was glad when she died, but as she lay dying he spent the days at her bedside. 'His nights were spent walking and talking with Geoffrey Thompson, to whom he complained bitterly of the so-called God who would permit such suffering.'[8] Earlier, when his brother Frank died, Beckett walked and talked with the same friend, 'lashing with frenzied invective at the ugliness and injustice of the world and the stupidity of God and man alike.'[9] These insights into Beckett, whom one assumes to be an agnostic, bear out the argument stated earlier, that it is not the alleged meaningless of Christian beliefs or the impossibility of proving the existence of God but the fact of suffering which is the most powerful factor making for disbelief in God. It's not logic but anger which makes some of the most sensitive and honest souls rebel. I once received a letter from someone who used to be a believing, practising Christian. Referring to God, it said: 'He has no kindness, no justice, no sympathy with or comprehension of the weariness and unhappiness of human life; he is a callous, indifferent, mocking, destructive tyrant—nothing more than an Amin or Ivan the Terrible on a larger scale.'

Few Christian utterances give the impression that they have grasped the strength of this moral anger. I once did a series of articles for a church newspaper. In one article I described an incident in the last war when Evelyn Waugh and F. E. Smith (later Lord Birkenhead), driven mad by the garrulousness of Randolph Churchill, took on a bet with him that he could not read the whole Bible through in a few days. Churchill accepted the challenge, but the purpose of the bet failed for he could not resist making comments, of which the most frequent was, 'God! Isn't God a shit!'[10] But when the article appeared in print, the last phrase had been changed to, 'of which the most frequent was one casting doubts on God's goodness'. Someone in the paper had felt that the readership could not cope with the thought that some people felt God was a 'shit' and had taken it upon themselves, without consulting the writer of the article, to substitute for the original a phrase in which every drop of anger had been mangled out.

The anger people feel before human suffering is not an empty gesture, a mere shaking of the fist at heaven. The anger makes the person want to do something to stop the suffering. This is the second mark of 'true unbelief': the person accepts responsibility. An emphatic 'No' to heaven intensifies the awareness that we have to stand on our own two feet and that, if suffering is going to be reduced, it will be through human effort. In one of Albert Camus' short stories, a ship's cook takes part in a religious procession and, because of a vow he once made to God, he carries a huge stone. Suddenly he stumbles and falls. It's too heavy for him. Then an agnostic engineer who has been watching comes forward, picks up the stone and carries it himself, but not towards the temple—away, in another direction altogether. Then when he finally flings the stone down, Camus writes, 'with eyes closed he joyfully acclaimed his own strength; he acclaimed, once again, a fresh beginning in life'.[11] The story was obviously a kind of parable for Camus, in which he expressed his conviction that in the end religion is no help and we have to shoulder the burden of life ourselves. But we not only accept responsibility for our own life; we should recognize and respond to the cry of the suffering of other human beings and commit ourselves to doing something about it.

It's a thesis he worked out most movingly in the person of Dr Rieux in *The Plague*. At one point Dr Rieux is asked if he believes in God. Camus wrote:

His face still in shadow, Rieux said that he'd already answered: that if he believed in an all-powerful God he would cease curing the sick and leave that to him. But no one in the world believes in a God of that sort . . . Anyhow, in this respect Rieux believed himself to be on the right road—in fighting against creation as he found it.[12]

Later Rieux and Father Paneloux have to spend the night listening to the death agonies of a child. Rieux lets out a burst of anger but Paneloux chides him, saying that what they witnessed was as unbearable to him as it was to the Doctor but that through grace he still managed to have faith. Rieux then says: 'It's something I haven't got; that I know. But I'd rather not discuss that with you. We're working side by side for something that unites us—beyond blasphemy and prayers. And it's the only thing that matters.' The doctor and the priest discuss further, Paneloux suggesting that Rieux too is working for man's salvation. But the doctor insists that his concern is with man's health; this comes first. It doesn't matter whether or not he believes. ' "What I hate is disease—as you well know. And whether you wish it or not, we're allies, facing them and fighting them together." Rieux was still holding Paneloux's hand. "So you see"—but he refrained from meeting the priest's eyes— "God himself can't part us now." '[13]

What comes across from this dialogue, even in its truncated form as quoted above, is the priority of human compassion over religious faith, of morality over religion. It's not that Rieux is opposed to religion, or closed to the possibility of himself believing. He is in fact open. but nothing can take priority over the task of trying to alleviate human suffering. 'It's the only thing that matters.' In their common task the priest and the doctor are united 'beyond blasphemy and prayers'. Even God himself can't part them.

The third characteristic of 'true unbelief' appears paradoxical, a contradiction of the initial moral protest against God. It consists of a sense of the worthwhileness of human endeavours, a refusal to be put down by life and a determination to make something of the opportunities it offers. The way this characteristic reveals itself in a particular person will depend upon a number of factors, not least his psychological makeup. Camus, who was forever grateful for the continuous sunshine in which he had been brought up as a child, spoke of his 'appetite for life'. It's a feeling that came across strongly in his youthful essays of 1935–6, which in later years he wanted to have reprinted, despite their clumsiness, just because they expressed something important to him which, despite everything, he had not lost. In the 1958 preface to the essays he wrote:

'There is no love of life without despair of life', I wrote, rather pompously, in these pages. I did not know at the time how right I was; I had not yet known the years of real despair. These years have come, and have managed to destory everything in me, except, in fact, this uncontrolled appetite for life ... the famished ardour that can be felt in these essays has never left me.[14]

In Samuel Beckett this characteristic expressed itself rather differently. Beckett had a tyrannical mother. It was only very late in life that he was able to escape her hold on him, and she left him with a crippled psyche. The line of his which more than any other sums up his emotional outlook is, 'Life is a punishment for having been born'.[15] Yet there is about Beckett a fierce integrity. The one thing that has really mattered to him is his writing. He has wanted to write something truthful about life. And he said once: 'I could not have gone through the awful wretched mess of life without having left a stain upon the silence.'[16] The phrase 'a stain upon the silence' is a typical Beckett way of speaking about, and undermining the value of, something that does in fact matter desperately to him. But it need not blind us to the fact that something has mattered to him. He has neither committed suicide nor sold out. He has kept faith to the end. In this there is some implicit recognition of the value of the human struggle.

The painter Francis Bacon had an equally bleak view of human life. In many of his paintings there seems an uncanny resemblance between human beings and slabs of raw meat at the butcher's: 'Man now realises that he is an accident, that he is a completely futile being, that he has to play out the game without reason.'[17] But despite this view of man, despite a daily consciousness of the shortness and apparent futility, not everything is futile. Something can be wrested from life in and through the struggle. Bacon says: 'My kind of psyche, it's concerned with my kind of—I'm putting it in a very pleasant way—exhilarated despair.'[18] Again, the phrase 'exhilarated despair' contains an implicit recognition that it is better to have lived than never to have lived at all. The same sense comes across in Bacon's view of art: 'We do know that our lives have been thickened by great art. One of the very few ways in which life has been really thickened is by the great things that a few people have left.'[19] The metaphor of thickening is used in such a way as to imply that it is better for life to be thick than thin; that the artist who through his work is helping to thicken it is engaged on something worthwhile. The wrong conclusion should not be drawn from these quotations from Camus, Beckett and Francis Bacon. No attempt is being made to say that deep down they really believe in God. There is no legerdemain being attempted. Rather, this is one of the characteristics of 'true unbelief' which the believer must listen to and take seriously. We might think that, logically, unbelief ought to lead to total despair, but even in people who temperamentally are depressed the despair is never total. There is despair and not despair at the same time.

'True unbelief' obviously does not exist in a pure form in any one person. What has been sketched out is to some extent a composite picture. But only to some extent. The three characteristics are all present to some degree in both Camus and Beckett. The first priority of a steward of the mysteries will be to listen to such voices, really to listen, and feel the moral force, the moral persuasiveness of the views they convey. The second priority will be to say something, to reply to such voices. But how? That is the question to which all this essay leads up. How can the Christian faith be stated to people like Camus and Beckett (and these are representative figures; no doubt others could have been chosen) in such a way that it does not suffer by comparison with the moral fervour and dignity of the views it opposes? It's not simply a question of the intellectual problem of how to reconcile the existence of human suffering with a God of love.

Perhaps all that can be said has been said by people like John Hick and Austin Farrer. We can only be grateful for the work that they have done—work that is essential for a credible Christian view of existence. But it's not simply the intellectual problem. It's the moral passion and power of 'true unbelief' that has to be reckoned with. Christians have not on the whole comprehended the fact that there are strong moral arguments against their position. They tend to assume that if Christianity isn't true, at least it is the most moral view of the world going. But this can be disputed. Alec Vidler has pointed out that it was not the rise of science or biblical criticism that turned people like George Eliot away from Christian faith. Rather: 'What it called upon them to believe, with such confidence of its superiority, struck them as morally inferior to their own ethical ideals and standards.'[20] The question then is this. Having really listened to and felt the force of voices of people like Camus and Beckett, how can the Christian faith be stated in such a way as to come across as a *morally*

convincing, *morally* compelling alternative? Before human suffering, faced with a person whose anger leads him not just to protest
but to commit himself to the alleviation of this suffering, a person
who, despite everything, is determined to live and live with
courage, what can be said?

TWO

Ivan Karamazov's Argument*

This article will not consider the problem of evil in its entirety. It is concerned only with the argument put forward by Ivan in Book Four, Chapter Five of Dostoevsky's novel *The Brothers Karamazov*[1] and with certain recent treatments of that argument. Ivan presents his case against God by giving descriptions of children suffering. He knows there are many forms of evil in the world but this seems to him the clearest instance of an evil which nothing can justify. He tells several stories, all of which can be paralleled outside the pages of a novel and then one final tale is told, about a retired general who set his pack of borzoi hounds on a boy who had accidentally injured one of them: 'They hunted the child down before the eyes of his mother, and the hounds tore him to pieces.'

Ivan draws two conclusions from this story. First, it would be wrong, under any circumstances, for the mother to forgive the general for what he had done to her child. Ivan says he can imagine, and indeed longs for, a future state in which the lion will lie down ith the lamb, in which those who have been murdered rise up and embrace those who have murdered them. But this would involve a forgiveness that it could never be right to offer:

> I do not want a mother to embrace the torturer who had her child torn to pieces by his dogs! She has no right to forgive him! If she likes, she can forgive him for herself, she can forgive the torturer for the immeasurable suffering he has inflicted upon her as a mother; but she has no right to forgive him for the sufferings of her tortured child. She has no right to forgive the torturer for that, even if her child were to forgive him![2]

Ivan's objection to forgiving the torturer is a profoundly moral protest which has to be taken with great seriousness. Most of us have grown up with the idea of forgiveness. We take it as a matter of course. But should a Jew who has lost his whole family in a concentration camp forgive those responsible? Forgiveness for the perpetrators of such deeds suddenly seems an affront to the memory of those who are loved; a denial of their preciousness. It's too easy, too cheap. Yet forgiveness is central to the Christian faith. John Hick meets Ivan's point by suggesting that the general who is eventually forgiven will have been changed and perfected through

* Article in *Theology*, March 1978

his remorse. Forgiveness in that case is not morally reprehensible.[3] Moreover, an anlaysis of what Ivan actually says reveals an inconsistency. He envisages a situation in which some forms of forgiveness are possible, for the mother has forgiven the general for harm done to her personally and the serf boy himself has forgiven the general. What he objects to is the mother forgiving him for the suffering inflicted on her son. However, is such a refusal to forgive really the expression of love it purports to be? If the son has forgiven the general then the mother's love for her son in this situation would most naturally take the form of sharing his attitude. A persistent refusal to forgive could only call into question her love for her son. Ivan's attempt to arm himself beforehand against ever offering forgiveness in such a situation, despite its impact as a moral protest against a too easy acceptance of evil, is on analysis merely the appearance of love masking a perversion of it.

The second conclusion that Ivan draws from his stories about suffering children is that no heaven, however blissful, could make up for what has happened:

> If the sufferings of children go to make up the sum of sufferings which is necessary for the purchase of truth, then I say beforehand that the entire truth is not worth such a price . . . We cannot afford to pay so much for admission . . . It is not God that I do not accept Alyosha. I merely most respectfully return him the ticket.[4]

Ivan does not deny the possibility of a future life. He does insist however that each individual who has ever lived must participate in it. He will not have, he says, his suffering serving as manure for the future harmony of someone else. He allows for heaven. His protest is that this future good is not worth the price. It cannot justify the suffering that has gone before. Once again what we have is a moral protest. Ivan believes in God but on moral grounds he doesn't want to have anything to do with him.[5]

Contrary to Ivan, however, human experience suggests that a worthwhile end, once achieved, does usually make the arduous journey to it appear in a different light and painful memories, though not obliterated, do fade. An engaged couple, meeting after a long period of separation, are caught up in the delight of one another's presence. A woman who has had a difficult pregnancy goes into raptures over her new child. An Olympic medallist stands on the rostrum with a sense of total thrill. Such moments are ecstatic. In them we are taken out of ourselves. It would be a strange person who at such a time started rooting up bad memories, who tried to revive past feelings of frustration, pain or deprivation. For we can become totally absorbed in something outside ourselves; caught up in sheer delight. Heaven, on one ancient view, is thought of as a vision, an endless enchantment. We will be taken out of ourselves by that sublime conjunction of beauty and goodness which is the Divine Glory. The question 'Was it all worth it?' implies that the years of separation, the difficult pregnancy, the endless pacing round the track in mid-winter, can somehow be put in the scales and weighed against the joy to be found at the end of the road. But when experiencing the joy, that question does not arise. Part of what it is for that moment to be ecstatic is that such careful calculation cannot be taken seriously. 'Were you worth it?' says the mother gazing at her new babe, 'Were you worth all those months lying in bed?' But it is not a question she bothers to answer except with a bigger hug.[6]

It's on the journey itself that the question presses us hard. Pacing round the roads in winter cold thinking of friends huddled over their fires the runner often asks himself 'Is it all worth it?' In relation to life as such what this question in fact amounts to is 'Am I glad to be alive?' Malcolm Muggeridge once wrote 'I believe with a passionate, unshakable conviction that in all circumstances and at all times life is a blessed gift.'[7] But not everyone shares this feeling. Some commit suicide. Many more, particularly when they are old, long to be out and away from it all. Suicide is the fundamental problem of life, said Camus, and if he is right it indicates how finely balanced is the answer. Yet if some have on their minds the question 'Is there any good reason why I should not commit suicide?' others are more impressed by another question: 'Why is it that the majority of people don't in fact commit suicide?' No doubt many don't consider it because they shut out all large questions. They intuitively feel the truth of Camus' statement that 'Beginning to think is beginning to be undermined'.[8] For most of us the sheer animal will to stay alive has much to do with it. But there is more to it than this. David Storey, who has an essentially tragic conception of life, has written that his characters 'have an appetite for life, a refusal to be put down by anything, simply a refusal. They survive despite the tragedy. It's like a flower growing in a bed of concrete.'[9] People accept life as a challenge and though they would not often put it as such, a moral challenge. They battle on with an underlying motto 'It's a great life if you don't weaken.' Moreover they witness in the most profound and practical way possible to their intuition that, despite everything, the experience of living is worthwhile. They continue to bring children into the world.

Ivan asserts that no future good can outweigh present suffering. But at the end of the creative process, when God will be all in all, each person will be so drawn out of themselves by the divine source and focus of all that they have regarded as good, true and beautiful, that the question 'Is it worth it?' will not arise. Though the question does arise whilst we are *in via*, for some people in the most agonizing way, the majority of people have 'a refusal to be put down by anything, simply a refusal.' They do not sit down and calculate the pains and pleasures of their life, balancing one against the other. They choose to live with a courage that transcends this way of thinking. But Ivan has not finished. 'Tell me frankly, I appeal to you—answer me:' he says to Alyosha,

> imagine that it is you yourself who are erecting the edifice of human destiny with the aim of making men happy in the end, of giving them peace and contentment at last, but that to do that it is absolutely necessary, and indeed quite inevitable, to torture to death only one tiny creature, the little girl who beat her breast with her little fist, and to found the edifice on her unavenged tears—would you consent to be the architect on those conditions? Tell me and do not lie![10]

At the centre of the debate on religious language in the 1960s was Anthony Flew's analysis of the assertion 'God loves us as a father loves his children.'[11] Flew argued that this proposition had to be qualified to such an extent that it became meaningless. Basil Mitchell and Ian Crombie, taking up Flew's challenge, maintained that we are not in a position to decide finally that God is unloving, for we don't have the complete picture. Only at the end of the creative process, when the work can be seen as a whole, will the purpose of everything become clear and God's ways be seen to be good. D. Z. Phillips maintained however that if this is indeed the case then God, far from being justified, would be shown to be evil. Certain actions are intrinsically evil. Murdering the innocent is wrong, whatever the consequences. Moreover we usually judge that if such murder is premeditated it is more heinous than a crime of passion. A child dying of cancer is bad enough, he says, but if this had been planned from all eternity, nothing could be worse. Nothing could be more evil than a God who planned a world in which such things happen, says Phillips, explicitly aligning himself with Ivan, whom he quotes. Mitchell and Crombie believe that God must be held responsible for the evil in the world but say that we must wait until we resurrect from the dead to hear God's defence. We *are* told, however, that the defence is to be a parading of consequences. No more need be said. God is condemned, for we believe that no consequence could justify torturing children to death.[12]

Phillips himself then offers a form of belief which he thinks is not open to Ivan's accusation. He argues that the relationship between events and religious faith is not one of inference. If a human being gives us a present we thank him. If he spits in our face we are not grateful. But in our relationship with God we don't infer from good experiences that he is loving and from bad experiences that he is malevolent. 'When the believer thanks God for his creation, it seems to be a thanksgiving for his life as a whole, for everything, meaning the good *and* the evil within his life, since despite such evil, thanking God is still said to be possible.'[13] The example of Job is then set before us as a man to whom everything possible disastrous happened and who still managed to say 'The Lord gave and the Lord has taken away, blessed be the name of the Lord.' In short 'the essence of the believer's belief in divine goodness consists precisely in the fact that the meaning of life does not depend on how it goes'.[14]

Phillips' account of religious belief avoids a head-on confrontation with Ivan Karamazov but it is defective both as a form of Christian faith and as a sensitive response to life. First, whilst a particular event or experience does not logically imply any one view of God, the course of events, taken as a whole, is certainly either conducive to faith or undermining of it. A series of disasters can gradually erode faith until there comes a point where the believer no longer interprets them as a testing of faith but wakes up to find he has no faith at all. 'It's like living in a Hardy novel' said someone recently and Freud expressed the same sombre view when he said that 'Dark, unfeeling, and unloving powers determine human destiny.'[15] The Christian does not wish to deny the facts which give rise to such assertions. He knows those for whom Beckett's line 'Life is a punishment for having been born' seems true.

Second, what enables a person whose life has been very unhappy to retain some kind of faith is the fact that their belief is more than Phillips' Wittgensteinian sense of the mystical evoked by the sheer existence of things. It will include certain definite assertions about the creation of an autonomous order by a good God and a future glorious consummation brought about by that same God. In a detective story all the evidence seems to point in one direction but the good detective has a puzzled hunch that the truth is somewhat different. Howard Root once suggested that the Christian is like this detective. So much of the evidence points against the possibility of there being a good God. The Christian has an intuition, based on certain neglected facts, that the true story is somewhat different. He does not deny the suffering in the world or pretend it is other than it is. He may admit a *prima facie* case against the existence of a loving creator. But he believes there is a larger picture which includes an ultimate state of affairs in which sorrow and crying will be no more.

Third, Phillips commends the attitude of Job; but this is not the only response to suffering and it may not be a helpful one. 'The Lord gave and the Lord has taken away' overlooks the fact that much that happens is clean contrary to the will of a loving creator. To pretend otherwise is to blunt one's responses and end by calling evil good. A young child dies and the parents say 'I suppose God must have wanted her in heaven.' They strive heroically to take what they suppose must be the Christian attitude. But it may be better from every point of view to admit that a tragedy is a tragedy.

Phillips' attempt to sidestep Ivan's accusation is a failure. So also, for different reasons, is that of Dorothee Soelle. Like Ivan and Phillips she too rejects the idea of an all-justifying future. 'The God who causes suffering is not to be justified even by lifting the suffering later. No heaven can justify Auschwitz. But the God who is not a greater Pharaoh has justified himself; in sharing the suffering, in sharing the death on the cross.'[16] According to Dorothee Soelle's analysis both Ivan and Alyosha reject justification by a future good. The difference between them is that Ivan is still metaphysically orientated in rebellion against God. Alyosha on the other hand, has rejected metaphysics and is earthly in his solidarity.[17] He shares the suffering of others and in that sharing God is present. But this rejection of traditional theism and confining of God, without remainder, as it were, to Christ on the cross, will not stand up to any analysis, philosophical or theological. We would not think much of a surgeon who undertook an operation without any thought about whether the outcome was likely to be successful and who then in the middle of the operation cut himself open as an act of solidarity with the patient. No more is it possible to trust a God whose *sole* quality is sharing our suffering. Further a metaphysical attitude is not *per se* anti-human. Many of those like Ivan, with a strong sense of rebellion against whatever

17

might lie behind the world, have been driven by a passionate desire to alleviate human suffering. Others, like Christ, with a trust in a heavenly father, have shown no less concern to meet human need. Exemplary though Dorothee Soelle's positive point is, namely we are to share the suffering of others as God in Christ shares ours, this is not all there is to be said either about God or suffering.

When it comes to the detailed reasons why Phillips, and others, agree with Ivan, there are two steps in the argument. First, it is maintained that there are certain classes of action, for example, murdering the innocent, that are intrinsically wrong. Such actions are wrong whatever good consequences might flow from them. Second, the suffering of innocent people is classified as an intrinsically evil act brought about by God. 'God is condemned' writes Phillips, 'for we believe that no consequences could justify torturing children to death.' But the use of the phrase 'torturing children' prejudges the issue. Torturing children is indeed intrinsically wrong but is a God who creates a world in which the innocent suffer guilty of such a crime? Clearly the answer is 'No'. There is an ancient, difficult to justify, but valid distinction between the intended and unintended consequences of an action. It has been used in moral theology when discussing the case of a woman who has an operation to save her life which also results in the abortion of her child. It is a distinction that has been much used in the ethics of war since the time of Vitoria in the sixteenth century. A direct attack on a military target might have certain side effects, the killing of civilians who live near the target area for example. It has usually been held that such deaths are unintended and do not count as murder. People suffer in the world for one of two reasons, either because other people have freely willed something that is harmful or because of accidents in the processes of nature. God willed to create man free and God willed to make man part of a material universe that combines structure and flexibility, the conditions which make organic life possible. But God does not intend the evil acts and the accidental suffering consequent upon such creation.

It might be argued that though God did not intend the suffering in the world, he foresaw that it would come about. This must be admitted. Even if God is not credited with a simultaneous apprehension of all time; even if he has limited himself to our ignorance before the exact details of the future, he would have known the probable consequences of creating such a world as ours. In some sense God foresaw what would happen. But to foresee is not to intend and whether God was justified in creating our world must depend upon whether the ultimate good outweighs the predicted evil. Here we take up an earlier point. The consummation of the creative process will come about when every creature who has ever lived is caught up in the Divine vision and lives a life of unbroken thanksgiving. God, in contemplating the creation of a universe, will have been confident that such an outcome could eventually be achieved. To talk in this anthropomorphic way of God rationally calculating the costs and benefits of creating a universe is crude in the extreme. But it is no more crude than creation conceived of as a kind of 'play'. We expect human beings to try to be rational and responsible before they act, to weigh up carefully the advantages and disadvantages of what they intend doing. God's creation of a universe is a great deal more than this but it is not less.

On a first reading of *The Brothers Karamazov* many are almost thrown off balance by the impact of Ivan's moral protest against God. Some, such as Phillips and Soelle, have tried to avoid his accusation by offering an alternative to traditional theism. Such attempts fail. Faith in God includes certain definite assertions, one of which is that the creative process has a transtemporal goal in which God will be all in all.[18] Ivan's question about the relation between this goal and the suffering experienced on the way to it cannot be avoided. The contention of this chapter is that if the accusation is faced, it can be lived with—in hope.

THREE

Evidence for God's love*

'Don't kill me mum.' These were the last words of an eight year old boy as his mother pushed him under the water in the bath and drowned him. Some years before this she had killed her two yong babies but it was thought, mistakenly, that she was now in her right mind and her older boy was safe. Such incidents which, alas, we can read about every day, rock any religious faith we might have to the foundation. How on earth can there be a God of love behind a universe in which such appealling things happen?

The case against the idea that there is a power of love behind the universe is very strong. Indeed someone has suggested that the situation is like a detective story. All the evidence appears to point to a particular culprit but the good detective, by using his intelligence, is able to see that the situation is very different. So it is in life. On the surface all the evidence seems to point against the possibility that love created the universe. Droughts, famines, car crashes, murders, cancer, mental illness, senility—all these add up to a formidable case to answer. Yet, by careful thought this case can be answered and in the course of answering it surprisingly strong evidence *for* the idea of a God of love emerges.

The price of freewill

First, an obvious point. Much suffering in the world is caused by the negligence, weakness and deliberate wrong doing of human beings. If it is the will of God to create free beings, as opposed to robots or puppets, this is the price he and we have to pay. It is true that some philosophers have suggested that God could have created us free in such a way as we always freely chose to do right. On this view God would be like a hypnotist who told us all under hypnosis how we should act. We would think we were deciding things for ourselves but in fact we would have been programmed by God. It would have been quite possible to create a universe in which this happened. But there is one fatal flaw. God himself would know he had cheated. He, at least, would know that we were not acting with genuine freedom but only in response to suggestions given us under hypnosis.

If we value being able to make up our own minds and make our

* From *Beyond Reasonable Doubt*, edited by Gillian Ryeland (Canterbury Press 1991)

own decisions in life then we too have to pay the price of living in a world in which this is possible. We cannot have it both ways. We cannot both be free and have a world in which wrong choices do no damage. This point, if accepted, has wide implications. For much more suffering in the world is attributable to human beings than we sometimes allow. Take the millions of starving. The fact is that there *is* quite enough food in the world for everyone. But through millions of wrong choices which have brought about the rigid political and economic structures in which we live, there are mountains of surplus food in Europe and America, whilst those in Africa starve to death. Similarly, take the question of earthquakes. The rich can afford to live in earthquake-free areas or in reinforced houses. It is the poor who cannot move or protect themselves. It is the poor who suffer.

Disease and earthquakes

So a great deal of suffering in the world is caused by human beings. But not all of it. There is disease. There are natural disasters. Two points can be made about this. First, God does not simply make the world. He does something much more sophisticated. He makes the world make itself. He gives everything in the universe, from the sub-atomic particles of which matter is composed, through electrons, atoms, cells up to multi-cellular structures like ourselves, a life of its own. In fact, when we think about it, a life of our own is the only kind of life we could have. If we did not have a life of our own we would not exist at all and this is true of the atom and the amoeba as much as of us. God has given the basic elements of matter a life of their own and has weaved the universe from the bottom upwards through the free interplay of millions of forces. In all this interplay what we call accidents occur the whole time. But accidents are not in themselves harmful. Take the question of volcanoes and earthquakes. These occur because the star called earth, on which we live, has reached a particular stage in its cooling. This is also the stage which made it possible for life to emerge. If the earth was still molten there would be no life. It has in fact cooled enough to allow a crust to form, on which life has been able to develop. But because it is a crust and not a solid ball the inner plates of the earth are still free to slide about a little, and the molten material inside the earth can on occasion find a way out of the crust. There is nothing wrong with these movements and eruptions in themselves. They are just examples of the millions and millions of clashes and combinations that occur every second at every level of the universe. They are not essentially different from the billowing of clouds or the movements of water in a stream.

God and the laws of nature

The second point is that in order to exist as the kind of creatures we are, capable of thinking and choosing, we need a relatively stable environment. I plan my day and make decisions in it on the basis of certain well-founded assumptions, that the sun will come up, that the laws of gravity will operate, that water will boil at a certain temperature and freeze at another one. The consequences of what I do, putting on the electric kettle or putting water in the freezer, are predictable. This means that there is a very strict limit on what God can do in the way of disrupting these scientific laws without frustrating his whole purpose in making the universe in the first place. It might be amusing to live in an Alice in Wonderland type of world but our amusement would only last a few seconds. If we suddenly started to shrink in an uncontrollable way or float up to the ceiling we literally would not know whether we were coming or going. If we were born into that kind of environment we would never learn to think at all. For thinking necessitates continuity between one day's experience and the next. If a child went to school and was told that the sign 'A' symbolized an 'aa' sound and the next day was told that the same sign really indicated a 'zz' sound, that child would never learn to read, for learning involves building on present experience in a predictable way. So it is with our environment as a whole. Sometimes we long for God to 'intervene' to stop some terrible accident in a miraculous way, but where would it stop? Suppose you are driving along and a young child runs out in front of the car. Normally you would hit the child but a miracle occurs and you pull up short in ten feet instead of the expected thirty feet. That would be wonderful. But what about the car just behind you? In order to prevent that car bumping into you, another miracle would have to occur. And what about the car behind that one? In other words a single alteration of the laws of nature (which are only laws in the sense that they are observed regularities on the basis of which we can make predictions) would have ramifications throughout the universe. And would it be fair to limit the miracle to one tiny point? If a miracle was performed to enable the first car to pull up in a few feet but not the second one, the driver of the second one could very well claim that it was unjust, for he had been driving along at the correct speed allowing for a proper stopping distance at that speed. He had not taken into account that a miracle would occur just in front of him—and why should he?

The self-limiting of God

This is not in any way to deny that God works in his universe. According to Christian belief he is at the very heart of things, closer to us than our own breathing. Furthermore, he works out his purpose through us, particularly when we co-operate with him in prayer. Indeed prayer itself may allow God to work through us in his universe in mysterious ways that we are not fully aware of. Nor is it to deny that full-blooded miracles, in the sense of a suspension of the laws of nature, may sometimes occur. The point is that there is a very severe limit to what God can do in this way without spoiling what it is all about—namely bringing into existence creatures like you and me, who are capable of thinking for ourselves and making real choices. For in order to exist as the kind of people we are, we need an environment characterized by continuity, stability, regularity and predictability.

The question arises, however, why did God make us as part of a material world? Much suffering arises from the fact that we are vulnerable creatures of flesh and blood, set in an environment whose regularity often seems very hard, as when a river floods and drowns many people. Why did not God simply create us as free spiritual beings like angels? No one really knows the answer to that question except God. All we can do is guess. The best guess comes from Austin Farrer. He argued that God bound us up with a physical universe in order to preserve our freedom in relation to himself. If we had been created like angels and set in the immediate presence of God we would have no freedom to respond to him or not. We would be drawn by his incandescent beauty and holiness like moths to a candle or metal filings to a magnet. So, in order that we might have real freedom of manoeuvre, God put us at a distance from himself—not a physical distance, because that is impossible, as God is closer to us than we are to ourselves—but a distance of knowing. He made us physical beings in a physical world to act as a kind of veil between us and himself. The result is that on this earth we have no immediate and overwhelming knowledge of God. Furthermore, we are born with a strong drive to preserve our life in being. We only come to a knowledge of God at all in so far as we are capable of growing out of our self-centredness and are willing to live before one who, by definition, makes a total difference to our lives. The knowledge of God is rarely overwhelming and inescapable. For most people there is only a flickering, dawning awareness which is always related to our willingness to know and love God. In this way God preserves our freedom and ensures that the pilgrimage we make is our own journey. (This guess has two implications, both of which I accept. First, angels are not as free as human beings. They are totally transparent to the bidding of God. Second, there was no fall of angels, for they were created perfect in the immediate presence of God.) We, however, have not been created perfect. We have instead been created with the possibility of achieving perfection of a different (and higher) kind than the angels. And we have not been created in the immediate presence of God. We have been made in such a way that we have to make our journey towards him.

So God has created a physical universe, which makes itself from the bottom upwards in ever more complex forms of life, until *we* emerge, as part of that physical universe, yet with the possibility of developing as rational, moral and spiritual beings; half ape, half angel, as Disraeli put it. The physical universe is characterized by reliability and predictability. We are now, for example, beginning to be able to predict hurricanes, earthquakes, and volcanoes, and to take steps to avert their worst effects on us.

The actions of God

But what, we might say, is God doing in all this? First, God is holding the whole universe in being and enabling each tiny constituent part of it to go on being itself. We tend to take this for granted. But why should each electron, atom and cell of the universe both be there and go on retaining its essential characteristics in such a way that it can combine to form higher forms of life? Religious believers claim this is so only because God, the source and fount of all being, holds everything in existence and does so in a way that reflects his own constancy. For the laws of nature, which we think of as so hard and impersonal, almost as an iron neccesity, in fact reflect God's undeviating constancy and faithfulness. When the steam arises from a boiling kettle, or rain drops fall from the sky or a breeze dries the washing, these are expressions of the faithfulness of God, his steady constancy, his utter reliability.

Second, God himself feels the anguish of the universe. It is of the very nature of love to enter imaginatively into the situation of others and, to some extent, feel what they feel. God who is perfect love knows every point of the universe from the inside and bears it within his heart. The word sympathy comes from two Greek words meaning 'to suffer with'. God suffers with his creation. When Jesus was tortured to death this was an expression, in human terms, of the pain God bears eternally.

Third, God is ceaselessly at work bringing good out of evil. When a tragedy occurs he inspires first sympathy and then practical action. He never stops in his work of making accident and disaster yield some good.

Fourth, the purpose of God cannot finally be defeated. Christ died a terrible death on the cross apparently feeling that God had abandoned him. 'My God, my God why hast thou forsaken me?' But God raised him from the dead to live for ever in a new kind of way altogether, as an ever present spiritual presence. The purpose of love cannot finally be defeated.

Fifth, God has promised us an eternal existence with himself. He knows each one of us through and through and he will recreate our real self in a form appropriate to an eternal existence. Heaven lies ahead for those who will appreciate it.

A God of love

The case against the idea that there is a God of love behind the universe is very strong. Indeed so strong that it is only on the basis of these five points, taken together, that it is possible to hold such a belief. Belief in eternity can hardly be an optional extra, for example, when so many people die young with their potential unrealized. If there is no further state beyond this life for them to develop in, how can we believe there is a God of love? Similarly, if Christ was not raised from the dead how can we believe either in him or the God in whom he trusted? For he trusted his heavenly father to the bitter end, even through the darkness of despair. It is only on the basis of these five points that we can believe that love made the world.

But these five points are also the evidence *for* the love of God. They provide not only the case for the defence but evidence for positive belief. The evidence that there is a God of love is based on our belief that the world has a genuine independence. We are not a dream of God or simply an expression of his body. His love is so great that he has made a world with a life of its own and brought to the light of consciousness creatures who even have the power to frustrate his purpose. But this is not an indifferent, impassive God. God bears our travail and anguish within himself. So much so that he has come amongst us and experienced as a human person the worst that life can do. Yet this is not a God who was irresponsible enough to make a world over which he would lose all control. Making the world was a huge risk but it was a risk he took in the confidence he could bring it to its natural fulfilment. Of this the resurrection of Christ is the expression and pledge. God's love cannot be defeated. He raised Christ from the dead and he will recreate each one of us anew for an eternal existence. As a father gives his children good gifts, so God will share with us his own immortality made manifest in Christ. This is very powerful evidence *for* the love of God. Believing in a God of love does not mean that horrible things do not happen. They do happen, all the time, for the reasons outlined earlier. The evidence for a God of love comes from a different source, from the five points just stated.

Is it worth it?

Although it is possible to understand some of the reasons why, if God was going to make creatures like us, the world has to have more or less the character of the world we know, it is still possible to wonder whether it is all worth it. 'Don't kill me mum.' Was God really justified in creating a world in which he knew such things would happen? For even if there is an eternity ahead of that murdered child, nothing can change the fact that he was killed by his own mother and that he knew what was happening to him. This is the question of Ivan, one of the brothers in Dostoevsky's novel, *The Brothers Karamazov*. After recounting various stories of cruelty to children he asked if God was justified in making such a world. He then went on to argue that whatever harmony might be achieved in some heavenly future, nothing could justify such cruelty to children on the way. It wasn't that he disbelieved in God, he said. He just wanted to return his ticket. This is a powerful point, yet at least three things can be said which put a somewhat different perspective on the matter.

First, the question of whether life is worth it or not is a question each one of us has to answer for himself. No one can reply for us and we cannot presume to answer for them, however ghastly their circumstances seem to us. For when we come across someone in hospital, perhaps paralysed from the neck downwards, our instinctive reaction is that we could not bear to live life under such conditions. We would rather be dead. Yet often such people show extraordinary courage and even cheerfulness, enhancing life for others in a most moving way. Whether, despite everything, life is worth living is a question only they can answer.

Second, the courage and endurance which so many show in life seem to witness to the fact that something desperately important is at stake in human life, that it is not simply a matter of weighing up the pleasure against the pain. If it was simply a matter of weighing up the pleasure against the pain, far more people would commit suicide. But the vast majority of people do not commit suicide. They go struggling on with humour and fortitude, their lives, as someone once said, like flowers growing in a bed of concrete. In D. H. Lawrence's novel, *Sons and Lovers*, Paul Morel visits his mother, who is dying of cancer, and she chides him because his life is all struggle. She says she wants him to be happy. But Paul says that there is something more important than happiness and unhappiness; he wants to live. By that he did not mean live it up. He wanted to live with all the couarge and creativity within him.

Third, there are sometimes experiences in human life when a glorious goal makes the difficult journey to it seem worthwhile, as when a runner after years of hard training wins a gold medal at the Olympic games. Or there are times when a glorious experience can make the pain of the past drop away. As when an engaged couple who have been separated for a year and only able to communicate by 'phone and letter come together again. All the pain of missing one another and the inevitable misunderstandings fade into the background.

If at the end of the whole creative process, beyond space and time, when, as St Paul put it, God is all in all, everyone who has ever lived is able to bless God for their existence, then the unbiased critic must admit that God was justified in taking the risk of creating a universe. For all who have gone through the experience will say for themselves 'Praise the Lord O my soul, all that is within me, praise his holy name'. This would be heaven. Of course suffering will not be totally forgotten. In the stories of Christ's appearance to his disciples, the wounds remain. But they are healed and transfigured, taken into a new, deeper reality in which they too have a part to play. This vision of an ultimate state of affairs in which all is well is a hope. But it is a hope that is witnessed to not only by the Christian faith but by the practical example of countless millions of people, of all faiths and none, who live lives with great courage. For they seem to have an intuitive sense that something vastly important is at stake in all this human travail. In old fashioned language, what is at stake is the making of our eternal souls.

A practical answer

On Karl Marx's grave in Highgate cemetery are carved his famous words 'Philosophers have only interpreted the world, the point is, however, to change it'. Christians have much sympathy with that statement. For they do not offer a philosophical answer to the problem of suffering, as though it were something to be resigned to. They offer a vision of an ultimate state of affairs in which suffering as we know it no longer exists, a state of affairs which has to be worked for. It is true that the new heaven and earth of which the Bible speaks go beyond our space and time but they have to be reached for and built up on this earth. The answer to the problem of suffering is not an idea or a theology but an actual state of affairs, which does not yet exist, but which offers us a vision of what, under God, can come about if we co-operate with God in his work. There are some very important practical implications of this.

First, suffering is contrary to the will of God. In the Gospels Jesus is shown healing the physically and mentally sick, casting out demons, calling sinners to change their ways. His ministry is an invasion of the forces of goodness and light against all that blights and hurts human life. There may be a sense in which God is responsible for everything, in that he created the universe. But a sharp distinction has to be made between what God directly wills and what he merely permits as part of his overall purpose. So a parent may be responsible for giving his child permission to drive the family car. But he in no sense wills the subsequent accident that unfortunately occurs. God wills the universe to exist, he lets it be with a life of its own. But he does not will suffering; on the contrary, he opposes it. Christ, the image of God, brings life and health. So Christians, following his example, have founded hospitals, leper colonies, hospices and all manner of institutions dedicated to relieving the sick.

Second, God is ceaselessly at work bringing good out of evil and we are called to co-operate with him in this task. For it is the particular work of God not only to oppose all that mars human life but to make what mars our lives yield some good fruit. So sickness can bring about sympathy and practical support from friends and a deeper understanding of life from the sufferer. Here we have to be very careful. Whilst it is true that many good qualities and actions can come out of sickness or tragedy, God does not design horrible situations in order to bring this good out of them. Such a god would be intolerable. If a friend tripped us up on the stairs and broke our leg in order to see whether we would develop qualities of patience and endurance under adversity we would not think much of his or her friendship: indeed we would not call him or her a friend. So with God. God, like a good friend, wants things to go well with us. He is not about to pull the carpet from under us to see how we will react. For good breeds more good than evil can. A comfortable home, with enough to eat, caring parents and an interest in sport or culture is much more likely to give children a chance to develop as healthy personalities than a home that is impoverished or stricken in one way or another. The parents in such a home may be very caring but if they are continually worried about money, have little time to give to their children because they have to work so hard, if they live in poor physical surroundings or are stricken with mental illness, then the children are likely to be affected. Good breeds more good than evil can. It is the particular mercy of God to make even evil yield some good.

Everyone knows someone who under adversity has developed admirable qualities. We have all been involved in tragic or difficult situations which have brought the best out of people. This is all summed up in some lines of the poet Edwin Muir. He contrasts our sad world with the apparently perfect conditions of the garden of Eden, but concludes:

> But famished field and blackened tree
> Bear flowers in Eden never known.
> Blossoms of grief and charity
> Bloom in these darkened fields alone.
> What had Eden ever to say
> Of hope and faith and pity and love . . .
> Strange blessings never in Paradise
> Fall from these beclouded skies.[1]

There is a tightrope to walk here. God does not will suffering. On the contrary he wills us to relieve and eliminate it, so far as we can. Yet out of suffering can come hope and faith and pity and love. God did not design the beclouded skies in order that the strange blessings might fall from them. Yet fall they do, making life look very different. The weighing of goods and evils is notoriously difficult and should not be done. A husband who has just lost a dearly loved wife does not want to be told that he has become a much deeper, more understanding person as a result. He would rather have his wife back. A man whose son has been killed in a motor bike accident may spend the rest of his life helping youth clubs and do much good work. But he would rather have his son back. Yet, if there is an eternal destiny, the good which people see coming out of evil will one day find its proper place. For if we have been made to grow more and more like God, so that we can live with him in the communion of saints, the deepening of a person in a bereavement or the good work that people undertake as a result of tragedy are considerations of ultimate significance.

Living in faith

The thoughts put forward here are only of very limited use and no use at all when a person is in anguish. When a person is afflicted with physical or mental pain they want understanding and practical help. They do not want religious consolation or attempts to 'justify the ways of God to men'. Nevertheless, there is a limited use for the kind of considerations adduced here on other occasions. For, as has been admitted, the case against the idea that love made the world is a formidable one. Unless something sensible is said, faith can ebb away and hope die. There is no intellectual solution to the problem of suffering and certainly no knock down arguments. All that is possible is to say enough to go on living in faith and hope and love. For, paradoxically, the very strength of the case against the notion of a God of love reveals more clearly the evidence *for* a God of love. This evidence, as considered earlier, has five features. First, God has given us a real independence. He has *created* us rather than dreamt us. Second, God himself feels our anguish with us. Third, he is ceaselessly at work forcing even evil to yield some good. Fourth, as the resurrection of Christ reveals, his purpose cannot finally be defeated. And fifth, God has promised us an eternal existence, if we are ready to receive it. A character in a novel by Rebecca West says at one point, 'What's the good of music if there's all this cancer in the world?' To this someone else responds, 'What's the harm of cancer, if there's all this music in the world?' Music can lift people into a dimension in which life seems very different. This is even more true of the love of God. A knowledge of the love of God does not stop tragedy being tragedy or suffering suffering. There is no glossing over, no pretending that all is for the best. For manifestly all is not for the best; a great deal is for the worst. But the love of God, of which we all have some practical proof in the sheer existence of our own being, but which is definitively disclosed in the life, death and resurrection of Christ together with the promises to us inherent in Christ, is a kind of music which makes us see, in our best moments, what really matters and what does not matter quite so much.

There is no intellectual solution. Instead the Christian faith offers a vision of what the love of God is in the course of achieving. We are called to co-operate with that love by relieving suffering, eliminating its causes in poverty and disease and by responding to things going wrong in as constructive and positive a way as possible. For so it is that God's purpose is furthered. A sense of how much suffering there is in life can lead us to deny our maker or to care for his world. The more we care, the more conscious we will be of the affliction which besets us. But the more we care the more certain we will be that the world which is afflicted is good. And in caring we will be at one with the caring of God.

FOUR

Attitudes to death in the twentieth century*

Dr Johnson once walked in the grounds of his old college at Oxford, Pembroke, with a friend. In his *Life of Johnson*, Boswell recorded:

> Dr Johnson surprised him not a little, by acknowledging with a look of horror, that he was much oppressed by the fear of death. The amiable Dr Adams suggested that God was infinitely good. *Johnson*, 'That he is infinitely good as far as the perfection of his nature will allow, I certainly believe; but it is necessary for good upon the whole, that individuals should be punished. As to an individual, therefore, he is not infinitely good; and as I cannot be sure that I have fulfilled the conditions on which salvation is granted, I am afraid I may be one of those who shall be damned.' (looking dismally) *Dr Adams*, 'What do you mean by damned?' *Johnson* (passionately and loudly), 'Sent to Hell, Sir, and punished everlastingly.' *Mrs Adams*, 'You seem, Sir, to forget the merits of our Redeemer.' *Johnson*, 'Madam, I do not forget the merits of my Redeemer, but my Redeemer has said that he will set some on his right hand and some on his left.'— He was in gloomy agitation, and said, 'I'll have no more on't.'

If we are to contrast attitudes towards death in the twentieth century with those of previous ages, the first point we notice is the fading of any sense of divine judgement after death. The belief in purgatory, which arose in the eleventh century and so dominated the European mind until the Reformation and which is so vividly expressed in some of the wall paintings of our churches, no longer terrifies the imagination. It might be argued that Johnson's fear of divine judgement was unusually strong because of his fierce sense of inner self demand or what the Freudians would call 'a strong super ego'. However, a belief in a God who sentences people to everlasting punishment remained firmly part of Christian ortho-doxy right through the nineteenth century. The great Christian social theologian, F. D. Maurice, was sacked from King's College, London for denying the everlastingness of hell. In Newman's *The*

* From *A Necessary End*, edited by Julia Neuberger and John A. White (Macmillan 1991)

Dream of Gerontius which was first published in 1865, the soul of Gerontius has to face the prospect of demons who mock him, judgement and purgatory. *The Dream of Gerontius* was immensely popular even before Elgar wrote the music, which received its first performance at the Birmingham Festival on 3 October 1900.

All this, like so much else, was changed with World War I for the nation could hardly allow the Church to consign literally millions of brave young men, who had died for their country, to yet another torment. They had suffered enough, they had lost everything without even the chance to make much of anything, they must have gone straight to something better—or so the logic of compassion urges. The twin pressures of bereavement and patriotism made the mention of hell or even of an intermediate state rare on the lips of preachers. Bishop Winnington-Ingram, the then Bishop of London, reassured the nation.

> Those dear young men they are not dead. They were never more alive than five minutes after death . . . they love still those they have loved on earth, and they live a fuller life than this, a more glorious life.

Death was simply the 'gate of life', a phrase often used. Christ was depicted as the great comrade waiting the other side to welcome the boys home. This attitude was not confined to the established Church. Cardinal Bourne said about the war, 'God has peopled Heaven with saints who, without it, would hardly have reached Heaven's door-sill.'

A belief that death opened the way to a fearful judgement gave way to a belief that death was but a door into a world that was kinder than the ravaged violent earth. This later view is well expressed in some words of Henry Scott Holland, distinguished Canon of St Paul's and Regius Professor of Divinity at Oxford from 1910 until his death in 1918. Scott Holland once wrote, in words that are often quoted today at memorial services·

> Death is nothing at all. I have only slipped away into the next room. I am I and you are you. Whatever we were to each other that we are still. Call me by my own familiar name. Speak to me in the easy way you always used. Put no difference into your tone. Wear no forced air of solemnity or sorrow . . . Life means all that it ever meant. It is the same as it ever was. There is absolute unbroken continuity. What is this death but a negligible accident? I am but waiting for you for an interval somewhere very near just round the corner. All is well.

The second major shift of emphasis has been away from concentration on the next world to preoccupation with this one. Two major figures both reflect and help to account for this change, Marx and Freud. Marx was not in fact as hostile to religion as is sometimes supposed. However, he did believe that the human hope which was expressed in religious hope for heaven is a falsification, a misplacing of a hope which should properly be directed towards a transformed earth. As is well known he called religion the opium of the people but the passage in which that expression appears is worth quoting in full, in order to grasp the force of what Marx said. In his *Critique of Hegel's Philosophy of Right*, he wrote:

> Religious suffering is at the same time an *expression* of real suffering and a protest against real suffering. Religion is the sigh of the oppressed creature, the sentiment of a heartless world, and the soul of soul-less conditions. It is the *opium* of the people.

Although there are not many classic Marxists around, his criticism of religious hope has entered deeply into the consciousness of twentieth-century human beings. Very many people, who are far from calling themselves Marxists, see it as the proper and urgent task of human beings to change social and political conditions on earth. Together with this they very often regard hope for a life after death as at best a distraction from, or at worst an obstruction to, the prime task.

The same point was made by Freud in rather different terms. He accounted for religion in a number of different ways but one of these was to regard it as the product of wishful thinking, a view that is well summed up in a lapidary statement of Iris Murdoch: 'All that consoles is fake.' Freud, with characteristic eloquence, wrote:

> Of what use to him is the illusion of a kingdom on the moon, whose revenues have never been seen by anyone? As an honest crofter on this earth he will know how to cultivate his plot in a way that will support him. Thus by withdrawing his expectations from the other world and concentrating all his liberated energies on this earthly life, he will probably attain to a state of things in which life will be tolerable for all and no one will be oppressed by culture any more. Then with one of our comrades in belief, he will be able to say without regret—let us leave the heavens to the angels and the sparrows.

If we want to obtain the full force of the contrast, we have only to compare the hymns written in the nineteenth century with hymns written in the last decade. The former focus on the joys of heaven and how to attain them, the latter on tasks to be done on this earth and how to achieve them.

These two fundamental shifts of emphasis, the fading of any sense of divine judgement after death and the transfer of interest from the next world to this one, have left a widespread sense of unease and uncertainty about the place of death in human existence. As is well known, for so many death has become a solitary, hidden experience. There are virtually no public mourning rituals now. There remains a wistful hope for some kind of continued existence after death but no lively belief in its certainty or even probability. This may be understandable enough in the population as a whole. However, what is somewhat more surprising is how contemporary Judaism sits light to the prospect of life after death and what a high percentage of Christian church-goers share the current scepticism. Public-opinion polls carried out a few years ago reveal not only widespread disbelief in the possibility of a life after death but also that this disbelief is shared by many regular church-goers. So we have a society in which death is not regarded as a gateway to either hell or heaven. It is simply there, full of foreboding but not properly faced except in some artistic works such as the plays of Samual Beckett.

At this stage, it might be worth indicating some developments in Christian theology that have taken place in recent decades. First, there has been a demise in talk about the soul. This has come about partly as a result of philosophical scepticism and partly because of a recovery of a more Hebraic way of thinking. Philosophers have been unable to give much sense to the idea of a soul conceived of as a box inside a box inside a box. It is true that there has been a reaction in some quarters, with a call to retain 'soul talk'. It has been urged that soul talk, though not referring to some invisible essence of the human being, is nevertheless essential to refute all forms of reductionism. In order to counter views which see human beings as simply a series of chemical processes or complex cells, talk about the soul reminds us that the human person must be seen as a whole and that the whole is more than the sum of its parts. But this demise, or at least reinterpretation, of language about the soul has gone together with a new emphasis upon the value of Hebraic as opposed to Greek ways of looking at the human being. The Hebrews did not think of human beings as essentially souls imprisoned in bodies. Rather, they thought of human beings as psychosomatic unities. God took the clay of the ground and breathed on it and man became a living being. The Hebrews thought of human beings as a unity of body, mind and spirit.

35

Second, and not unconnected with the first point, it has become usual to contrast the way in which Socrates and Jesus approached their respective deaths. Socrates died calmly, looking forward to the release of the eternal soul from its prison in the body. Jesus was 'very sorrowful, even to death' and, according to Luke, with his sweat like great drops of blood falling to the ground, prayed three times in the Garden of Gethsemane that the cup of suffering and death might be removed from him, 'Abba, Father, all things are possible to thee; remove this cup from me'.

Similarly, St Paul viewed death as 'an enemy'. This attitude has surprising resonances in some modern literature.

Reflecting on his father's dying, Dylan Thomas wrote those lines which have since become well known:

> Do not go gentle into that good night,
> Old age should burn and rave at close of day;

Simone de Beauvoir quoted these words on the first page of her book about the death of her mother, published in 1964, and ironically entitled *Une Mort très Douce* (*A Happy Death* in the English version). The theme of the book is stated in the final words:

> There is no such thing as a natural death: nothing that happens to man is ever natural because his very presence calls the world in question. Every man is mortal; but for every man his death is an accident and even if he knows of it and consents to it, an untimely violence.

Canon Henry Scott Holland also held death to be an accident, but a 'negligible accident' not *une violence indue*, not an outrage as Simone de Beauvoir held.

Third, and again not unconnected with the previous two points, there has been a recovery of the depth of meaning in the symbol of resurrection. For most of its history the Church has combined the Greek and Hebraic way of looking at what happens after death. It was held that at death the immortal soul was released from the body but that, except in the case of the blessed Virgin Mary, who was assumed body and soul into heaven, the soul had to wait for its reunification with the body until the general resurrection of the dead at the end of time. Then the actual physical corpuscles of its own body would be revivified and transformed. Few today could go along with this belief, however many paintings of Stanley Spencer are set before us for our edification. But this does not mean that talk about resurrection has no point. It remains a vital Christian symbol, indicating first of all that whatever lies beyond, we will be more truly and richly ourselves than we are now. We will not simply be wispy shades or ghosts. Furthermore, the symbol brings out the point that as this life is sheer gift, so whatever lies beyond is, no less, the gift of God. We go into the darkness of death and it seems the end of all that we are. But God knows us through and through, and that essential being which is each one of us he recreates or reforms in a form and manner appropriate to an eternal existence. We have no right to this, we do not automatically go on in however attenuated form. But we trust that he whose touch we have known now in raising us out of self-preoccupation and despair will touch us again to revivify our essential being for eternity. In some such way those Christian theologians who retain a faith that is recongizably Christian would express the resurrection hope.

It is true that Christian hope for eternal existence has been down-played in many, perhaps most, Christian circles. However, it is not discarded even in those theologians most anxious to emphasize the role of Christianity in transforming this world. The Tübingen theologian Jürgen Moltmann, for example, in his influential *The Theology of Hope*, whose thrust is to nerve us for action in changing the social and economic conditions in which so many live lives of poverty and oppression, yet maintains that we must have hope, not only for the poor on earth but also hope in the face of death.

Liberation theologians, as the phrase suggests, see the Christian faith as that which liberates us not only from what constricts our personal existence but from all those social, economic and political ills which frustrate that human fulfilment which God has in mind for each one of us. The thrust of liberation theology is to ground and inspire Christian solidarity with and work for the poorest and most oppressed people of the earth. The Vatican, through The Sacred Congregation for the Doctrine of the Faith, has issued two documents on liberation theology. Despite the desire of the press to polarize liberation theologians and the Vatican, the Vatican, whilst making perfectly justifiable criticisms of some forms of liberation theology, is essentially sympathetic to what the liberation theologians are trying to achieve. However, the Vatican documents quite rightly realize that the quest for true justice must include a hope for eternal existence. As *Liberatis Conscientia* puts it:

For true justice must include everyone; it must bring the answer to the immense load of suffering borne by all the generations. In fact, without the resurrection of the dead and the Lord's judgement, there is no justice in the full sense of the term. The promise of the resurrection is freely made to meet the desire for true justice dwelling in the human heart.

Winston Churchill once said: '. . . there may very well be two worlds, but I prefer to take them one at a time'. The way the modern Christian Church expresses the Christian hope is certainly stronger than that but is not totally unrelated to the priorities that Winston Churchill indicated. It might be put thus. We are to work for the transformation of this world. Under God, our efforts to do so will find their proper fulfilment, if not in this world then in the next.

The attitude C. S. Lewis takes is an interesting contrast with this approach. C. S. Lewis was rather late in coming to a belief in a life after death. When he was a student at Oxford he came to know an old Irish parson, dirty, gabbling and tragic, who had long since lost his faith but retained his living. His only interest in life was the search for evidence of human survival about which he talked non-stop. He did not seek the beatific vision for he did not believe in God. He didn't even seek reunion with his friends. All he wanted was some assurance that something he could call himelf would outlive his bodily life. Lewis said that this state of mind appeared to him as the most contemptible that he had ever encountered and the whole question of immortality became disgusting to him. The result was that when Lewis eventually came to believe in God, it was some time after that before he could reconcile himself to a belief in heaven. Yet when he did come to such a belief, it was at the foreground in both his popular writings on theology and his imaginative literature. Towards the end of his life he was accused of placing too much stress upon this aspect of the Christian faith. But, as he said:

> How can it loom less than large if it is believed in at all? If that other world is once admitted, how can it, except by sensual or bustling pre-occupations, be kept in the background of our mind?

> (*Prayer, Letters to Malcolm*, Collins, p. 120)

C. S. Lewis is still very influential in some quarters and his books have sold many millions. However, the centrality of the hope for immortality in his thinking has not on the whole been shared by professional theologians. They, as I have tried to show, state the matter somewhat differently. Lewis is instructive by the contrast he makes with professional theologians, who retain a hope for eternal life but who do not isolate it from hope for a better earth.

Given these changes of attitude, the fading of any real sense of divine judgement after death, the shift in emphasis away from the next world to this world, and within theological circles an approach to death which recognizes its proper fearfulness and, whilst retaining hope in the face of death, does not make immortality the be-all and end-all of Christianity, what today do we mean by a 'good death'? How can we talk about a 'good death' in a way that remains true to Christian faith and yet which can also engage the sympathy of that wider circle which have no consciously articulated faith?

What then is meant by a 'good death' in our time? First, the management of pain. This is not my sphere, so I do not intend to say anything about it except that I am grateful that through good medical care, the right doses of the right drugs administered at the right times, it is possible to keep patients even in the terminal stages of a distressing illness out of acute pain.

Second, a 'good death' is one in which one is able to face up to all those disturbing and unsettling feelings about oneself and others. This, along with so much else, has, as we know, been pioneered by the hospice movement, originating from the work of Dame Cicely Saunders, at St Christopher's. The hospice movement has enabled many patients to deal with the sometimes inevitable guilt, depression and family discord that occur in the crisis of death. Counselling is made available, though not pressed, so that the family is enabled to travel together. Within this context patients can search for meaning in a climate of openness and trust. The hospice movement has tried to establish, alongside its committment to excellence in practice, the affirmation of the individual with all their hopes and fears and a concern for the bereaved family as a whole.

The unsettling feelings which people experience in the approach to death have many facets. But one of them is certainly the sense of loss. In some ways the Bible can be considered as a story of loss, of people being given a land and then losing it, of being given a monarchy and then losing it, and so on. From this point of view Jesus comes as the combination of the sense of loss, both his own sense of loss as his hopes for the Kingdom of God appeared not to be realized and the sense of loss of his disciples after his crucifixion. It is true that the New Testament puts into the mouth of Jesus predictions about his resurrection. However, most New Testament scholars regard these as expressions of the mind of the Church, wise after the event.

39

A 'good death' is one in which we are enabled to face our negative feelings, in particular our attitude to death itself. There is a long and honourable religious tradition on the theme of preparing for death, on dying before we actually die. The old Prayer Book litany prayed that we may be delivered from 'battle, murder and sudden death'. The theme of leaving time to prepare is never very far away in Graham Greene's novel *Brighton Rock*. Much of this may have had to do with preparing to meet one's Maker suitably contrite and believing. However, the twentieth century can see also in this tradition another wisdom. Doctors know better than anyone the shock of a sudden death. Death, however much expected, is always in some sense a shock. Yet a long illness gives not only the person who is dying but, no less important, family and friends time to adjust and accomplish much emotional business in the period before death finally comes.

A 'bad death' is one in which one dies alone. Of course, there is a sense in which everyone is alone at the end. However, a 'good death' is one in which one has the companionship of other people both in the preparatory period and during the period of passing itself. Here again the hospice movement and hospitals that have been influenced by it have been so helpful in giving, wherever possible, the necessary support and companionship. One of the wonderful features of accounts of the death of saints, of which there are so many in Christian literature, is the description of beloved friends crowding round the bedside weeping, praying, saying farewell and, as often as not, recording a sense of the dying one being welcomed to the other side by a no less loving fellowship. They were communal events. By way of contrast, I was struck by the loneliness of the self-inflicted deaths of Arthur Koestler and his wife in 1983. On rational grounds they opted for euthanasia. But it seemed so sad and isolated.

Then, a 'good death' is one which is fully integrated into, and in some sense is, a proper flowering of the person's life. One of the people who seemed to achieve this was, surprisingly, D. H. Lawrence. As he lay dying of TB in 1929, still only in his early forties, Lawrence wrote what must be the most positive poems on death of our century. In 'Shadows' he expresses a biblical faith in one who allows us to sink into oblivion in order to raise us to new life:

> I am in the hands of the unknown God,
> he is breaking me down to his own oblivion
> to send me forth on a new morning, a new man.

Yet it is what is almost the theme music for this sequence that I specially want to note. Another poem begins:

> Sing the song of death, O sing it!
> For without the song of death, the song of life
> becomes pointless and silly.

'Sing the song of death'; this, coming from Lawrence, above all the man of life about whom Frieda wrote, 'Right up to the last he was alive and we both made the best of our days, then he faced the end so splendidly, so like a man.' It is the fact that this song of death comes from Lawrence that is so impressive. Others have welcomed death, none more so than Stevie Smith. Her final lines:

> Come, Death, and carry me away . . .
> Come, Death. Do not be slow,

express a lifetime's longing for oblivion.

Lawrence's whole life, on the other hand, was a protest against that kind of attitude; yet it was he who said: 'without the song of death, the song of life becomes pointless and silly'. In order to sing that song more is required than being able to see death as a way out or through. The gifted preacher and theologian Austin Farrer pointed to that more. In a sermon preached some time during the 1950s when a mission was going on in Oxford University, Austin Farrer considered the problem of our nice worldly friends. Are they to languish for ever in hell? How absurd it seems when we are all laughing together over a pint of beer in a pub:

> Man's destiny consists of two parts: first we live and then we die. In the eyes of God our dying is not simply negative, it is an immensely important and salutary thing; by living we become ourselves, by dying we become God's if, that is, we know how to die; if we so die that everything we have become in our living is handed back to the God who gave us life, for him to refashion and use according to his pleasure.
>
> God desires that we should grow, live, expand, enrich our minds and our imaginations, become splendid creatures. He also desires that we should die, should be crucified on the cross of Christ Jesus, should surrender all we have and are to him; and he desires that we should die that death spiritually before we die it physically. Well now, what after all are we to say about our dear, delightful unconverted friends? We must say that so far as their lives are wholesome or truly human, they are splendid manifestations of the power to live; but that they have not yet

learned to die, they have not made even the first step along that more difficult path which Jesus Christ opened up for us.

A moving statement, yet those of us who are less sanctified than Austin Farrer still want to ask: 'Why should I surrender all I am to him? Why should I hand back to God everything I have become in living?'—questions that lead us to the heart of faith. First, because surrender is an acknowledgement of the highest, a discovery via our hints and guesses of a worthy object of our longing, the source and standard of all we hold to be true and good and beautiful. Second, because we come to see that our very being, all that we are, flows from that spring. Third, because though we spring up *ex nihilo* and return to nothing, though we come from the dust and return to the dust, the mouth which breathed us into life and sustains us in being utters the word of promise: not less, but more. Yet we cannot receive this more except we live in accord with reality, in particular the reality that we are receivers, dependent moment by moment for our existence on a source beyond ourselves. We receive a self and surrender a self, hearing the promise that we will receive again more than we handed back.

We live and grow and become a self and our whole being cries out against the loss of that self. Yet the Christian faith invites us to make that loss a consciously willed love of God and man. Few people manage to get the balance right. The Jesuit theologian and anthropologist, Teilhard de Chardin, with his passionate affirmation of all that made for life on the one hand and his creative acceptance of death on the other, was of the few. He believed in the divinization of our activities, in a communion with God through our human strengths. In contrast, however, to the current view of life as a process of physical growth followed by physical decline, Teilhard saw it as a process of growth followed by the possibility of further growth through what he called the divinization of our passivities. It is a difficult vision to sustain, and when faced by horrible illness or humiliating death in those we know, it must sometimes seem impossible. Everything within us that is healthy, that loves life, rages against the forces that diminish us. Yet Teilhard believed that the forces of diminishment take us to a deeper communion and this was his prayer in *Le Milieu Divin*:

> It was a joy to me, O God, in the midst of the struggle, to feel that in developing myself I was increasing that hold that You have upon me . . . Now that I have found the joy of utilising all

forms of growth to make You, or to let You, grow in me, grant that I may willingly consent to this last phase of communion in the course of which I shall possess You by diminishing in You.

... grant, when my hour comes, that I may recognise You under the species of each alien or hostile force that seems bent upon destroying or uprooting me. When the signs of age begin to mark my body (and still more when they touch my mind); when the ill that is to diminish me or carry me off strikes from without or is born within me; when the painful moment comes in which I suddenly awaken to the fact that I am ill or growing old; and above all at the last moment when I feel I am losing hold of myself and am absolutely passive within the hands of the great unknown forces that have formed me; in all those dark moments, O God, grant that I may understand that it is You (provided only my faith is strong enough) who are painfully parting the fibres of my being in order to penetrate to the very marrow of my substance and bear me away within Yourself.

This brings out the point that, for a Christian, death must in the end be not only an act of self-surrender but a form of trust and an expression of self-offering. Jewish mothers used to teach their children to go to sleep with the words of the psalm on their lips, 'Into thy hands I commend my spirit.' It was, according to Luke, with these words that Jesus himself died, 'Father into thy hands I commit my spirit.' Trust, self-surrender, self-offering, a handing-over of ourselves as totally as possible.

Two years before he himself died in 1983, Bishop John Robinson preached at the funeral of a girl of sixteen who had died of cancer. In his sermon, John Robinson said that 'God was to be found in the cancer as much as in the sunset.'

As he himself was dying of cancer he told people how that statement had come true for him. It does not mean, he stressed, that God sends cancer to test or try us; such a God would be intolerable So what did he mean? First, it set him thinking about the cause of cancer. He didn't know the cause but he did know that hidden resentments and unresolved conflicts within us sometimes make their presence felt through physical illness. His cancer made him look at what he called his unfinished agenda and to face, come to terms with, and, stronger than that, embrace things about himself he had tended to hide away. This is the spirit of God, who searches us out and knows us, leading us into the truth about ourselves and a true love of ourselves. Second, he became aware of the many people who cared for him. No doubt, he said, it was all there before, but as a result of the cancer he had become aware through the giving and receiving in his relationships with his family and friends of grace upon grace. Third, when he was given only a few months to live he re-examined his priorities and decided to do only what really mattered. He went on holiday with his wife; he finished off some scholarly work and above all he tried to make his life really life; life with a capital L and not mere existence. This life, which the New Testament calls 'eternal life' is begun, continued but not ended now. It is not ended with death but it has to begin and develop now.

In these three ways John Robinson said he had found God in his cancer as much as in the sunset. John Robinson's death was a good death not only for the reasons discussed earlier but because he discovered meaning and purpose in the process of dying itself. (The above summarizes Eric James, *A Life of Bishop John A. T. Robinson* (Collins 1987), pp. 304–9.)

Our attitude to the prospect of what might happen after death is very different in the twentieth century from all preceding centuries, at least in Europe. Nevertheless, death is no less with us and the problem and opportunity of helping people in the different circumstances of our time to achieve a good death is very much with us. The Christian faith has still, I believe, many insights to contribute to this task.

I am a child of the twentieth century and, therefore, these swirling currents in our understanding of death have inevitably affected me. I am also, by conscious choice, an inheritor of the Christian tradition and so I want to be shaped by its central beliefs. I am with all this a particular person with a particular psychology, and so these cultural shifts and religious beliefs will take effect in me in a particular way. So where does that leave me in my personal approach to death?

First, I do not fear death itself. Unlike some people I love the dark. The dark for me does not kindle anxiety or fear but a sense of peace and oblivion, in the positive sense that D. H. Lawrence used the word; oblivion as a passage to fresh life, whether after sleep or the sleep of death. Second, however, I do fear the process of dying. The fear of pain is strong. So I cannot but be grateful for living in the twentieth century, with its drugs and sophisticated terminal care. But it is still the process of dying rather than the fact of death itself which scares me.

What of the hereafter? A belief in the hereafter is fundamental to my belief in God. I find it difficult to comprehend how people can believe that there is a loving God whilst treating a belief in the afterlife as a kind of optional extra. For me the Christian faith stands or falls as a whole. The existence of so much human anguish and suffering poses such a large question mark against the existence of a loving God that it is only with the full panoply of Christian faith, including the hope of eternity, that one can live with (not answer) the question. So the traditional four last things, death, judgement, heaven and hell, are as real today as they ever were, though one might interpret them somewhat differently from our forebears in the medieval or Reformation periods.

The God in whom I believe will not sentence me to hell. However, in the light of absolute truth, I will see myself as I am and that will surely be a painful purging process. In 'Little Gidding' in his *Four Quartets*, T. S. Eliot writes about the gifts reserved for old age:

> And last, the rending pain of re-enactment
>> Of all that you have done, and been; the shame
>> Of motives late revealed, and the awareness
> Of things ill done and done to others' harm
>> Which once you took for exercise of virtue.
>> Then fools' approval stings, and honour stains.
> From wrong to wrong the exasperated spirit
>> Proceeds, unless restored by that refining fire
>> Where you must move in measure, like a dancer.

As we move into the nearer presence of God the re-enactment will be no less painful and the refining fire no less fiercely beautiful.

God will not sentence me to hell because he has shown me in Christ that his love will never let me go. Whatever agonies of self-knowledge I may have to undergo his hand will hold mine and lead me through. About heaven, it is foolish to speculate. All images are inadequate. I am content with the words of the Collect in the Book of Common Prayer:

> O God who hast prepared for them that love Thee such good things as pass man's understanding; pour into our hearts such love toward Thee, that we, loving Thee above all things, may obtain thy promises, which exceed all that we can desire; through Jesus Christ our Lord.

How can these things be, when there is nothing in the way of hard evidence? Yet I am troubled less by Hume than by Marx. Pure philosophy in the end leaves metaphysical questions open. Marx, and others, pose a profound moral challenge. How can we talk about the afterlife in a way which does not detract at all from our efforts to improve life in the world? So I am challenged to keep my gaze on this earth, to let God work in and through me to alleviate suffering and enhance human well-being here and now. Nevertheless, there is hope. The Christian faith talks about this hope in terms of resurrection. I do not believe that my physical body will be resurrected as in some Stanley Spencer painting but the person I truly am will be re-created and re-formed in a manner appropriate to an eternal mode of existence. That is the truth that the doctrine of the resurrection of the body safeguards. I will be more richly myself then, with a greater capacity to express myself and communicate wtih God and others, not simply a wispy shadow. The immortal diamond that is really me will, in the resurrection, be for ever me.

> In a flash, at a trumpet crash.
> I am all at once what Christ is, since he was what
> I am, and
> This Jack, joke, poor potsherd, patch, matchwood,
> immortal diamond,
> Is immortal diamond.
>
> Gerard Manley Hopkins

Meanwhile, I hope to die as I seek to live, with trust in God, and self-surrender. As I know something of his goodness now I am expecting to know it more fully through the fire of judgement and resurrection.

FIVE

'Astride of a grave'— Samuel Beckett and Christian hope*

Samuel Beckett is of particular importance to Christians. This is not just because of his genius as a writer, though this in itself is enough to win our attention. It is because his central themes are those with which religion has traditionally been concerned and because his treatment of them raises a question-mark against every other version, particularly the Christian one.

At a burial, when the body is ready at the graveside, a priest using the 1662 Prayer Book says: 'Man that is born of woman has but a short time to live, and is full of misery.' If he is using the 1928 Book he might use these words from Psalm 103: 'The days of man are but as grass; for he flourisheth as a flower of the field. For as soon as the wind goeth over it, it is gone; and the place thereof shall know it no more.' This view of life underlies every line Beckett writes. One of his plays is called *Breath*.[1] These are the stage directions:

> CURTAIN
> 1. Faint light on stage littered with miscellaneous rubbish. Hold about five seconds.
> 2. Faint brief cry and immediately inspiration and slow increase of light together reaching maximum together in about ten seconds. Silence and hold about five seconds.
> 3. Expiration and slow decrease of light together reaching minimum together (light as in 1) in about ten seconds and immediately cry as before. Silence and hold about five seconds.

This play, which lasts thirty-five seconds, and which Beckett has described as 'a farce in five acts', hardly needs a commentary. But, as Ruby Cohn has written, it contains Beckett staple: 'symmetry, repetition, inversion, the wresting of sound from silence, a flicker of light against the dark, dying, but no definable death'.[2]

A sense of the brevity of life, which receives such simple but startling treatment in *Breath* permeates every play. In *Waiting for Godot* Pozzo says: 'They give birth astride of a grave, the light gleams an instant, then it's night once more.'[3] And shortly

* The Drawbridge Memorial Lecture delivered in the City of London, 1982

afterwards Vladimir takes up the image: 'Astride of a grave and a difficult birth. Down in the hole, lingeringly, the grave-digger puts on the forceps. We have time to grow old. The air is full of our cries.'[4]

We are born astride the grave. And during the brief flicker of consciousness which we call our life, the darkness of death shrouds us. *Endgame* takes place in a small room at the edge of the world. All life has gone or nearly gone. Some have taken the stage set to be a nuclear shelter. It isn't, but there is a sense of living through, or rather, dying through, the last minutes of time. Two of the characters on stage, Nag and Nell, are toothless old folk stuffed into dustbins. During the course of the play one of them, or perhaps both of them, dies. But it makes no difference; everyone is dying anyway. The play begins with Clov saying tonelessly, 'Finished, it's finished, nearly finished, it must be nearly finished.' In due course Hamm responds, 'Me—(he yawns)—to play.'[5] It is the last few moves of a game. Towards the end Clov hits Hamm with a dog and Hamm says, 'If you must hit me, hit me with the axe. (pause) Or with the gaff, hit me with the gaff.' Clov responds imploringly, 'Let's stop playing!' 'Never' says Hamm, and, after a pause, 'Put me in my coffin.' 'There are no more coffins', says Clov. 'Then let it end', replies Hamm.[6] In Christian history the preacher has tried to make people face up to the shortness of life and the inevitability of death, in order to summon them to their responsibilities before the God who will meet them after death to reward them according to their deeds. 'The end is nigh', say the placards, 'Prepare to meet thy God.' 'Live each day as if thy last', says the hymn. But the nearness of death in Beckett's plays is not something that people have to be reminded of. They are fully aware of the fact. Nor is it something they want to stave off. Death is near but still too far away; soon, but it cannot come too soon ('It must be nearly finished', says Clov.) Meanwhile there is the problem of getting through until it does come.

Our main device for getting through until the end comes is talking. In *Waiting for Godot* Vladmir and Estragon toss remarks back and forth like the circus clowns they in some way resemble. At one point they have a rapid-fire dialogue, with each sentence only six words or less. Then they run out of conversation and a long silence ensues. 'Say something', says Vladimir; 'I'm trying', replies Estragon, but there is another long silence. 'Say anything at all', says Valdimir in anguish. 'What do we do now?' responds Estragon; and so it goes on, in little burts of three or four sentences followed by silence. They then get going for a couple of pages, and after another silence Estragon remarks, 'That wasn't such a bad little canter.' 'Yes,' says Vladimir, 'but now we'll have to find something else.'[7] And so it continues.

In *Happy Days* the curtain goes up with Winnie in a heap of sand up to her middle and a hellish light. In the second act the sand is up to her neck. Winnie spends the whole play talking and occupying herself with the objects of her handbag which she lays out around her. Behind her, in a trench, for the most part unseen and silent, is her husband Willie. 'Is not that so, Willie, that even words fail, at times? (Pause. Back front) What is one to do, then, until they come again? Brush and comb the hair if it has not been done. Or if there is some doubt, trim the nails if they are in need of trimming. These things tide one over. (Pause) That is what I mean.'[8] The play opens with the words 'Another heavenly day' and Winnie saying her prayers, 'For Jesus Christ's sake Amen.' Again she prays, 'World without end. Amen,' and continues 'Begin, Winnie.' (Pause) 'Begin your day, Winnie.' And so, with the aid of encouraging clichés, prayers, snatches from hymns and the objects from her handbag, Winnie tries bravely to get through:

> 'Ah well—can't complain—no, no—mustn't complain—so much to be thankful for—no pain—hardly any—wonderful thing that—nothing like it—slight headache sometimes—ah yes—occasional mild migraine—it comes—then goes—ah yes—many mercies—great mercies—prayers, perhaps not for naught—first thing—last thing.'[9]

Graham Greene wrote once of 'our baseless human optimism that is so much more appalling than our despair', and the truth of this is apparent in every line of Winnie.

One of the ways in which Beckett characters get through is by telling their story, a tale which illuminates their own situation and lets through, in an oblique way, what they feel about it. 'What now? (Pause) What now, Willie? (Long pause) There is my story, of course, when all else fails.' And so she begins to tell her story about a girl called Mildred who had a doll, and who came downstairs one night. In telling the story she breaks off for a while to look at Willie who she suspects may be crying out. 'I do of course hear cries. (Pause. With finality) No no, my head was always full of cries (Pause) Faint confused cries.'[10] Then she talks about her song which she sings every day to help her keep her spirits up, before returning to her story:

> 'Suddenly a mouse ran up her little thigh, and Mildred,

dropping Dolly in her fright, began to scream. (Winne gives a sudden piercing scream)—and screamed and screamed (Winnie screams twice)—screamed and screamed and screamed and screamed till all came running, in their night attire, papa, mamma, Bibby and . . . old Annie, to see what was the matter . . . (pause) . . . what on earth could possibly be the matter?'[11]

The cries are there all the time. So is the hostility; hostility to the universe that causes such pain. In *Endgame* Nagg tells a story about a man who asks his tailor to make some trousers. Some days later he comes back and finds that the tailor has made a mess of the seat. The man is understanding and returns in due course to find that the tailor has made a mess of the crutch. Again he is understanding and comes back ten days later to find that the tailor has made a mess of the fly. And so it goes on. At last in exasperation the man says: 'There are limits. In six days, do you hear me, six days, God made the world. Yes, Sir, no less, Sir, the WORLD! And you are not bloody well capable of making me a pair of trousers in three months!' (Tailor's voice, scandalised): 'But, my dear Sir, look! (disdainful gesture, disgustedly)—at the world—(pause)—and look—(loving gesture, proudly)—at my TROUSERS!'[12] This story, though seriously meant, is light-hearted in its tone. *Endgame* also has another story, in which the merciless element in life is laid bare in a much harsher way.

Religious imagery, and references to religion, play a large part in Beckett's work. At the beginning of *Waiting for Godot*, for example, the two tramps suddenly turn to the Gospels. Vladimir says: 'Two thieves, crucified at the same time as our Saviour. One.' But he is interrupted by Estragon: 'Our what?' 'Our Saviour. Two thieves, one is supposed to have been saved and the other . . . damned.' 'Saved from what?' says Estragon. 'Hell', answers Vladimir[13] who continues to puzzle about the fact that only one of the four Gospels reports the story. It matters to him that it is true, that one of the thieves was saved. Their life is a confused, hellish waiting for they-know-not-what; but something that might save them. Meanwhile they suffer. 'But you can't go barefoot!', blurts out Vladimir. 'Christ did', responds Estragon. 'Christ! What's Christ got to do with it? You're not going to compare yourself to Christ!' 'All my life I've compared myself to him', says Estragon. 'But where he lived it was warm, it was dry!' says Vladimir. 'Yes, and they crucified quick'[14] responded his companion. Life is a waiting, a waiting for someone to come and put things right; but that person does not seem to come. We are in a state from which we need saving, but there does not seem to be a saviour. We suffer and it's not over. Religious imagery is used to heighten the aspects of our human situation for which religion has traditionally provided a solution. But no solution is offered. Indeed the possibility of a solution looks unlikely. So the religious references, which arouse expectation, in fact underline our predicament and intensify the awareness of our need.

In *Not I* all the audience sees is a luminous mouth in the middle of a darkened stage and a shadowy figure in the corner who hardly moves. The mouth talks very rapidly, in staccato fashion. The effect is extraordinarily powerful. After ten minutes I had to look away and I wonder if I would have been able to last for more than the twenty-minute length of the play. The effect is difficult to describe—words like panic, tension, terror, come to mind. The mind, which is projecting itself through this mouth, could be losing consciousness, as a result of drugs, or because the person is dying. On the other hand it could be coming back into consciousness. Certainly it is coming back into the non-stop flow of words. The mouth tells its story. Abandoned by both mother and father, she was brought up in an orphanage. Nothing of note happened until coming up to seventy, the traditional allotted span, when on an early April morning all went out. She began to think she had died. The script says: '. . . for her first thought was . . . oh, long after . . . sudden flash . . . brought up as she had been to believe . . . with other waifs . . . in a merciful . . . (brief laugh) . . . God . . . (good laugh) . . . first thought was . . . oh, long after . . . sudden flash . . . she was being punished . . . for her sins.'[15] Then a few lines further on the same reference to what she had been taught as a child is repeated with the same laughs. A few pages later, there is the dialogue, which again is repeated: 'Seventy? . . . Good God! . . . On and on to be seventy . . . something she didn't know herself . . . wouldn't know if she heard . . . then forgiven . . . God is love . . . tender mercies . . . new every morning . . .' Out of the mouth pours a torrent of tight, taut words. The text refers to the experience of losing consciousness and regaining it again; and what happened on that April morning is being relived. If it is an experience of dying it is also an experience of coming to consciousness. And all the suffering of going impregnates the experience of coming . . . The title is *Not I*, and the mouth is desperately trying to confine the stream of consciousness to talk about itself only in the third person, to avoid being 'I'. The terror reveals the suffering, not emphasized but implied in almost every line. 'Dusk . . . sitting staring at her

hand . . . there in her lap . . . palm upward . . . suddenly saw it wet
. . . the pain . . . tears presumably . . . hers presumably . . . no-one
else for miles . . . no sound . . . just the tears . . . sat and watched
them dry . . . all over in a second.' Also on the stage there is a
helpless figure who three times moves slightly. This is what the
stage direction says: 'Movement; this consists in a simple sideways
raising of arms from sides and their falling back, in a gesture of
helpless compassion. It lessens with each recurrence till scarcely
perceptible at third. There is just enough pause to contain it as
MOUTH recovers from vehement refusal to relinquish third
person.' Traditionally, dying is a time when the soul comes in
judgement before God. But in *Not I* this may also be an experience
of being born, or at least of coming to self-consciousness. In any
case, it is an experience which is resisted; in which Mouth suffers
and, as a result of which the reference to a merciful God brings
forth a bitter laugh; and about which the unknown hearer makes
gestures of helpless compassion. *Not I*, like all Beckett plays, is
many-layered, and it resists easy summary. But there is no
doubting the centrality of religious imagery and ideas.

In Beckett's play entitled *Play* three characters sit in urns. A
spotlight focuses on each face in turn and is the signal for the
person to speak. They are two women and a man who has been
involved with both of them. They each rehearse the story of what
has happened to them from their own partial point of view, a
sentence or two at a time, when the spot switches to the next. It
could be some kind of judgement. Certainly they are conscious of
going through something, of being answerable: 'Is it that I do not
tell the truth? Is that it? That some day somehow I may tell the
truth at last and then no more light at last for the truth?'[16] But the
eye that observes them is, as they gradually realize, mindless—
'Mere eye. No mind. Opening and shutting on me', says the man.
'Am I as much . . . am I as much as . . . being seen?'[17] In *Not I*
Mouth had a sense of being judged, of being answerable. This
theme here is more explicit; of being answerable but with no one
apparently to be answerable to. The spotlight is not the light of
Christ but the flicker of consciousness with its baffled suffering
sense of being answerable to someone or something. Although the
characters have died and are in urns, and it seems like Sheol or
purgatory, Beckett is not giving us his idea of what happens after
death, any more than Sartre was in *Huit Clos*. We have here
something related to the life we know now; and this life is not just
one that the characters would like to end; it is one they wish had
never been: 'Yes, peace, one assumed, all out, all the pain, all as if

. . . never been . . . no sense in this, oh I know . . . none the less one assumed peace . . . I mean . . . not merely all over, but as if it . . . never been . . .'[18]

The underlying assumption of all Beckett's plays can be brought out by two contrasting quotations. Malcolm Muggeridge once wrote: 'I believe that at all times and in all circumstances life is a blessed gift.' Beckett has written: 'Life is a punishment for having been born.' In *Endgame* Hamm puts his hand against the wall of this enclosed room and says, 'Old wall! Beyond is the . . . other hell'.[19] But what about the traditional consolations of life, available to all, believer and non-believer alike, human love and art? The characters in Beckett's plays need one another. Estragon says to Vladimir: 'Don't touch me! Don't question me! Don't speak to me! Stay with me!'[20] Winnie in *Happy Days* needs Willie, even though he utters only one grunt in the whole play. Being with another person is marginally less hellish than being on one's own. But these relationships are characterized by patterns of torment-ing and being tormented. Amongst the belongings in Winnie's handbag in *Happy Days* is a revolver. As the poet Browning, with his mixture of doubt and religious comfort, was there for Victorians to quote, so is Winnie's Browning revolver. She brings it out and says: 'You'd think the weight of this thing would bring it down among the . . . last rounds. But no, it doesn't. Ever uppermost, like Browning.'[21] At the end of the play Wille crawls out of his trench and up the heap of sand. He reaches out his arm to Winnie and they both look at each other. The revolver is on the sand between them. In *Not I*, Mouth tells the story of her conception and start in life: 'Parents unknown . . . unheard of . . . he having similarly . . . eight months later . . . almost to the tick . . . so no love . . . spared that . . . no love such as normally vented on the . . . speechless infant.'

What about art? Beckett's chracters tell stories which illuminate their situation. Their stories are one of the devices which keep them going. When all else fails there is still their story to tell. Is that Beckett's view of art, of his own art? He has said: 'I couldn't have done it otherwise. Gone on, I mean, I could not have gone on through the awful wretched mess of life without having left a stain upon the silence.' 'A stain upon the silence.' No more significance than that? But both love and art hint at more. In *Krapp's Last Tape* a man on his sixtieth birthday is speaking into a recording machine and playing back old tapes. Every year he has recorded himself a birthday message, a review of how he has got on in the year, and now he is commenting on his previous views of himself. It is an ingenious device. Once again the religious themes are present—the three-score-years-and-ten nearly over; the review of the life; twice Krapp sings: 'Now the day is over, night is drawing nigh, shadows of the evening steal across the sky.' The play focuses on the replay of what Krapp recorded on his thirty-ninth birthday, and on his present attitude to what he was then. In that year he exults for what he calls 'a moment of vision, a miracle . . . for the fire that set it alight'. It was, he says, 'clear to me at last that the dark I have always struggled to keep under is in reality my most . . .' then he switches off impatiently and winds the tape forward. His voice on the tape speaks of a relationship with a girl: he is lying with her in a punt and they decide they cannot go on: 'He lay there without moving. But under us all moved, and moved us, gently, up and down, and from side to side.'[22] Krapp reviewing his life is a mixture of savagery and regret for this crucial year. It contained a beautiful moment of love. Times of happiness in Beckett's plays are rare. The occasional lyrical moment is quickly snuffed in the all-engulfing darkness. But here love is deliberately put aside for the pursuit of the artistic vision, a vision which, on the approach of death, he feels has not been fulfilled. At the end of the tape he stands motionless and silent.

I suggested at the beginning that Beckett offers a particular challenge to Christians. This is, first, because of the view of human existence that is implicit in all his writings. It is, as I have tried to show, a view in which religion is taken seriously but in which there is none of the traditional religious consolation. Rather the reverse, the religious themes and imagery serve to heighten the awareness of our horrific state. Beckett in his own life has suffered much. He had a powerful mother from whose emotional clutches he took a long time escaping. He has obviously been through long periods of depression. It was many years before he achieved any degree of success. And he is obviously a kind man, highly sensitive to suffering in others. When his mother was dying this is how Deirdre Blair, his biographer, describes the effect on him:

> His days passed in an exhausting, crushing depression brought on by long hours at her bedside. His nights were spent walking and talking with Geoffrey Thompson, to whom he complained bitterly of the so-called God who would permit such suffering.[23]

This theme, the suffering of mankind, permeates all the plays. 'There's something dripping in my head', says Hamm in *Endgame*, 'a heart, a heart in my head.'[24] And there are bitter laughs at the thought of a loving God in *Not I* and elsewhere. Krapp's tape reviewing his life has the line: 'Sneers at what he calls his youth and thanks God it's over. (pause). False ring there. (Pause). Shadows of the opus . . . magnum closing with a—(brief laugh)—yelp to Providence.'[25] And the stage direction reads, 'Prolonged laugh in which Krapp joins'.

This is the first question mark raised against Christian hope. The second is the compelling power with which Beckett writes about it. Ruby Cohn has written, 'Beckett is an important writer because he writes about important experiences that *precisely* convey their meaning.'[26] He uses everyday language: (almost the whole of *Happy Days*, for example is made up of clichés,) which Beckett orders into an object of great beauty. This beauty is related to the intensity and sensitivity with which Beckett himself experiences life. The effect on others can be overwhelming. Billie Whitelaw, who gave the first, incredible performance of Mouth in *Not I*, has said: '*Not I* came through the letter-box. I opened it, read it and burst into tears, floods of tears. It had a tremendous emotional impact upon me.'[27] George Devine wrote of Beckett: 'This man seemed to have lived and suffered so that I could see, and he was generous enough to pass it on to me.'[28]

The challenge then is simply to feel life, in all its glory and horror, with something of the intensity and sensitivity of Beckett—and to communicate a more hopeful vision. Life is as brief, painful, tragic and absurd as Beckett conveys it. But if people are more usually right in what they affirm than in what they deny, there may be something else to be affirmed. The task is to communicate it, and that means first, and most important of all, to experience it, with something of what Ruby Cohn has called his precision, that is his sensitive honesty.

There is a profound *challenge* to Christian hope in Beckett. But is there any *support* for it? First despite the antagonism shown to God, or at least the idea of a merciful God, the question of God is never quite closed. It is a measure of Beckett's genius that you cannot say for certain, on the basis of his plays alone, that he is an atheist. This is partly because of the many layers of meaning that are present. 'The meaning', if there is such a thing, cannot be pinned down. If you think you understand a play, you can go back to it and discover you have misunderstood it; that another meaning suggests itself. It is this continuously suggestive power which the plays have that makes the question of God not finally closed. There is mystery in them, as in life itself, so that every interpretation opens out into the possibility of another somewhat different one.

Second, there is the strange paradox that despite everything

Beckett's characters do not commit suicide. Camus said that the great problem in life is suicide. Perhaps the more interesting fact is that most people do not kill themselves. Beckett's characters are tempted to. Vladimir and Estragon in *Waiting for Godot* talk about hanging themselves from the tree, but get in a muddle about who should go first. Winnie has her Browning revolver. 'You remember Brownie, Willie, I can see him (pause) Brownie is there, Willie, beside me.'[29] In *Endgame* Hamm says, 'it's the end of the day like any other day, isn't it, Clov?' 'Looks like it', replies Clov. 'What's happening, what's happening?' asks Hamm, and Clov answers, 'Something is taking its course.' 'All right, be off . . . I thought I told you to be off', says Hamm, and Clov replies, 'I'm trying. Ever since I was whelped.'[30] The going-off refers to Clov leaving Hamm, but there is also the hint of leaving the life which they regard as hell. But they allow things to take their course. Why should they struggle on? No reason is given.

Third, there is, despite the harshness, hardness and grotesqueness of many of the scenes and of some of the dialogue, an underlying compassion. A helpless compassion, as indicated in the gesture of the shadowy figure in *Not I*, but still a compassion. Winnie, in *Happy Days*, is not a figure of fun. As the horror grows in the audience as it senses her plight, the mortality we all share, and the desperate attempts to keep going with a brave front, the pathos is intense. You don't admire Winnie, but neither is she the product of cynicism. Pity is too weak a word for her predicament (also ours), but something akin to it is called forth by her struggle to keep going.

Finally, perhaps, Beckett's art itself is a sign of hope—the fact that out of all that he has experienced himself and been sensitive to in others, he has produced works of art which will undoubtedly endure. Once Harold Pinter suggested to Beckett that his writing was a constantly courageous attempt to impose order and form upon the wretched mess mankind has made of the world. 'If you insist on finding form, I'll describe it for you,' Beckett replied. 'I was in hospital once. There was a man in another ward, dying of throat cancer. In the silence I could hear his screams continually. That's the only kind of form my work has.'[31] Nevertheless the form of Beckett's work, the dense poetic texture, the ordering of experience that he thinks of as absurd, is what makes it art.

Some words that Beckett used about his old master Joyce have often been used about Beckett himself: 'Here form *is* content, content *is* form.' Literally speaking, this remark is not true either as a generalization or about Beckett. All art has some content, and, as

I have shown, Beckett's plays have recognizable themes running through them. But these themes are inseparable from the way they are expressed, and it is this, the form, in which Beckett's genius is revealed. The form that Beckett uses is a simple one, repetition. Ruby Cohn has analysed the plays in detail and isolated many different kinds of repetition—simple doublets, that is, a word or sentence repeated immediately in order to sow doubt or express hesitancy; interrupted doublets; distanced doublets, echo doublets, triplets and refrains. In *Waiting for Godot*, for example, the dialogue 'Let's go. We can't. Why not? We're waiting for Godot. Ah.' recurs six times, and each word in the sequence occurs in other groups. One play, *Play*, is repeated a second time straight through, and then begins a third time, indicating that this is a pattern that recurs without end. Endless repetition can convey a sense of the futility of life:

> Vanity of vanities! All is vanity . . . The sun rises and the sun goes down, and hastens to the place where it rises. The wind blows to the south, and goes round to the north; round and round goes the wind, and on its circuits the wind returns . . . All things are full of weariness; a man cannot utter it . . . What has been is what will be, and what has been done is what will be done; and there is nothing new under the sun. (Eccles. 1.2, 5–6, 8–9)

And it is this biblical writer rather than any other that Beckett seems close to. Porter Abbott has written that repetition can mean, 'no conclusion (and hence no redemption), or it can mean renewal'.[32] The dominant effect of Beckett's repetition is no conclusion, and hence no redemption. But, as always with Beckett, it is never as simple as that. *Not I* ends: 'God is love . . . tender mercies . . . new every morning . . . back in the field . . . April morning . . . face in the grass . . . nothing but larks . . . pick it up'—words which have been repeated before, and which, you are led to believe, will be repeated again. What is picked up? It may be flowers, words, a body, a spirit, her return to consciousness, her telling of her story. There is endless repetition but it is part of the mystery with which Beckett leaves us—that the possibility of renewal cannot be totally ruled out.

In the Old Testament, God is the creator who imposes order on chaos. He shapes the primaeval chaos into life and then conscious life. An artist, through his attempt to impose form and order on experience, shares a similar vocation. The beauty of Beckett's works is, for those who are predisposed to see it, a sign of the capacity of creatures to share in their creator's power and skill. It would be absurd of course to try and make Beckett a crypto-Christian, an anonymous believer. And nothing of the kind is being attempted. But the mystery in his plays is akin to the mystery of life itself, with their door not finally closed; the way the characters struggle on without killing themselves; the compassion and the art itself, with its unique blend of truthful insight and poetry, are for the believer signs which are underpinned and have their proper place in a view of the world that includes more than Beckett brings into his plays. Augustine once wrote: 'Do not despair; one of the thieves was saved. Do not presume; one of the thieves was damned.' Reading Beckett's plays, a person is not likely to presume. And although the element of despair is always close to the surface hope is not finally quenched. In the 1662 burial service, the minister is bidden to pray: 'We give thee hearty thanks, for that it hath pleased thee to deliver this our brother out of the miseries of this sinful world'. Beckett's world, grim and bleak as it is, would have been recognized by the writer of that prayer. And if it does not have the hope of that prayer, neither does it completely extinguish that hope.

SIX

'Away grief's gasping'—
The note of hope in Hopkins'
anguish*

Recent writing on Hopkins has been marked by a stress on the unhappiness of his life. This is so, for example, in Robert Martin's biography,[1] which emphasizes the loneliness of Hopkins and the roots of this in his repressed homosexuality. In no way do I wish to belittle or underestimate the anguish which Hopkins often felt. For someone who is suffering there is nothing worse than an attitude of 'It's not nearly as bad as you think' and we do the dead a disservice to take up that attitude towards them. It is clear to even the most untutored reader that the Sonnets he wrote in Dublin were indeed, as he said, 'written in blood'.[2] The pain in them can be felt. Nevertheless, this mental suffering needs to be put in perspective, not least into the perspective of his own consciously accepted Christian discipline in its Ignatian form.

My concern is with the final Dublin years, from 1884 until his death five years later in 1889. More specifically I am concerned with the poetry of that period. What I have to say is not biography, though it will draw on biography. It is not literary criticism, though it will draw on such criticism. If it is a theological evaluation, it is such of a particular kind. As a Catholic and a Jesuit Hopkins went regularly for confession and spiritual direction. If he brought those last poems to his director and that director was a sensitive and wise soul friend, also schooled in Ignatian spirituality, what would he say to Hopkins? In setting up this perspective I am not, I believe, being presumptuous because this was the one, above all others, that Hopkins accepted.

The suffering was real and had a number of causes. First, as Robert Martin brings out so well, Dublin at that time was an unattractive city, shabby, crowded and poverty stricken.[3] Hopkins wrote to Bridges to say that it was as smoky as London and covered in soot. His sister said that Hopkins 'was made miserable by the untidiness, disorder and dirt of Irish ways, the ugliness of it all'. Hopkins was acutely sensitive to surroundings, to the environment and the squalor seeped into his soul. There was inadequate public draining, resulting in numerous diseases and this was clearly a

* The 1992 Annual Lecture of the Gerard Manley Hopkins Society, delivered at St Asaph

cause of the typhoid which killed him. For the college in which he lived was poor, uncomfortable and had no decent sanitation.

Secondly, there was the burden of a vast, inhuman amount of marking to do. Every year he had to set papers and then mark between 1,300 and 1,800 scripts. Even for someone who flicked through exam papers this would be a gigantic task. But Hopkins was not only intellectually finely tuned, he was hyper-conscientious. People told of seeing him in the middle of the night with a towel round his head. His letters are full of the numbers loaded on him. But it wasn't just the numbers. It was that, as a highly creative mind, he saw no value in this kind of learning. Someone once defined a lecture as that which passes from the notes of the lecturer to the notes of the student without passing through the mind of either. That was not Hopkin's method of lecturing and his students derided him because it wasn't, but it was what the system expected and threw up in exam papers. It was, wrote Hopkins, 'great, very great drudgery'.[4]

Not surprisingly, Hopkins was not a successful teacher. His classes erupted in uproar. His fellow Jesuits found him a little odd, eccentric. Not surprisngly, the surroundings, the burden of work, the lack of satisfaction in his teaching brought about a succession of minor illnesses which aggravated his general debilitated condition. He had trouble with his eyes and numerous other physical complaints. Yet none of this gets to the heart of his unhappiness, which I will consider in more detail when I come to the poems. Nevertheless, this oppressive scene needs to be balanced. It was not the whole picture.

Hopkins may have seemed odd but he was kindly treated by his Jesuit brethren. Beginning with Robert Bridges there has been an attempt to blame the Jesuits for Hopkins's troubles. In fact, as Martin writes: 'The society seems to have done all it could to take care of him, short of giving him permanent sick leave, which would obviously have been of little help.'[5] Amongst the Jesuits in Dublin was a particular friend, Robert Curtis, about whom Hopkins wrote: 'He is my comfort beyond what I can say and a kind of Godsend I never expected to have.'[6] Hopkins went on delightful holidays, sometimes in the company of this Robert Curtis. They shared a passion for walking and swimming and like Hopkins Curtis was clever and well-read.

Then, although his brethren had not the remotest undrstanding of the calibre of Hopkins's mind and spirit, and on occasion laughed at him, they were not entirely unappreciative. When R.W. Dixon went to Dublin four years after Hopkins's death, he found that one of the priests who had known him well 'had a great opinion of Gerard, without, I think, knowing of his genius. He spoke of him as a most delightful companion, and as excellent in his calling, and so on . . .'[7] In one of the Sonnets of Desolation Hopkins emphasizes that he is a stranger, cut off from his family by religion, from England by its lack of appreciation of his creative thought and from Ireland by both his Englishness and his political views: 'Now I am at a third remove', he writes. But we need to give full force to the line that continues, 'Not but in all removes I can / kind love both give and get.'[8]

In his letters he does from time to time unburden himself and give us a glimpse of the inner strain. But this is in part what letters to friends are for. And those same letters show the most amazing interest in life, in all its aspects. They are full of judgements about poetry and poets, about painting, etymology and science. There are cheerful letters to his family. In particular, there is a growing enthusiasm for the details of musical composition. Not long before he died he had said, almost in passing, in a letter to Bridges: 'I am ill today, but no matter for that as my spirits are good.'[9] When Hopkins's father went to Dublin after his death he 'found golden opinions on all sides and devoted friends'[10], as he wrote in a letter to one of Gerard's school friends. The fond wish of a father of course, but still to be taken into account.

That is, at it were, the setting provided by his letters and the evidence of others. We now need to look in more detail at the poetry. I will take it in the order as set out in the edition of the poems by Gardiner and Mackenzie and as usually accepted.

On 17 May 1885 Hopkins wrote to Bridges: 'I have after a long silence written two sonnets, which I am touching: if ever anything was written in blood one of these was.'[11] On 1 September 1885 he wrote to Bridges: 'I shall shortly have some sonnets to send you, five or more. Four of these came like inspirations unbidden and against my will.'[12]

'Carrion Comfort' has been taken as evidence that Hopkins comtemplated suicide. Perhaps he did. What is quite clear, however, is that he firmly rejected this course, as well as the despair which gave rise to the thought:

Not, I'll not, carrion comfort, Despair, not feast on thee;
Not untwist—slack they may be—these last strands of man
In me or, most weary, cry *I can no more*. I can;
Can something, hope, wish day come, not choose not to be.[13]

Hopkins asserts that however oppressed he feels by melancholy he can still 'not choose not to be'. By use of the double negative he indicates both the extent of the depression and the firmly disciplined, affirmative will to choose life. It brings to mind Paul Tillich's *The Courage to Be* where he writes that 'even in the despair about meaning being affirms itself through us. The act of accepting meaninglessness is in itself a meaningful act. It is an act of faith.'[14] Hopkins is more positive and less paradoxical but what both have in common is the discovery of meaning in the depths of depression. Camus once wrote that the major problem of life was suicide, by which he meant whether or not we should commit the act. Some of the contemporaries of Hopkins appear to have thought the same. On 24 April, 1885 Hopkins had written to a friend of his, Baillie, mentioning two of his Oxford friends who had recently committed suicide: 'Three of my imtimate friends at Oxford have just drowned themselves, a good many more of my acquaintances and contemporaries have died by their own hands in other ways. It must be, and the fact brings it home to me, a dreadful feature of our days.'[15] It is against that background that we can see the strength and force of Hopkins's deliberate 'not choose not to be'.

He goes on in 'Carrion Comfort' to write of the apparent terror of God, his lion-like limbs and his tempest. Hopkins wonders why God should be like this to him. The obvious answer is that it is a kind of winnowing: 'That my chaff might fly; my grain lie, sheer and clear.' Rather surprisingly, the poem goes on beyond that answer. It is that in all his turmoil and travail his heart 'lapped strength, stole joy, would laugh, cheer'. There seems an echo here of Psalm 84.5–7, which in the Book of Common Prayer version reads:

> Blessed is the man whose strength is in Thee: in whose heart are thy ways.
> Who going through the vale of misery use it for a well: and the pools are filled with water.
> They will go from strength to strength:

Yet again, however, Hopkins moves on in a surprising way. Who should we cheer? God who flung him down or Hopkins himself who fought God? There is no pious resignation here. This is an extraordinarily modern note, with its sense of the dignity of the human struggle, even in its rebellion against fate and God. This willingness to argue with God recurs later in

> Thou art indeed just, Lord, if I contend
> with Thee; but, sir, so what I plead is just.[16]

Such boldness to have it out with God is there in the Hebrew Scriptures in Abraham, in Job and in the developed Jewish tradition. It has come to be a commonplace of Christian spirituality in the last two decades. But it is freshly modern in Hopkins. 'Carrion Comfort' ends: 'Of now done darkness I wretch lay wrestling with (my God!) my God.' The image is derived from Jacob's wrestling all night with God recorded in Genesis. The 'my God!' in brackets is particularly fine. It expresses astonishment that it is God with whom he is wrestling, and also religious acknowledgement, as in Thomas's 'My Lord and my God'.

To say that this poem has its origin in the temptation to despair, says nothing. It is an extraordinarily fine exploration that takes us surprising step after surprising step, each one revealing the dignity and strength of the subject.

'Carrion Comfort' contains a reference to 'that year of now done darkness'. It refers to a darkness in the past and could, therefore, as some have argued, be placed after the other poems. The next poem, however, takes us to the heart of the whirlwind.

> No worst, there is none. Pitched past pitch of grief,
> More pangs will, schooled at forepangs, wilder wring
> Comforter, where, where is your comforting?[17]

It contains the famous lines:

> O the mind, mind has mountains; cliffs of fall
> Frightful, sheer, no-man-fathomed. Hold them cheap
> May who ne'er hung there.

The first line, 'No worst, there is none' could have come straight from Samuel Beckett. We feel the pain of Hopkins in almost every line. Robert Martin writes that the poem 'advances the argument until he has to acknowledge that only the destruction of the individual can save him from self torment' [18] But this is not the full truth of the last two lines. Hopkins writes:

> Here! Creep,
> Wretch, under a comfort serves in a whirlwind: all
> Life does end and each day dies with sleep.

Hopkins, like Lear, to whom scholars have found a number of references in this poem, stands in a great storm. But the poem is less about self-destruction than it is about survival. Mountaineers in bad weather put up a tent or creep under a rock. Hopkins sees sleep, the foretaste of a greater sleep, as a way of surviving the storm of self-torment and destruction. It is true that sleep in such circumstances is a blessed relief. But it is also a way of hanging on, of surviving until another day when things might be better. It is the technique of a person who knows what they can and what they cannot manage: 'Nor does long our small / Durance deal with that steep or deep', and who chooses the only possible way of surviving.

The next poem begins:

> To seem the stranger lies my lot, my life
> Among the strangers.[19]

Hopkins feels removed from his parents by religion, from England because they have not appreciated his creative thought and from Ireland where he is an Englishman whose views do not chime with either side. Hopkins refers to England as the wife of his creating thought. On this Martin comments:

> Inevitably, the word 'wife' stands out for the reader, and it becomes clear that this is in part a poem about human relations as well as divine, and that Hopkins has drawn his metaphors from his deep absorption with his own loneliness when those nearest to him were otherwise engaged.[20]

The charge that Hopkins is absorbed in his own loneliness will be considered later. The reader does of course notice the reference to 'wife' but the suggestion that the force of the poem lies in the experience of loneliness hardly does justice to its climax. Although Hopkins is cut off from other people in so many ways he can in all situations 'kind love both give and get'. The conclusion reads: 'Only what word

> Wisest my heart breeds dark heaven's baffling ban
> Bars or hells spell thwarts. This to hoard unheard,
> Heard unheeded, leaves me a lonely began.

The deepest source of his frustration and anguish is his failure to be published and the lack of recognition of his creative writing. As is well known he could not get 'The Wreck of the Deutschland' published. His most discriminating friends, Bridges and R.W. Dixon, could not understand some of the poetry that meant most to him. Even the scholarly articles he wrote as Professor of Greek could not find an outlet. His political views were unheeded.

Although Hopkins renounced the writing of poetry when he became a Jesuit and started writing again almost by accident, it is clear that after his religious faith the creative side of his nature, expressed especially in his poetry, meant more to him than anything else in his life. His letters are full of discussions of poetry and music, with perceptive judgements about other poets. As a Jesuit he had renounced worldly fame for himself, as the famous prayer of St Ignatius puts it: 'Teach us, good Lord, to labour and not to ask for any reward, save that of knowing that we do thy will.' Nevertheless, he recognized the need for others to have public recognition. He wrote to Robert Bridges in surprisingly forthright terms:

> By the bye, I say it deliberately and before God, I would have you and Canon Dixon and all true poets remember that fame, the being known, though in itself one of the most dangerous things to man, is nevertheless the true and appointed heir, element, and setting of genius and its works. (The manuscript originally read 'necessary' rather than 'true').[21]

He goes on to say that although art and fame might not matter spiritually in the ordinary way of events Christ's words about virtue apply to the work of artists of all kinds: ' "Let your light shine before men that they may see your good works (say, of art) and glorify your Father in heaven." (That is, acknowledge that they have an absolute excellence in them and are steps in the scale of infinite and inexhaustible excellence).'

That is a high doctrine of art and its recognition. One he had renounced for himself but which he saw as, if not absolutely necessary, nevertheless the true medium for poets. As a Jesuit Hopkins followed the path of self denial, even to the point of refusing to write poetry for much of his time as a religious; but it is clear that is where his emotions were still invested. His wisest words were hoarded 'unheard' or if they were heard they were 'unheeded'. This above all is his anguish.

The poem beginning 'I wake and feel the fell of dark, not day', is the most terrible of the terrible sonnets. There is no glimmer of light.

> I am gall, I am heartburn. God's most deep decree
> Bitter would have me taste: my taste was me;
> Bones built in me, flesh filled, blood brimmed the curse.
>
> Selfyeast of spirit a dull dough sours. I see
> The lost are like this, and their scourge to be
> As I am mine, their sweating selves; but worse.[22]

There is here a sense of self-disgust: 'their sweating selves'. But the particular poignancy and anguish of this for Hopkins is that he, more than anyone, had valued the self and his sense of self. As a result of the influence of Duns Scotus at Oxford he had come to exult in the individual and the particular, especially the individual self. Everything in nature does its own thing, as people used to say, and this includes us:

> Each mortal thing does one thing and the same:
> Deals out that being indoors each one dwells;
> Selves-goes itself; *myself* it speaks and spells,
> Crying *what I do is me: for that I came.*[23]

What he writes in this poem is of one piece with his meditation on the *Spiritual Exercises* of St Ignatius Loyola. Here he follows through the argument from creation to creator but in a highly distinctive way. He is less concerned with creation in its generality than with the individual. It is because each individual is so uniquely unique that we look for that which is even more uniquely unique, God, as the only possible source and cause. Hopkins writes:

> When I consider my selfbeing, my consciousness and feeling of myself, that taste of myself, of I and *me* above and in all things, which is more distinctive than the taste of ale or alum, more distinctive than the smell of walnutleaf or camphor . . . nothing else in nature comes near this unspeakable stress of pitch, distinctiveness and selving, this selfbeing of my own.[24]

It is against the background of this intense sense of self, not we might note in a selfish or self-absorbed way but as a heightened awareness of what it is to be us and no one else that we must see the horror of this poem. Hopkins, so conscious of the dinstinctiveness of his self, tastes only bitterness, sourness, sweating anguish. This is indeed hell. 'The lost are like this.'

'Patience, hard thing!'[25] begins the next poem. But the word 'patience' is related to the Latin root *patior*, meaning I suffer. Therefore to pray for patience is to pray for war and wounds. Patience is also the name of a rare dock leaf. Rare patience roots in a particularly harsh soil: deprivation and setbacks. Here also ivy grows:

> Natural heart's ivy, Patience masks
> Our ruins of wrecked past purpose. There she basks
> Purple eyes and seas of liquid leaves all day.

This image has been much admired. The ivy basking in the sun forms a kind of ocean through which we can see the wreck. Some commentators have concentrated on the fact that ivy is poisonous.

But ivy is a traditional Christian symbol of everlasting life. Furthermore, although the beauty of ivy can have a certain menace about it, the purple berries and leaves shining in the sun have a rich and strange beauty about them, as Munch depicted so well in one of his pictures.

Beneath the ocean we can hear the timbers of the wreck: 'Our hearts grate on themselves'. Nevertheless, although we rebel against this, that same rebellious will bids God to bend us to him even so. No one can fail to discern the pain and the sternness in these images.

> And where he is who more and more distils
> Delicious kindness?—He is patient. Patience fills
> His crisp combs, and that comes those ways we know.

The reference is to honeycombs and distilling, that is, pressing the honey out of them. Out of this hard won patience comes delicious kindness. For God himself is patient and he it is who fills these honeycombs with his peace and presence. Hopkins knew this from the lives of the saints and in his own experience: 'That comes those ways we know.' St Ignatius in his *Spiritual Exercises* had written: 'Let him who is in desolation strive to remain in patience, a virtue contrary to the troubles which harrass him; and let him think that he will shortly be consoled.'[26] There may not be much sign in the poem that Hopkins himself had yet experienced the consolations of patience. Nevertheless, as Norman Mackenzie has rightly pointed out, this poem represents an advance upon the blackest of the other dark sonnets because instead of concentrating on the blackness of the way it focuses forward on the route along which in God's good time the ability to surmount frustrations will come.

In July 1886 Hopkins had written to Richard Dixon to console him for not being elected to the Chair of Poetry at Oxford. He points out: 'that life is short and we are lucky to get even a short spell. The lives of the great conquerors were cut short. Above all, Christ our Lord: his career was cut short.'[27] Robert Martin comments on this letter that Hopkins 'was beginning to console himself with that most dangerous of comforts, that it is better to fail than to win, and for his example he chose Christ'.[28] This may be the most dangerous of doctrines. Nevertheless, it is worth considering the paragraph in full. What Hopkins wrote was:

> Above all Christ our Lord: his career was cut short and, whereas he would have wished to succeed by success—for it is insane to lay yourself out for failure, prudence is the first of the cardinal

virtues, and he was the most prudent of men—nevertheless, he was doomed to succeed by failure; his plans were baffled, his hopes dashed, and his work was done by being broken off undone. However much he understood all this he found it an intolerable grief to submit to it. He left the example: it is very strengthening, but except in that sense it is not consoling.

It is crystal clear from this paragraph that Hopkins was fully aware of the dangers of invoking failure and that it should not be sought for its own sake. Christ would have wished to succeed by success—it is insane to lay yourself out for failure. He was a prudent person and prudence goes for success. Being human he found it an intolerable grief to submit to failure. Nor is there any false consolation in this doctrine. It is strengthening but that is all. The sanity and balance of this paragraph stand in startling contrast to the judgements of some recent commentators on Hopkins with their continual harping on his disappointment and sadness. Hopkins felt all the anguish of his wrecked past purposes. But as a Christian and a Jesuit he persevered in the way of patience, knowing God is patient and experiencing at least something of the consolation that comes from the way of obedience.

Psalm 19 would have been well-known to him. It refers to the statutes of the Lord in words echoed in the poem that begins: 'Patience, hard thing!': 'More to be desired are they than gold, yea, than much fine gold: sweeter also than honey and the honeycomb.'

The next poem continues, however gradually, the emergence from the darkest dark. It adopts the tone of a kindly confessor and counsellor:

> My own heart let me have more pity on: let
> me live to my sad self hereafter kind.[29]

Hopkins had once described a friend as a 'self-tormentor'. It was this to which he himself was prone. He brought into his Roman Catholicism all the self scrutinizing rectitude of high Victorian Anglo-Catholicism. This self-tormenting left him like a blind man in a dark dungeon or all thirst in a world of wet; desperate, longing and helpless. It is not only the tone of this poem, full of pity, that is striking. It is the movement from addressing the heart in the third person in the first verse: 'My own heart let me have more pity on', to the identification with the suffering in the second verse: 'I cast for comfort I can no more get', on to the third verse in which he addresses the soul directly:

Soul, self; come, pour Jackself, I do advise
You, jaded, let be; call off thoughts awhile
Elsewhere; leave comfort root-room;

The message he gives his sad self is one basic to life, let alone the
Christian life. If we strive too hard for a particular experience we
are likely to lose it. If we let go and trust the unexpected then
surprising blessing can come. Only God knows the time and the
size of this joy. But it is like the smile of the sky that we see between
mountains sometimes which 'lights a lovely mile', as Hopkins put
it.

Hopkins wrote a few more poems before he died in 1889. 'Tom's
Garland', in which he enters into the despair and rage of the
unemployed; 'Harry Ploughman'; 'Epithalamion', which is full of
sensuous delight in nature and male bathing but which fails to
finish its stated theme of seeing this as an image of married love; a
rather bitter one in which he gets his moods in perspective by
seeing the distorted reflection of his face in a spoon; a poem of
apology and explanation to Robert Bridges; and three others that I
will discuss.

First, the poem he was asked to write in honour of St Alphonsus
Rodriguez, a labourer of the Society of Jesus in Majorca. Over the
years Christian theologians have discussed whether Christian
martyrdom or the inner spiritual struggle is more valiant.
Alphonsus Rodriguez underwent the latter. A lay brother who
lived from 1533 to 1617 in Majorca and who for forty years was the
hall porter of the Jesuit College in Palma, he yet underwent
fearsome spiritual travail. Outwardly his life seemed so serene on
this beautiful and temperate island. But his spiritual writings,
which would have been known to Hopkins, relate fierce struggles.
In 1888 Alphonsus Rodriguez was canonized and for the celebra-
tion of his first feast day on 30 October Jesuits in other provinces
were asked to send tributes. It was this that evoked the poem by
Hopkins. It begins by recognizing the honour that is flashed off
exploit, whether of soldiers in battle or of martyrs. But the inner
struggle is no less heroic. For God's struggle with creation, though
hidden, ends triumphant. The forty years that Alphonsus
Rodriguez spent as a door-keeper were not wasted:

But be the war within, the brand we wield
Unseen, the heroic breast not outward-steeled,
Earth hears no hurtle then from fiercest fray.
Yet God (that hews mountain and continent,
Earth, all, out; who, with trickling increment,

69

> Veins violets and tall trees makes more and more)
> Could crowd career with conquest while there went
> Those years and years by of world without event
> That in Majorca Alfonso watched the door.[30]

It is a poem which reflects Hopkins himself fully committed to the path of inner discipleship, and to a scale of Christian values which could reveal this inner discipline as triumphant though hidden. I like the way that the poem leaves the readers, as does Edward Thomas's 'Addlestrop', at once focused and lingering, highly particular, and yet opening up to the eternal:

> Those years and years by of world without event
> That in Majorca Alfonso watched the door.

The complaint that good people suffer whilst the wicked prosper is one often heard in the Bible, particularly in the psalms. Hopkins takes words from Jeremiah 12.1 to make one of his finest poems:

> Thou art indeed just, Lord, if I contend
> With thee; but, sir, so what I plead is just.
> Why do sinners' ways prosper? And why must
> Disappointment all I endeavour end?[31]

He goes on to contrast nature blossoming all around him with his own barren state:

> Birds build—but not I build; no, but strain
> Time's eunuch, and not breed one work that wakes.
> Mine, O thou Lord of life, send my roots rain.

The sense that from a creative point of view he was producing nothing worthwhile expressed in the image of being a eunuch is one which recurs in Hopkins. Modern critics have made much of it. He first used it as an undergraduate, lamenting the unfruitfulness of his life without Dolben. On 1 September 1885 he wrote to Robert Bridges that it wasn't so much the thought that none of his work would see the light of day that really depressed him but the failure of his creative spirit: 'If I could but produce work I should not mind its being buried, silenced, and going no further; but it kills me to be time's eunuch and never to beget.'[32] Again: 'All impulse fails me: I can give myself no sufficient reason for going on. Nothing comes: I am a eunuch – but it is for the Kingdom of Heaven's sake.' Robert Martin emphasizes the use of sexual metaphor to describe the barren state of his soul.[33] But sexual metaphor, we might remark, is used throughout the Bible. What is more remarkable than the image is the fact that though Hopkins felt totally uncreative he was in fact producing some of his finest works. It is ironic that one of his most enduring poems would be based on the conviction that no work of his would ever endure.

This brings us to the heart of the divine paradox, the divine irony of Hopkins. For in 1918, nearly thirty years after his death, Robert Bridges published a collection of Hopkins's verse. Poets were impressed and began to be influenced. Critics soon held him as one of the greatest of modern poets, quickly given his place in the great tradition. The source of his deepest frustration and unhappiness is the sphere of his lasting fame. Earlier he had complained of heaven's baffling ban which had kept his creative words bursting inside him: 'This to hoard unheard, heard unheeded, leaves me a lonely began.' But his words have been both heard and heeded. Many years before Hopkins had written so lightly:

> Shape nothing, lips; be lovely-dumb:
> It is the shut, the curfew sent
> From there where all surrenders come
> Which only makes you eloquent.[34]

He had lived out that life of surrender, that lack of publication, that lack of recognition, that lack of understanding. But from that surrender there came an eloquence that has enthralled the world. It would not, we think, have surprised Hopkins totally, though he would not have claimed fame for himself. But it was the heart of his faith that a life of obedience, a life surrendered trustingly to God would, in God's time, in time or out of time, bring forth God's fruit.

The final poem that I want to consider is 'That Nature is a Heraclitean Fire and of the Comfort of the Resurrection'. The first part is taken up with a wonderful evocation of the movement and vitality of nature, the clouds moving in the sky, the light filtering through the trees, the wind blowing everything about and drying up the mud. This sense of the aliveness of nature is like Van Gogh's landscapes. But this continuous movement is not straight description. It is also an image of nature as a great bonfire. Ancient philosophers speculated about the composition of the basic elements of nature. Heraclitus, one of the pre-Socratic philosophers thought that the substrate or underlying matter of the universe was fire. Everything was fire in a constant state of change. He alludes to a constant change of state occurring in the elements, a downward movement causing fire to transmute into sea, which in turn condenses into earth; and an upward return movement which the earth rarifies into water and that again separates out into clouds of moisture and the fire of which even the sun and the stars are made. Hopkins depicts the upward cycle in nature. Sun, fire and the wind are drying the storm-flooded ground. In contrast to this upward movement, however, stands man, a spark in this bonfire destined for a tiny glow before going out: 'Man, how fast his firedint, his mark on mind, is gone!' Then Hopkins brings Paul's view of the resurrection into the picture: 'Behold, I show you a mystery: we shall not all sleep, but we shall all be changed, in a moment, in a twinkling of an eye . . . For this corruptible must put on incorruption and this mortal must put on immortality.' (1 Cor. 15.51–53):

Man, how fast his firedint, his mark on mind, is gone!
Both are in an unfathomable, all is in an enormous dark
Drowned. O pity and indignation! Manshape, that shone
Sheer off, disseveral, a star, death blots black out; nor mark
      Is any of him at all so stark
But vastness blurs and time beats level. Enough! the Resurrection,
A heart's-clarion! Away grief's gasping, joyless days, dejection.
      Across my foundering deck shone
A beacon, an eternal beam. Flesh fade, and mortal trash
Fall to the residuary worm; world's wildfire, leave but ash:
      In a flash, at a trumpet crash,
I am all at once what Christ is, since he was what I am, and
This Jack, joke, poor potsherd, patch, matchwood, immortal
    diamond,
      Is immortal diamond.[25]

Human beings can be described from different points of view. We are a jack of all works, a bad joke, a piece of broken pottery, an ill-matched piece of cloth (or in Elizabethan parlance a fool), a jagged fragment of splintered wood. Yet we also have or are divine soul, immortal diamond, which is revealed after the fire in all its glorious beauty.

'Jack' is a word that Hopkins used a number of times to describe human beings. He had no illusions or pretensions about what, considered from many angles, we are. But he was also conscious of his unique individuality known to himself and known to God. He had once written a lovely hymn:

      Thee, God, I come from, to Thee go,
      all day long I like fountain flow
      From thy hand out, swayed about
      Mote-like in thy mighty glow.[36]

The poem on the resurrection, written in Dublin in 1888, shows no diminution in Hopkins's powers as a poet. His sense of nature, his capacity to intertwine fresh imagery with profound reflection is at its height. His faith is full blooded and expectant. Nor does this poem lend itself to the criticism of a Freud or a Marx that it is looking for an illusionary compensation in another world. It is this world that is celebrated, human beings here and now that are affirmed, but human beings properly understood as unique selves or souls with the capacity to become like Christ. One cannot help noticing that Robert Martin's biography with its emphasis on Hopkins's loneliness, repressed homosexuality and unhappiness does not even refer to this poem. Yet the consensus of critical judgement is that it is one of his finest creations.

I stress that I do not in any way underestimate the periods of anguish in the last years of Hopkins. My point is that we need to see this in the perspective of his consciously accepted discipline as a Christian and a Jesuit. From this point of view the sonnets, though terrible indeed, betray a mind that is totally sane and faithful. When biographers and critics ignore this dimension they are inclined continuously to misinterpret, to get him wrong, as Eric Griffiths showed in such a masterful way in his review of Martin's biography.[37] Griffiths argues that Hopkins was not being evasive, as though he had something shameful to hide. On the contrary, he was conscious that his life was hid with Christ in God, as Paul put it. Hopkins wrote to Robert Bridges on religion: 'It is long since such things had any significance for you. But what is strange and unpleasant is that you sometimes speak as if they had in reality none for me . . .'[38]. Eric Griffiths comments, 'He may say the same to his biographer'.

'Away grief's gasping, joyless days, dejection.' We may wish that Hopkins had experienced more human happiness: but that he knew Christian joy I have no doubt; a foretaste of that revealing of the immortal diamond, which was his own unique, suffering, struggling, amazingly creative self.

SEVEN

The resurrection in some modern novels*

In Iris Murdoch's novel *The Good Apprentice* one of the characters is asked his view of Christ. He replies:

> I have to think of him in a certain way, not resurrected, as it were mistaken, disappointed—well, who knows what he thought. He has to mean pure affliction, utter loss, innocent suffering, pointless suffering, the deep and awful and irremediable things that happen to people.[1]

This view, which reflects Iris Murdoch's own position in her philosophical essay *The Sovereignty of Good*[2] and which is derived from a particular reading of Simone Weil, presents a moral challenge to theologians that is too little considered. It may be put in this way. How can the resurrection of Christ be so affirmed that it can be clearly seen to be *morally* congruous with our deepest feelings about suffering? Like the character in Iris Murdoch's novel, most people can see the moral appeal of a Christ who shares in the worst affliction of humankind. But how can his triumph over suffering be presented in a way that is sensitive to people experiencing 'the deep and awful and irremediable things'? Or so that it does not take away from the profound effect of a Christ who shares our bitter anguish? I suspect that underlying many of the radical interpretations of the resurrection of Christ there lies this question. For if the resurrection is understood simply as a matter of 'seeing' the suffering love of the cross to be triumphant, this has great moral appeal.[3] The affliction, Christ's and ours, is in no way diminished. It is simply understood in a different way, as a moral victory. The problem is how to state a more traditional view of the resurrection in such a way that it can be assented to on moral grounds (as well as historical ones) and which does not come across as a happy ending brought about by a *Deus ex machina*. Historical questions cannot be ignored and they must be answered honestly. But too often unrecognized assumptions and presuppositions push the scholar in a particular direction. There are

* From 'If Christ be not risen . . .', edited by Elizabeth Russell and John Greenhalgh (St Mary's, Bourne Street 1986)

assumptions about what is or is not possible. There are also assumptions about what is morally of a piece with our deepest insights about human suffering. It is best if these assumptions are taken out and examined. In particular it is important to see whether a traditional view of the resurrection can be stated in a way that is morally sensitive. If this is so, then there may be less unconscious pressure to look to a radical interpretation. It is therefore worth looking at the work of some novelists who have incorporated the resurrection into their work, to see how they have considered the matter. There is a particular kind of moral sensibility that makes for a great novelist, an imaginative sympathy, a sensitivity to the most delicate nuances of human feeling. At the least we can say that if a good novelist cannot write about the resurrection in such a way that carries moral conviction, no one can.

There is also another problem. The Gospels depict a risen Christ able to come and go as he wills. He is not simply a resuscitated corpse like Lazarus but nor on the other hand is he only a vision in the minds of his followers. Depicting this on the stage is obviously difficult; the imaginative novelist, however, is not limited by physical retraints. In the popular stage production *Godspell* Jesus was depicted as a clown. In contrast to the philosophers of the world with their portentous sayings and ponderous ways Jesus was all light and laughter. After his death the audience was invited onto the stage and the bread of the last supper was shared round. All partook and the singing and clapping went on. This was a neat way of meeting two difficulties. There was no physical resurrection to be shown. The resurrection was the spirit of Jesus living again in the audience as they took the bread and were caught up in his *élan* and *joie de vivre*. Presenting the resurrection in this way also solved the problem of how to make the resurrection morally congruous with the cruci-fixion. Life, death and resurrection were of a piece, in the same style. But suppose we wish to depict, like the Gospel writers, a raised and glorified body? And suppose we wish to do this without in any way cheapening the reality of Christ's affliction or ours? One way would be to look to the novelists. Encouragingly, and perhaps somewhat surprisingly, a number of major modern novelists have, in their various ways, dealt with these questions. I propose to consider three themes. First, the conviction of a redemptive power at work in the world; a power intimately connected with the historical Jesus. Second, the belief that this power is released into the world by a Christ-like death and third,

75

an exploration of how this redemptive power is related to an author's whole understanding of human life.

First, the conviction of a redemptive power at work in the world, a power intimately connected with the historical Jesus. I begin with Tolstoy's novel called *Resurrection* whose publication in serial form began in 1899. The plot can be simply told. A young aristocrat Nekhlúdoff seduces a peasant girl, Katisha Máslova. As a result she conceives, is thrown out of her employment and becomes a prostitute. Then, as a result of a false charge being brought against her, she is put into prison. There, some years after the seduction, Nekhlúdoff sees and recognizes her. He is overcome with remorse, tries to obtain her release and fails. When she is sentenced he follows her to Siberia. The book is a massive indictment of Russian society at the time, particularly its judiciary and prison service. It is also about Nekhlúdoff's and Máslova's rebirth to a different kind of life. Inevitably the understanding of this life reflects Tolstoy's personal and social preoccupations. There is a strong contrast between the flesh and the spirit, in an un-Pauline sense, so that resurrection means overcoming sexual desire, regarded as evil. More centrally it meant that men should always acknowledge that they were sinning and, as a result of this, should refuse to condemn anyone else. Criminals should not be sentenced but forgiven and released. At the end of the novel Nekhlúdoff is given a New Testament. He reads it all through the night, and he is overcome with the thought that the Sermon on the Mount could be literally put into practice:

> He did not sleep all night, and as it happens to many and many a man who reads the Gospels, he understood for the first time the full meaning of the words read so often before but passed by unnoticed. He drank in all these necessary, important, and joyful revelations as a sponge imbibes water . . . The Master's will is expressed in these commandments. If men will only fulfil these laws the kingdom of heaven will be established on earth, and men will receive the greatest good that they can attain.
>
> 'And so here it is, the business of my life. Scarcely have I finished one, and another has commenced'. And a perfectly new life dawned that night for Nekhlúdoff, not because he had entered into new conditions of life, but because everything he did after that night had a new and quite different significance.[4]

I begin with Tolstoy's *Resurrection* primarily because it provides a contrast with a better, profounder novel written earlier by Dostoevsky. Dostoevsky's *Crime and Punishment* whose first instalments appeared in 1866, and on some of whose themes one suspects that Tolstoy drew, brings out rather better than Tolstoy's novel the idea of a redemptive *power* at work.

Raskolnikov, the main character in *Crime and Punishment* is a strange perverse creature who longs to be a Napoleon figure, beyond good and evil. For no reason at all he murders two old ladies. Eventually his feelings of guilt lead him to admit the crime but not before he has met Sonia, who befriends him. The turning point for Raskolnikov is when Sonia reads to him the story of the raising of Lazarus. Then, in Siberia, where Sonia has followed him, he too reads the New Testament, indeed it was the same copy in which Sonia had read to him the story of the raising of Lazarus, and he wonders if her convictions can be his. The novel ends suggesting that as a result of this posibility there is a new story ahead, 'the story of the gradual regeneration of a man, the story of his gradual passing from one world to another, of his acquaintance with a new and hitherto unknown reality'.[5]

There are two immediate contrasts to be made with Tolstoy's treatment of the same theme. First, there is more emphasis in Dostoevsky on the existence of a transcendent order into which Raskolnikov has been reborn. Secondly, his regeneration is brought about not only by the New Testament but by the power of Christian love working through Sonia. Sonia has been reduced to prostitution by the poverty of her family. But, in all her degradation and humiliation, she is kept going by her faith. It is the risen Christ working through her faith, her love and her prayers, that is the main instrument of Raskolnikov's regeneration. The main contrast, however, that I want to draw attention to is the fact that in Tolstoy's *Resurrection* it is obedience to the tenets of the Sermon on the Mount that is decisive, in *Crime and Punishment* it is resurrection grace and power breaking through the Lazarus story that is crucial. The whole scene is most tense and dramatic, though there is only space to quote a few words. Raskolnikov is urging her to read:

> 'Come on, read! I want you to!' he insisted. 'You used to read to Lisaveta, didn't you?'
>
> Sonia opened the book and found the place. Her hands trembled, her voice failed her. Twice she tried to read without being able to utter the first syllable.
>
> ' "Now a certain man was sick, named Lazarus, of Bethany..." '

she forced herself to say at last, but, suddenly, at the third word her voice rang and snapped like a string that had been screwed up too tightly.[6]

Raskolnikov knew that in reading Sonia was exposing her very heart, what was deepest and most precious for her: 'But at the same time he knew now, and he knew it for certain, that, though she might feel upset and worried . . . she herself was most anxious to read to *him*, and to him alone, and to make sure that he *heard*, heard it *now*.'

Eventually Sonia manages to continue reading:

' "Jesus said unto her, *I am the resurrection and the life*; he that believeth in me, though he were dead, yet shall he live: and whosoever liveth and believeth in me shall never die. Believest thou this? She saith unto him" ' (and as though drawing her breath painfully Sonia read slowly and distinctly the verse to the end, as though she were herself making a public confession of her faith): ' "Yea, Lord, I believe that thou art the Christ, the Son of God, which should come into the world." '

What is central to this novel is Christ as the resurrection and the life, working through the faith of Sonia, to raise Raskolnikov to new life.

In the end we cannot separate the moral claim of the gospel and the grace of the gospel. To know divine love is to know what love asks of us and to know what love asks of us is to know that it is love that asks. Furthermore, when the Church has averted its eyes so much from the claims of the Sermon on the Mount, it is right that prophetic figures like Tolstoy should direct us to them. But Dostoevsky's emphasis is truer both to life and the Christian life than that of Tolstoy. This may be reflected in the fact that Tolstoy himself was caught up in the most tragic and appalling contradictions and hypocrisies, whereas Dostoevsky achieved near sainthood. It may also be reflected in the fact that *Resurrection* is a much less satisfactory novel, with the Christian message tacked on at the end with little relationship to the story that had gone before. By contrast *Crime and Punishment* is a unity and its resurrection theme integral to the whole. In this novel the resurrection power of Christ, working through the faith and love of Sonia and communicated through the gospel story as she reads it, is the prior and fundamental reality. It is this resurrection power that makes it possible for Raskolnikov to discover and live in a new reality and begin to meet the ethical claims of that reality.

It is no accident that this emphasis on the resurrection power of Christ should be there in a Russian novel. For the resurrection is a present living reality for Orthodox thought in a way that it has never quite been for the Western Church. In the Western Church the stress has been on the death of Christ as the means of our redemption: in the Orthodox Church it is on the resurrection. I turn now to two more recent novels where the theme of resurrection is apparent, Patrick White's *Riders in the Chariot* and William Golding's *Darkness Visible*. Both are difficult novels, dense if not obscure in places. But in both there is a redemptive power let loose in the world as a result of a Christ-like death.

Riders in the Chariot is set in Australia. The climax of the novel comes when Himmelfarb, a Jewish refugee from Germany, is strung up in a mock crucifixion. The main theme of the book is the indivisibility of evil in the killing of Christ, Nazi Germany and Australian suburbia. Shortly after the mock crucifixion Himmelfarb dies. But his death is not the end. Strange things happen. But what things? Two ladies talking together after the events are at pains to emphasize there was no miracle: 'Only, there was no miracle. Definitely no miracle!'[7] Mrs Colquhoun was almost shouting. And there was indeed no miracle in the world of public events; or not that the readers can discern. But as a result of the death something happens to each of the four main characters. Each of the four has, throughout the novel, a mystic vision derived from the Book of Ezekiel, but for each of them their insight and way of life that ensues from it is very different. Miss Hare, who lives in a large, empty house, has a mystic communion with sticks and stones and animals. Alf Dubbo is a half-aborigine who expresses his faith in paint. Mrs Godbold is a solid, kindhearted washer-woman. Himmelfarb himself is a practising Jew, who may be the expected Messiah. After his death, in which the other three are all involved in an inner, spiritual way, even though some of them are not physically present, they each in their different ways come to personal fulfilment. Alf Dubbo completes his painting then dies of TB. Miss Hare has a mystic vision. Himmelfarb dies at peace. Mrs Godbold, a rock of love, continues to be a rock of love. Towards the end Mrs Godbold goes into church:

> So, at last, the figure of her Lord and Saviour would stand before her in the chancel, looking down at her from beneath the

yellow eyelids, along the strong, but gentle beak of a nose. She was content to leave then since all converged finally upon the Risen Christ, and her own eyes had confirmed that the wounds were healed.

That evening, as she walked along the road, it was the hour at which the other gold sank its furrows in the softer sky. The lids of her eyes, flickering beneath its glow, were gilded with the identical splendour. But, for all its weight, it lay lightly, lifted her, in fact, to where she remained an instant in the company of the living creatures she had known, and many others she had not. All was ratified again by hands.[8]

All the four main characters have a vision of a transcendent, spiritual realm. Each of them is on the edge of ordinary society, despised or disregarded by the pushers and thrusters. Each of them is mystically bound up with the death of Himmelfarb and the events following his death are conscious echoes of the crucifixion story. Another Jew, who has been involved in a kind of betrayal, commits suicide. Mrs Godbold, as she does her washing, remembers the deposition. What distinguishes the four is a failure in wordly terms that opens them up to receive the reality of the spiritual world, a failure brought to a climax at death. Himmelfarb, as he lies dying, thinks of his father, 'Always separate during the illusory life of men now they touched, it seemed, at the point of failure.'[9] Then he thought of his wife and what she stood for and had tried to convey to him: 'It seemed to him as though the mystery of failure might be pierced only by those of extreme simplicity of soul, or else by one who was about to doff the outgrown garment of the body. He was weak enough, certainly, by now to make the attempt which demands the ultimate in strength.'

This mystery of weakness, of failure, which comes to its appointed focus in death, is shared by the four riders in the divine chariot. The death of Himmelfarb, his extreme point of human failure, seems to allow the power of a transcended order to flood into the world and affect the lives of others living as he did, in such a way as to help bring them to their appointed spiritual fulfilment. Indeed for all of them in their different ways the words of Paul are true:

> For his sake I have suffered the loss of all things, and count them as refuse ... that I may know him and the power of his resurrection, and may share his sufferings, becoming like him in his death, that if possible I may attain the resurrection from the dead.[10]

In our mundane way we ask what is the relationship between the death of Himmelfarb and what happens to the other three. The very denseness and difficulty of the writing, particularly in the last few chapters, suggests that there is no mundane answer. The suburban ladies raise the question of miracle but there is no miracle they can see and they are anxious to deny that there has been one. But for those other riders in the chariot, something has certainly happened: happened to them and in them and through them. Miss Hare has a vision of her friend Himmelfarb, 'She stood in the everlasting moment.'[11] Alf Dubbo finishes off his picture of Christ, just before he himself dies: 'Once on emerging from behind the barricades of planes, the curtain of textures, he ventured to retouch the wounds of the dead Christ with the love he had never dared express in life, and at once the blood was gushing from his own mouth, the wounds in the canvas were shining and palpitating with his own conviction.'[12]

Mrs Godbold the rock of love, has her vision, but continues to serve on earth: 'She would lower her eyes to avoid the dazzle, and walk on, breathing heavily, for it was a stiff pull up the hill, to the shed in which she continued to live.'[13]

William Golding's *Darkness Visible* is the most ambitious of his novels and perhaps the most ambitious of all the books here considered. The central character is Matty, who emerges out of a fire in London's blitz most terribly disfigured. In hospital, adults 'hurrying to their own unfortunates, were repelled by the sordid misery in which Matty passed his days, and they flashed sideways at him an uneasy smile which he interpreted with absolute precision.'[14] At school he was terribly teased. At the ironmongers where for a time he had a job: 'He was perpetually employed and never knew that people gave him jobs to get him out of their sight.'[15] Matty's mind is a strange one, scarred as it is by his terrible experience but it formulates a pressing question, 'Who am I?' The question is never answered but Matty comes to reformulate it, 'What am I for?' and to feel that he exists for something. In scenes reminiscent of the wandering of the people of Israel Matty pursues his way before becoming an odd job man in a private school. Then, in a terrorist attack on the school, he is accidentally blown up and killed. Matty seems to become one of the flames in the fire, fire being a key image in the book. The flames of fire cause one of the terrorists, fleeing with a child, to let go of the boy who then escapes. But even more remarkable is what happens next. Whilst a child Matty had met a Mr Pedigree, a pederast. Mr Pedigree was revolted by Matty but Matty, through some strange misreading of the relationship, became devoted to Mr Pedigree. Mr Pedigree is caught up in a cycle which from time to time leads him to attempt sexual relationships with a child. At the time of Matty's death Mr Pedigree is in the grip of one of his compulsive cycles and is waiting outside a public lavatory for some children. Matty appears to him in a vision of gold to free him from his enslavement:

> He came slowly to Mr Pedigree who found his approach not only natural but even agreeable for the boy was not really as awful to look at as one might think, there where he waded along waist deep in gold. He came and stood before Pedigree and looked down at him. Pedigree understood that they were in a park of mutuality and closeness where the sunlight lay right on the skin.
>
> 'You know it was all your fault Matty.'
>
> Matty seemed to agree; really the boy was quite pleasant to look at![16]

As in *Riders in the Chariot* there is a contrast between two worlds. When the terrorists attack the school in order to kidnap the children the media is focused upon all the outward events. TV cameras and newspaper men are caught up in what is happening. The death of an obscure, strange odd job man is not noticed. But while the world watches these dramatic outward happenings another plot is all the time being worked our. Matty is an agent of redemption. He knows his life exists for something and his death releases him from the constraints of time and space for the redemption of Mr Pedigree. Matty becomes at once a flame of fire and a vision of gold.

The third theme I want to explore is the relationship between an author's understanding of resurrection and their wider concerns. In addition to the novels already mentioned I refer in particular to D.H. Lawrence's story *The Man who Died* and R.C. Hutchinson's novel *Rising*. In contrast to his popular reputation D.H. Lawrence was a religious man who wrote some of the profoundest poetry on death of our time. He also had a relationship with the Christian faith, albeit an ambivalent one. He was at once attracted and repelled by Christian concepts of virtue. In *The Man who Died* a man, who is obviously meant to be Jesus, regains consciousness in the tomb, the crucifixion not having fully killed him. He emerges and after a period with a peasant family goes to live with a priestess of Isis. Jesus, in the story, comes to re-evaluate his ministry and reject it as based on death. Through the healing hands of the goddess he comes to a new life of tenderness and touch. The priestess starts to anoint and rub his wounds and as she does so brings him to real life. They begin to talk about the woman in the gospels who anointed him with oil and Jesus reflects:

> I asked them all to serve me with the corpse of their love. And in the end I offered them only the corpse of my love. This is my body—take and eat— my corpse—
> A vivid shame went through him. 'After all,' he thought, 'I wanted them to love with dead bodies. If I had kissed Judas with live love, perhaps he would never have kissed me with death.'
> There dawned on him the reality of soft, warm love which is in touch and which is full of delight . . .
> And he in the recurring dismay of having died, and in the anguished perplexity of having tried to force life, felt his wounds crying aloud, and the deep places of the body howling again: 'I have been murdered, and I lent myself to murder. They murdered me, but I lent myself to murder.'[17]

Jesus feels sexual desire arising in him, senses death going and life coming. Afterwards 'in the absolute stillness and fullness of touch, he slept in the cave'[18] at one with the woman, the world and himself.

The story reflects a number of Lawrence's personal preoccupations, not least his own disillusionment with the role of prophet. He came to see, and therefore made Jesus see, that you cannot impose a new order on things. The value of *The Man who Died* from the standpoint of Christian theology is twofold. First, it forces Christians to think about celibacy and the prophetic role, in particular the prophetic role of Jesus in bringing in the Kingdom of God, and it makes us seek ways of talking about these things which are not open to Lawrence's strictures that they are simply disguised forms of death. Second, although we would want, on historical grounds, to reject Lawrence's reconstruction of the course of events, his theme can be affirmed as an aspect of or effect of Christian redemption. For Christianity, which believes that creation was made good; that God took flesh and dwelt among us; which believes in the resurrection of the body, is not stand-offish about the body. To live consciously and joyously as a physical being, as a body, not simply in its sexual aspects but in all its physicality, is part of redemption. There is a temptation to say that

if what Lawrence describes has a place in the Christian understanding of resurrection, it must be as the fruit of a prior spiritual
transformation. But it is wiser to heed the words of Edwin Muir:

> Whether the soul at first
> This pilgrimage began,
> Or the shy body leading
> Conducted soul to soul
> Who knows? This is the most
> That soul and body can,
> To make us each for each
> And in our spirit whole.[19]

Lawrence's approach to the resurrection story brings out starkly
how its interpretation is related to our whole understanding of life.
This is true of all writers. One value of Lawrence is that he throws
into relief some more traditional interpretations and shows them
as also making claims, if of a rather different kind. In R.C.
Hutchinson's novel *Rising* Sabino, a member of a leading South
American family, is sent with a private army to guard part of a
railway line that is being attacked by guerrillas. Earlier in his life
Sabino had sentenced a man from this area to be brutally tortured
to death. Now he finds himself, with a broken leg, captured by a
member of that man's family. He is expecting a similar long drawn
out death. But a strange experience happens to him. An Indian
surgeon comes to him and through the touch of his hands heals his
leg. They talk about the nature of healing and the surgeon says it is
necessary for Sabino to yield to affection, to yield to the healer who
cares for him. They begin to talk about the man whom many years
before Sabino had killed, or thought he had killed. Sabino looks at
the man before him and sees that same man of many years before.
Is it a dream or is it real?[20] Certainly his leg is healed. Sabino
comes back to his family. Unfortunately, R.C. Hutchinson died as
he was finishing the novel but he left notes on how he intended to
go on. Sabino is to realize, hard man that he is, the supremacy of
love, of Christian love: 'Only when he has realized that if . . . he
puts himself into the hands of the risen Christ as his follower, he
may do wrong again, he may even be proud and cruel again, but
never again will he be without the knowledge that, in his new life,
he can be forgiven and can find peace.'[21]

Another note added: 'We want, finally, a sense of things not
ending but freshly beginning.'

This novel makes clear what was perhaps more movingly
explored in Hutchinson's novel *Johanna at Daybreak*,[22] that redemp-

tion is fundamentally a moral matter, it is redemption of sinners. Sabino is a hard man who has tried to put at least one person cruelly to death. In *Johanna at Daybreak* the central character is a woman who has handed her husband and children over to the Nazis and who has to come, through divine judgement and divine forgiveness, to live with the fact. In *Rising* this redemption is initiated by the dream or reality of the person Sabino has tried to kill offering affection and healing. The *Rising* of the title has a threshold reference, to peasant risings, the rising from death, or apparent death, of the person Sabino sent to a cruel death and the rising to new life of Sabino himself. In this emphasis on moral redemption Hutchinson stands with Golding and Dostoevsky. This does not mean to say that the understanding of Patrick White and D. H. Lawrence is valueless. Far from it. White brings out the fact that redemption involves individual vocation, Lawrence the point that it should include an affirmation of and oneness with the physical. Yet both these are in fact manifestations of a redemption which is first of all moral redemption, for redemption, whichever way it is looked at, must have choice at its core and therefore also contrition, forgiveness and transformation by grace.

I began by suggesting that there were two problems that anyone who wishes to discuss the resurrection of Christ in traditional terms is faced with. First, if the resurrection cannot be neatly categorized as either physical or visionary, how can it be depicted in a way which carries conviction? Novelists, whose work is not bound by physical restraints and who can make use of the boundless power of the imagination, are here in a good position. What is noteworthy about the treatments considered is that they leave the sense of mystery about what exactly happened at the resurrection intact. The good ladies of the Australian suburbs want to talk about miracle and yet insist that no miracle has happened. That something has happened we are left in no doubt, but exactly *what* is known differently to the people to whom it has happened and known by them at their points of deepest conviction. Even in *Darkness Visible*, which comes closest to a visible manifestation, the blown-up Matty takes shape both as a rescuing flame and as a vision to Mr Pedigree. In both these novels, however, what happens after the death of the Christ figure is not just a change in outlook in a few people. Something is released into the world by the death; a presence, a power, a person. In Dostoevsky the emphasis is different from that of White and Golding because he is not dealing with the resurrection as an event in history but with resurrection power as a present reality. In *Crime and Punishment* we see this reality, working through the faith and love of Sonia and becoming recognizable as such through the words of Scripture. Here the God who raised Christ Jesus from the dead, and who will raise us from death into immortal life, is experienced now raising us from the death of sin and despair. The same is true in Hutchinson's *Rising* where it seems to be deliberately unclear whether the man whom Sabino sent to his death is in fact physically alive, having survived death, or a vision of a risen presence. In either case it is a loving, healing, redeeming power personified that is at work. In none of these novels do the authors fail to convince, except in the case of Tolstoy, whose view anyway can be questioned on theological grounds. This is not, of course, in any sense proof that the resurrection of Christ happened, only that it can be presented by accomplished novelists in such a way that those who read the books experience the same degree of reality when resurrection is being described as when mundane facts are written about. The level of conviction does not falter when we move from crucifixion, which we know can happen, to resurrection.

The second problem concerned the moral congruity of the resurrection with our deepest insights about human suffering. How can we speak of it in a way that does not belittle the affliction of human beings, that does not appear morally cheap? It is easier to write a novel that deals only with the crucifixion.[23] We can respond to a God who shares our loss and woe. In the novels considered the resurrection of Christ is seen in intimate connection to the divine redemptive purpose. It may be that in recent years the resurrection of Christ has been seen too exclusively against the background of the crucifixion and not in this wider context. The earliest Christian preaching saw the resurrection of Christ as the beginning of the general resurrection. They preached not only that Christ was risen but that he would soon return to judge the quick and the dead. In early Christian art, particularly in its Eastern form, the resurrection is most intimately connected with the harrowing of hell. The great Byzantine mosaics and frescoes of the tenth and eleventh century show Christ rising from the dead and at the same time hauling Adam and Eve and the good men of old out of their grave.[24] In the Medieval West the harrowing of hell was also a major theme. For example, in *The Mysteries* a cycle of three mystery plays, it is the harrowing of hell that is the major theme in the last one. The resurrection of Christ occurs, but it is, as it were, an incident on the way to the raising of all the dead. In the novels discussed here the prime thrust of the action is the redemption of human souls. The risen presence and power at work to this end is, as it were, the incarnation carried on by other means. The resurrection of Christ is the essential point of transition, enabling the work of Christ to go on unconstrained by the limits of time and space.

This is not to deny that there are important historical questions to answer, for Christianity makes a claim about what happened in history. But when we are considering the moral significance and appropriateness of the resurrection these novels suggest that the resurrection has to be seen in a much wider context than the crucifixion. If the resurrection is isolated from the wider context it is easy to obtain the impression that it is simply a reversal of the crucifixion. Within the wider context it can be seen as an essential transition point in the carrying out of God's redemptive purpose for all of humankind.

There is another point. If divine redemptive work is a concept to which one can morally give assent then this calls into question some of the presuppositions that Iris Murdoch, amongst others, brings to bear. It forces one to ask whether there is not a victim mentality, a defeatist pathology that is influencing the whole way some people look at what is or is not morally appropriate. For a Christ who is all loss, all affliction, is morally appropriate to an age which can see nothing but loss and affliction. But the Christian faith has always been preached as good news about the ultimate triumph of divine love. An age which cannot conceive of the possibility of anything but tragedy will, understandably enough, have difficulty in grasping the moral appropriateness of the resurrection. Nevertheless that resurrection (as witnessed to by the novels discussed) calls into question the very assumptions by which we judge what is and what is not morally proper.

The novels considered here illuminate the resurrection of Christ in at least four ways:
1. They show that it is possible to write about the resurrection in a way that carries literary conviction. There is no unnatural break between the suffering and the triumph. All novel reading involves a suspension of disbelief. But no greater, or different, suspension of disbelief is called for in writing about the resurrection than in writing about the crucifixion.
2. They show that it is possible to write about the resurrection in a way that carries moral conviction, which does justice to our deepest feelings about human suffering.
3. They understand the resurrection against the background of a

divine redemptive purpose at work in the world. Except in the case of Lawrence, that is conceived of in fundamentally moral terms.

4. They lead us to question the presuppositions that we bring to bear in judging what is or is not morally appropriate. The novels are concerned with the *achievement* of redemption, with the *accomplishment* of the divine purpose of love. They lead us to ask why it is that so many today are drawn to a defeated Christ but not a victorious, glorified one.

Part Two

QUESTIONS OF PEACE AND JUSTICE

EIGHT

The Christian concept of peace*

Peace is the object of all the yearnings of mankind, religious and secular; a vision and a promise, a concept at once mystical and practical, supernatural and political. The very name of that concept—*Peace, Pax, Shalom*—tolls like a bell throughout Western theology and literature. Even the toughest agnostic is touched unexpectedly by those phrases in the Christian liturgy which play on all our profoundest longings; *'the peace of God which passeth all understanding . . .'*; *'My peace I give unto you . . .'* and by the vision, which has so tragically haunted Judaic and Judaic- inspired civilisations, of Salem, Jerusalem, the vision of peace. Concepts like this are not to be pinned down and labelled like entomological specimens by international lawyers or political scientists.

(Michael Howard)[1]

The concept of peace is not to be pinned down and labelled, so that passage warns us. Nevertheless, clarity demands that some attempt be made to define the main senses in which the word 'peace' has been used. Some of the acrimony in the debate about peace in recent years has been due to the simple (or wilful) confusion of different kinds of peace. Peace is a word that carries the longing of humankind. It is also a word that is used to describe a precise state of affairs, namely the absence of overt violence. Confusion is compounded by a lack of suitable terminology. Swedish distinguishes between *Frid*, peace of heart, and *Fred*, the absence of war between nations. Welsh too makes a similar distinction between *Tangnefedd*, inner peace, and *Heddwch*, the absence of violence. In English, the same word, 'peace', is used to describe different phenomena. Three main types of peace need to be distinguished and related to one another.

Shalom: the peace in which everything flourishes
This is a peace which envelops the whole of human life. It is not just the peace of solitary individuals but the peace of the whole community. It is not only an inward state but an outward condition. It embraces life in its totality, inward and outward;

* Lecture delivered at St Antony's College, Oxford on 9 March 1988

91

personal, social, political, economic and environmental. The root meaning of the word Shalom is 'whole' and it indicates well-being in its fullness, spiritual harmony and physical health; material prosperity untouched by violence or misfortune. Two particular aspects of Shalom can be noted. First, Shalom includes all that we mean by justice. In this life peace and justice often seem to be in tension. Sometimes we are offered the choice of striving for one or the other and it is not possible to have both at once. Again, in this life, different understandings of justice are often in conflict. But where there is Shalom, all that is indicated by true justice is present.

So it can be said that where God's justice is present, Shalom will also be present. Secondly, the realization of Shalom, in its fullness, belongs to the realm of hope. Throughout the Hebrew Scriptures there is a yearning for the time of Shalom, expressed in unforgettable images. This Shalom embraces the whole created order:

The wolf shall dwell with the lamb,
   and the leopard shall lie down with the kid,
   and the calf and lion and the fatling together,
   and a little child shall lead them.
The cow and bear shall feed;
   their young shall lie down together;
   and the lion shall eat straw like the ox.
The suckling child shall play over the hole of the asp,
   and the weaned child shall put his hand on the adder's den.
They shall not hurt or destroy in all my holy mountain;
for the earth shall be full of the knowledge of the Lord
   as the waters cover the sea.
(Isa. 11. 6–9. See also 65.25)

He shall judge between many peoples,
   and shall decide for strong nations afar off;
and they shall beat their swords into ploughshares,
   and their spears into pruning hooks;
nation shall not lift up sword against nation,
   neither shall they learn war any more;
but they shall sit every man under his vine and under his fig tree,
   and none shall make them afraid;
   for the mouth of the Lord of hosts has spoken.
(Mic. 4. 3–4. See also Isa. 2.4)

In the Hebrew Scriptures, as the two quotations suggest, this peace is sometimes envisaged as the abolition of war and the rule over the nations by Israel's messianic king and sometimes as a paradisal existence in which all forms of strife will have been removed. But both sets of images assume that Shalom in its fullness belongs to the eschaton, the final age, when God's just rule will transform and suffuse all things. Shalom is a longed-for peace. Can we hope for its appearance on earth? Or is it a peace that lies beyond the spatio-temporal order? Is it a peace that can be achieved in history or does its realization lie beyond history? What we can affirm is that Shalom is that state of affairs when God will be all in all, towards which the created order is being led; a vision which one day (within time or beyond time or both beyond and within) will be a reality.

Pax: when war is absent but coercion may be implicit or latent

Shalom is such a heady notion it is easy for theologians to overlook the vital need for Pax. Any country that has known war on its own soil, or which has been beset by civil strife, knows the great blessing of a simple cessation of hostilities. There is, writes Michael Howard, a bedrock meaning of peace, the simple absence of violence,

> especially random and endemic violence, from the society in which we live; the absence of armies traversing and re-traversing the land, burning, raping, plundering, killing, whether those armies are official or unoffical, organised and uniformed or mere robber bands; whether they inflict destruction with knives or from a safe distance with bombs. Peace is the simple assurance that one can sow a crop, with some hope of reaping it, build a house with good hope of living in it, raise a family, learn and pursue a vocation, lead a life which will not be interrupted by the incursion of violence, by physical destruction, wounding, maiming, torture, deaths.[2]

It is not to be thought that the people of Israel, in their longing for Shalom, were insensible of the benefits of Pax. On the contrary, on many occasions we read the phrase, 'And there was peace between Israel and . . .'. This is contrasted with another state signalled by a no less frequent phrase, 'And there was war between Israel and . . .'. Shalom of course includes amongst its benefits the absence of violence and sometimes, in their longing for a kinder future, it was security from the threat of harm that was to the fore:

> Thus says the Lord of hosts: Old men and old women shall again sit in the streets of Jerusalem, each with staff in hand for

very age. And the streets of the city shall be full of boys and girls playing safely in its streets.

(Zech. 8.4–5)

It is difficult to find an adequate one-line definition of Pax because a state of affairs where war is absent can also be one where coercion, in one form or another, is present. This coercion may be basic to keeping war at bay, as in a system of mutual deterrence, or its impact may be minimal. There is no war going on between the USA and the USSR but coercion, in the form of mutual deterrence, is fundamental to their present relationship, and, many would argue, to the absence of war. There is no war going on between the USA and Canada and the coercion implicit in their relationship is less obvious. But it is not totally absent, for Canadians are conscious of pressures of various kinds from their more powerful brother.

The extent to which one believes that coercion, in one form or another, is present in all relationships between organized groups, will affect the definition of Pax. If it is judged that coercion is always a factor then Pax will be defined as armed peace.[3] The problem with defining Pax simply as an absence of war or absence of violence, is that it ignores the many forms of implicit coercion. The *Pax Romana* did not feel much like peace to the Donatists in North Africa, or the *Pax Britannica* like peace to Zulus in South Africa. Indians in North America, Maoris in New Zealand, and Aborigines in Australia are at peace with their white populations. But few today would argue that it is a peace free of coercive elements. We read of Solomon that

he had peace on all sides round about him. And Judah and Israel dwelt in safety, from Dan even to Beer-sheba, every man under his vine and under his fig tree, all the days of Solomon.

(1 Kings 4.24–25)

A highly desirable state of affairs has been described. But the verse begins, 'For he had dominion over all the region west of the Euphrates'. The next verse adds that 'Solomon also had forty thousand stalls of horses for his chariots, and twelve thousand horsemen'.

The peace under Solomon, which later generations of Israelites tended to idealise and for whose restoration they prayed, was a peace based on dominion, a peace dependent on suppressing the opposition in the surrounding lands, a peace based on the strength of vast numbers of horses, chariots and horsemen.

Even when military might is not as blatant as it was under Solomon there are forms of coersion no less painful to those who suffer from it, forms of economic coercion that are virtual slavery. Sometimes those who speak vehemently for peace as an absence of war can be blind to hidden forms of economic coercion in society. It is difficult to find a definition of Pax which does not assume either that all Pax is coercive or that no coercion is present. The definiton chosen here *Pax: when war is absent* but *coercion may be implicit or latent* does not seek to prejudge any issue, simply to reflect the fact that a state of 'absence of war' may be one in which good will and economic co-operation are basic to the relationship and coercion is minimal or one in which war is kept at bay only by the mutual fear of the consequences of going to war.

Societies are held together by a mixture of coercion and consent. Neither, by itself, provides a strong enough adhesive. If income tax was purely voluntary, who would pay it? The minimal essential conditions for any kind of properly human life depend in part on the ability of the government to enforce its policies, whether or not everyone entirely agrees with them. This means, in specific terms, the presence of a police force, courts of law and the army. There can be no human community and therefore no properly human life without a measure of just and peaceable order. This is established partly by ensuring that, consent or no, it is not in the interest of individuals, or groups, or nations, to break the peace, disrupt the order or violate the norms of justice. Thus Pax has as its prime concern the absence of overt violence so that individuals can plan their lives on a predictable basis and pursue their goals un-hindered. The overt violence that has to be kept at bay is not simply that of the criminal elements within a population but the hired killers of oppressive dictatorships and the unprovoked aggression of invading force.

It is tempting to make a total distinction between the legally authorized forcible restraint necessary to hold a society together, and the kind of violence that may be unleashed by war. But the distinction is not absolute. The destruction caused by war may be horrifyingly greater than the legitimate pressure used by a state for internal control. Nevertheless, no state can create an oasis of peace in a world of unbridled anarchy. Its internal peace and order depends, in part, on the maintenance of a wider environment of peace and order. The power of strategies of 'non-violence' is sometimes appealed to. In certain contexts they can be highly effective, as Gandhi found in India and Martin Luther King in the USA. But 'non-violence' is often used for tactics which are in fact a mixture of pure persuasion and coercion by indirect means, for example strikes or boycotts.

Pax does not itself bring about that flourishing of the whole community which is defined as Shalom. It seeks to create and maintain the conditions without which there can be no opportunity for flourishing. Its purpose is similar to the 'Pax' which children call to one another after they have been fighting together. For one reason or another the children agree that they have had enough; it may be that they want to engage in some more enjoyable activity or it may be they are getting too hurt. Whatever the reason, in the interest of both parties, they agree to a cessation of rough and tumble.

Coercion, overt or implicit, is a permanent feature of sinful human existence. Individuals, groups and nations have an ineluctable tendency to pursue their own interests without taking the interests of others into account. Worse still, they can deliberately negate the interests of others. Sometimes this ruthless pursuit of self-interest at the expense of fellow creatures is clothed in moral rhetoric, political ideology or religious demagoguery. This is not simply a re-emergence of an animal instinct for survival. It is also a failure to come to terms with a desire to place ourselves at the centre not only of our own existence but that of others as well. Self-interest and the will to survive, which within limits are proper in themselves, become transmuted into the desire to dominate. It is for this reason that morality and religion can make matters worse as well as better. They can be abused to reinforce a sense of rightness and superiority over others leading, at worst, to a crusade mentality when the enemy is seen as God's enemy. True religion, by contrast, is rooted in repentence, not simply at an individual level, but at a cultural, racial and national level, leading to an awareness that even when there is 'just cause' there is frailty and sin on both sides. Armed conflict is not only due to differences of perspective, or even to differences of interest. There is also at root the desire to dominate or the will to survive. History can be read, with Marx, as a history of economic domination in certain forms. Economic power is not the only form of power, however, and financial thraldom is not the only form that domination takes. The tendency to dominate can be clothed in moral, religious or ideological rhetoric. True religion has much to say about this, both in exposing it and in leading us to repent.

Nevertheless, although true religion has this role it does not always exercise it; sometimes, as history reveals all too clearly, it makes matters worse. So religion considered as a human phenomenon cannot be relied on to keep the peace. If there is rampageous power it must be kept in bounds by checks and balances. In the world in which we live, a world in which power relationships have not been abolished, power must be balanced by power, lest one becomes a tyrant over other states: though this will not prevent it being a tyranny in its own borders. In a world where self-interest has not been transcended and where the self is always liable to become overweening, organized interest groups have to be tamed by keeping before them the consequences of unbridled pursuit of their aims. Pax at its highest, where the element of consent is large, partakes of Shalom. Where the element of consent is small, the role of coercion will be large. But whether large or small we need Pax, for without a just and peaceable order no other human enterprise is possible.

Inner peace

The longing for an inner peace or serenity, what Wordsworth called a 'Central peace, subsisting at the heart of endless agitation'[4] is widespread. It has also been disparaged as a luxury of the bourgeois class, the expression of an inner discontent that can be afforded only by those with an outer content in more than their fair share of this world's goods. From a Christian perspective this is only a portion of the truth. For the Christian faith offers an inner peace which is not to be accounted for wholly in sociological or psychological terms. It offers an inner peace that is a personal participation in Shalom; a fragmentary anticipation, by a particular individual, of that divine peace which one day will embrace the whole of existence. Shalom may be, in its fullness, a transcendent vision. But at one point at least it can always be apprehended by the individuals in their own personal lives, in whatever circumstances they find themselves.

This peace is, in essence, a fruit of the union of the human will with the divine will. For the Christian this union has been achieved, for all people of all times, by Jesus Christ. Our peace is a sharing in that unbreakable union he has eternally with the Father. In Christ there is a union of God and humanity, of earth and heaven, which can never be broken. Through faith and baptism Christians share in this union. So the Christ of the Fourth Gospel told his disciples:

> Peace I leave with you; my peace I give to you; not as the world gives do I give to you. Let not your hearts be troubled, neither let them be afraid.
>
> (John 14.27)

So it is that when the risen Christ in John's Gospel greets his disciples he says, 'Peace be with you'. This was the standard greeting at the time but its repetition in the resurrection stories in John 20 are a clear echo of the peace of Christ promised earlier. This is a peace integrally linked to the death and resurrection of Christ. Because he has descended into hell and been raised again there is indestructible union of God with people, through Christ, even for those in the midst of hell.

Paul makes the same point in his letters. He writes to Christians at Rome:

> Therefore, since we are justified by faith, we have peace with God through our Lord Jesus Christ.
>
> (Rom. 5.1)

Several times he reminds the recipients of his letters that peace is an essential aspect of the Christian life, a fruit of the Spirit, a result of our relationship with God through Christ. The writer of the letter to the Ephesians goes further than this and calls the gospel itself 'the gospel of peace' (6.15) and states that Christ 'is our peace' (2.14).

The quest for peace of mind and heart is there in all religions and is the great benefit held out by techniques of meditation and contemplation. The Christian emphasis is that this inner peace, which is in essence the union of human wills with the divine will, is present in Christ, not to be earned but to be received as a gift. This does not make the mystical quest null and void. On the contrary, the path of prayer is a way of receiving, at deeper and deeper levels of our being, what is offered in Christ. Nor is it to be seen apart from the sacramental receiving of that gift in Holy Communion. When Christians receive the sacrament there is a holy union, a holy communion. This union is the union of the divine and the human which those 'in Christ' share.

This inner peace can be grasped even in the midst of turmoil and conflict. For it is a peace that nothing can destroy. But it is not an alternative to Shalom or an attempt to escape the obligation to bring Shalom to bear on the whole of human existence. Shalom, in its fullness, lies in the future, for it is that union of all things with the creator which nothing can destroy. That union can be received now at a personal level. However, it is not an alternative to the whole but a sliver of the whole; a handhold in the inner life on what one day will embrace all life. Inner peace is a foretaste of what one day will include the whole of social, economic and political existence; and inner peace carries with it an obligation to work for the whole of which it is a part:

> We beseech thee, O lord our God, to set the peace of heaven within the hearts of men, that it may bind the nations also in a covenant which cannot be broken, through Jesus Christ our Lord.[5]

The God of peace

Peace in all forms, Shalom, Pax and inner peace, comes from God and is a gift of God. Peace is an essential characteristic of his being and it is from that being that we receive peace. Many times in Paul's writings he refers to 'the peace of God' or 'the peace from God':

> Now may the Lord of peace himself give you peace at all times in all ways.
>
> (2 Thess. 3.16)

This does not refer only to inner peace. The Hebrew Scriptures are no less clear in their affirmation that Pax, peace with neighbours, peace within the borders and at the borders, is a gift of God; and so of course is Shalom.

This raises again the general problem of the relationship between divine gift and human effort. That question is outside the scope of this chapter, but here as elsewhere they should not be seen as mutually exclusive. Our peace-making is nothing less than the gift of God in and through us. The gift of peace we pray for is also the peace we work for. We are conscious of needing the gift because we know that of ourselves we can do nothing that is lasting:

> *Nisi Dominus* Except the Lord build the house; their labour is but lost that build it.
>
> (Ps. 127.1 Prayer Book Version)

A single peace

Shalom, Pax and inner tranquility seem very different forms of peace. Yet within a Christian perspective they are integrally related to one another, as this ancient prayer makes clear:

> O God, who wouldest fold both heaven and earth in a single peace; let the design of thy great love lighten upon the waste of our wraths and sorrows; and give peace to thy church, peace among nations, peace in our dwellings and peace in our heart; through thy Son our saviour Jesus Christ.[6]

As already considered, inner peace is to be seen as a fragmentary anticipation of that Shalom which will one day embrace all things; a receiving in personal and at first inward terms of what will one day include all that is social and outward. Pax, too, although it contains elements in it derived from coercion and the fear of the consequences of certain actions, is not unrelated to Shalom, for Pax will include elements in it based on free consent, on mutual goodwill and the common good. Nevertheless, there are clearly special difficulties in thinking about the relationship between Pax and Shalom. These stem from the fact that in the state of affairs where Shalom takes full effect power relationships have been transcended, but in the world in which we live they are the fundamental feature of relationships between organized groups. Before that relationship is considered further, however, some mention must be made of the role of conflict in life and the notion of false peace, which figures in the Scriptures so prominently.

The role of conflict and the exposure of false peace
Most human being shy away from conflict and there is a tendency to think that conflict is incompatible with the Christian life. In heaven it may be different but conflict is a fundamental and proper part of earthly existence. It is through the possibility of conflict that individuals and groups have opportunity to share their perspectives, state their concerns and work for their interests. Without the possibility of conflict between different perspectives, concerns and interests this freedom would not exist.

There is of course both proper and improper conflict. There is the improper conflict that springs from the hearts of those out to make trouble; which springs from the malice that can wreck any human system. That is why, on a Christian view, practical arrangements for the ordering of human affairs can never be entirely separated from *ascesis*, the inner discipline or purifying of the heart, which seeks to ensure that those affairs are managed by people of good will rather than malevolence.

Then there is the improper conflict which, born of a mixture of legitimate self-interest and improper pride, seeks to resolve a particular conflict by force of arms when other means of redress are still open. It is part of the rationale of a democratic system that it enables conflicts to be resolved without resort to violence, through law and Parliament, which makes possible even the change of governments without recourse to violence.

Within the international order there do not yet exist totally adequate mechanisms for the peaceful resolution of conflict. The

United Nations recognizes this both in its support of peace-keeping forces and in its recognition of the right of self-defence as a last resort. When a nation defends itself against external aggression or when it rises up against an occupying power then that conflict, though tragic, is proper under the present conditions of human existence. Failure to resist or to take the necessary steps to offer adequate resistance can be a failure of responsibility; an acquiesence in a false peace.

There is peace of a kind to be had by shutting the heart and mind to all that disturbs. Clearly this kind of peace in a cocoon should have no part in the Christian life. Such a peace is to be had only by selling our birthright as human beings, as Wilfred Owen makes clear in his poem 'Insensibility':

> But cursed are dullards whom no cannon stuns
> That they should be as stones.
> Wretched are they, and mean
> With paucity that never was simplicity.
> By choice they made themselves immune
> To pity and whatever mourns in man.[7]

There is a false peace to be had by accepting social injustice. When Martin Luther King was in prison a group of white pastors wrote to him urging him to stop disturbing the peace. He wrote back that 'Peace is not the absence of tension but the presence of justice.' In South Africa many prayers are offered for peace on her borders. But the sons or grandsons of black members of those congregations where such prayers are offered may be on the other side of those borders praying for a peace that is the fruit of justice. That striving for justice is a greater contribution to Shalom than premature attempts to achieve a reconciliation based on injustice:

> For from the least to the greatest of them,
>   every one is greedy for unjust gain;
> and from prophet to priest,
>   every one deals falsely.
> They have healed the wound of my people lightly,
>   saying 'Peace, peace,'
> when there is no peace.
>   (Jer. 6.13–14. See also 8.11)

This kind of peace is likened to daubing over cracks with whitewash. The destruction of such whitewashed buildings is inevitable:

> Because, yea, because, they have misled my people, saying,

'Peace,' when there is no peace; and because when the people build a wall, these prophets daub it with whitewash; say to those who daub it with whitewash that it shall fall!

(Ezek. 13.10–11)

When Jesus came he brought the Shalom of the Kingdom of God. His birth was preceded by that of John the Baptist who came to prepare the way for one who would 'guide our feet into the way of peace' (Luke 1.79).

At the birth of the Messiah the heavens rang with the song:

'Glory to God in the highest, and on earth peace among men with whom he is pleased!'

(Luke. 2.14)

The disciples when they were sent out were directed to bring this peace to the houses where they were staying:

Whatever house you enter, first say, 'Peace be to this house!' And if a son of peace is there, your peace shall rest upon him; but if not, it shall return to you.

(Luke 10.5–6. See also Matt. 10.12–13)

This peace, this Shalom of God, which broke into the world in the person of Jesus, came into conflict with the corrupt practices and unjust structures of human existence. There could be no easy accommodation with the peace of men; conflict was inevitable. So we get the terrible words:

Do not think that I have come to bring peace on earth; I have not come to bring peace, but a sword.

(Matt. 10.34)

This brought anguish to the Son of God:

And when he drew near and saw the city he wept over it, saying, 'Would that even today you knew the things that make for peace! But now they are hid from your eyes.'

(Luke 19. 41–42)

The Christian vocation is not only to preach the peace of Christ but to expose false peace, a peace based on insensitivity and complacency; a peace rooted in injustice and suppression of dissent. Exposing this false peace inevitably leads to conflict. But this conflict is an essential prelude to that Shalom which is the product of justice; of a right relationship with God that is reflected in right relationships between human beings, not in domination but mutual respect and equality of concern.

Shalom and Pax

It has already been suggested that Shalom and Pax are not unrelated to one another, for in all forms of Pax there will be an element, however minimal, of free consent. Nevertheless, in this world there will often be a tension between them, because Pax makes use of, and rightly makes use of, elements of coercion to maintain order both within a state and between states. This tension is inescapable for the Christian, because in one sense the Kingdom of God has already come and yet its full consummation lies in the future. The rule of God has already taken form in this world in the life, death and resurrection of Jesus Christ. Yet Christians live between the times: between the time of his rising and his coming again. Every line of the New Testament reflects this tension. The presence of this tension is not due to á 'sell-out' to worldliness. On the contrary, it is a recognition of the legitimate, that is, God-given, claims of civil society. So long as God wills human life to continue, he wills human communities, for human beings are essentially social; there can be no human personhood without social life. This social life needs political structures and so long as life continues Christians have a duty, along with other citizens, of maintaining a just and peaceable order. As Augustine put it:

> Thus, the heavenly City, so long as it is wayfaring on earth, not only makes use of earthly peace but fosters and actively pursues along with other human beings a common platform in regard to all that concerns our purely human life.[8]

Ultimately a Christian's allegiance is to the one, undivided and unified will of God. Nevertheless, searching for this will in the actual conditions under which we live, a Christian becomes conscious of two sets of claims upon him, not just one. There are the claims that arise out of our membership of civil society and there are the claims derived from the demands of the Kingdom of God. The first set of claims, of 'our station and its duties', to use the phrase of A. D. Lindsay, is referred to by Paul in Romans 13. The other set of claims, that posed by the challenge of perfection, finds its most sublime expression in the Sermon on the Mount. Until the Kingdom of God comes in its fullness, that is so long as God wills human society to exist under sinful conditions, these two sets of claims will live in necessary tension with one another. Nevertheless, they are integrally related, that is, Shalom bears upon Pax in a number of ways.

103

First, Shalom provides a true vision, an ultimate standard in the light of which the whole of human life is to be seen and judged. It reveals our present forms of peace for what they are, sometimes a false peace based on injustice, sometimes Pax, a compromise made necessary by a sinful world.

Secondly, Shalom presents us with an obligation to work for this vision and to express it so far as we can under the conditions of sinful finite existence. Mention was made earlier of the way in which religion can be used to disguise and justify the drive to dominate others. But Christian faith keeps before us the vision of true religion, which works to break down the barriers which divide us and bring about reconciliation between warring parties. It has been argued earlier that in the world as we know it Pax may depend upon power being checked by countervailing power. But again, Christian faith bids us lift up our eyes to the horizon of the cross, where all human power is humbled before the self-emptying love of God. So we are called to work for reconciliation, even at great cost to ourselves. Such work is not in vain. For it is possible for there to be anticipations and signs of Shalom.

Inner peace can be such a sign. The commitment of a community to justice and reconciliation can be such a sign. The life of a Church built on a mutual forgiveness that is rooted in the forgiveness of God can be such a sign.

Shalom presents us with a vision of peace and justice that impels us to work for a transformed world. Not just in the inner life or the Church but in the whole complex of human political relationships, we look for and work for, transformation. Our prayer will be:

> Show us, good Lord
> the peace we should seek,
> the peace we must give,
> the peace we can keep,
> the peace we must forgo,
> and the peace you have given
> in Jesus Christ our Lord.[9]

NINE

Reinhold Niebuhr and his pacifist critics*

Reinhold Niebuhr had great admiration for the type of non-violent resistance practised by Gandhi. He believed that it had moral strengths[1] and that it was a particularly strategic instrument for an oppressed minority group. In 1932 he predicted: 'The emancipation of the Negro race in America probably waits upon the adequate development of this kind of social and political strategy.'[2] Furthermore, he thought that religion had a particular contribution to make to the development of this type of resistance.[3]

Niebuhr's positive evaluation of the techniques of non-violent resistance should not be overlooked. Nevertheless, he strongly objected to two confusions that had grown up around it. First, in his judgement, Jesus taught total non-resistance, rather than non-violent resistance.[4] Secondly, he denied that there was an absolute moral distinction between the use of force and the techniques of non-violent resistance. He noted that Gandhi's boycott of English cotton resulted in the undernourishment of the children of Manchester and the Allied blockade of Germany in the death of German children.[5] So instead of the terms 'force' and 'non-violent resistance', he preferred to distinguish between violent and non-violent coercion. Both were forms of coercion: and we need our eyes open to the way that coercion, particularly economic coercion, is already operative in society, and working to the benefit of the advantaged. Moreover, the attempt to make an absolute distinction led to the absurd position that the non-violent power of Dr Goebbels' propaganda was more moral than the military efforts of the Allies to resist Nazi tyranny.[6] So Niebuhr made two basic distinctions. First, between *non*-resistance and all forms of *resistance* and then between violent and non-violent coercion.[7]

More recently Ronald Sider and Richard Taylor have made a basic distinction between non-violent coercion and what they call 'lethal violence'.[8] They maintain that coercion is quite compatible with love and instance the disciplining of children and the use of

---

* From *Reinhold Niebuhr and the Issues of our time*, edited by Richard Harries (Mowbray 1986)

economic boycotts. These forms of coercion, they say, still respect 'the other person's freedom to say no and accept the consequences'. Lethal violence on the other hand is different, for then 'one cannot lovingly appeal to the other person as a free moral agent responsible to God to choose to repent and change'. As they write, 'It makes no sense to call a person to repentance as you put a bullet through his head'. Sider and Taylor's analysis is, however, confused. Consider three conditional sentences.

1. If you don't stop bullying your sister you will go to your room.
2. If you don't stop bullying your sister I will shoot you.
3. If you don't drop your gun I'll shoot it out of your hand.

The fundamental distinction is *not* between the first sentence and the other two, in both of which weapons are mentioned, but between (2) on the one hand and (1) and (3) on the other. The difference is that the coercion in (1) and (3) are proportionate whilst that in (2) is totally disproportionate. If a man is holding up a bank and the police burst in and tell him to drop his gun, their threat is the appropriate and proportionate response to the threat posed. It is the minimum use of coercion necessary to achieve a legitimate goal.

Did Jesus resist evil? Sider and Taylor, unconsciously following Augustine, point to Jesus' verbal denunciation of the Pharisees, his cleansing of the Temple and his remark at the trial when a soldier struck him, 'If I have spoken wrongly, bear witness to the wrong; but if I have spoken rightly, why do you strike me?'[9] They then argue that Christians *should* resist whilst at the same time being willing to suffer in the process. For loving means having 'the needs—not necessarily the wants' of the enemy in mind. This point, also made by Augustine in his commentary on the Sermon on the Mount, is surely correct. There is nothing worse for the aggressor than to allow him to get away with his aggression, for this simply reinforces the harmful tendency within him. For his own good, for the love of him, he has to be stopped. Sider and Taylor also admit that it is sometimes in the interest of the careless debtor to take him to court. So the authors are prepared to countenance the use of coercion. They maintain that discipline and boycotts are compatible both with the teaching of Jesus and the nature of love. They support disciplinary punishment (though not retributive punishment, which has to be left to God). They uphold the police and the courts, disassociating themselves from Tolstoy in this respect. They admire the British tradition of unarmed police and write, 'We would favour creative efforts to expand the many ways that police can use non-lethal coercion'.[10]

So do we all of course—but the crucial question—which they dodge—is what happens if the criminal is armed and refuses to give up his arms? They slip away with the remark, 'In any case, police work is radically different from warfare'. Is it? It is a question that will be considered later. But what their previous argument amounts to is that coercive resistance is compatible with love—up to a point. But what happens at that point—when a criminal refuses to give up his gun—we are not told.

There is, however, a question which Sider and Taylor do force the Niebuhrian to face. Is it possible to love someone at the same time as you put a bullet through their head? Leaving aside all other considerations, for example, weighing the life of the torturer against the person he is torturing, and considering only the enemy *per se*, is it possible to shoot and love at the same time?

One possible answer is to say that you are not shooting to kill. Your prime intention is to render the attacker harmless, to disable him, and this is so whether the enemy is a terrorist or a soldier. However, it may be pressing the principle of double effect further than it will go to say that killing is an unintended result in every instance. There *is* an important distinction between what is directly intended and what is foreseen but unintended. Nevertheless, in some instances, killing is so inevitable that it probably cannot be regarded as unintended in terms of the action involved.

Another possible answer is that just because a person is dead you do not have to cease loving him. On a Christian view personal identity exists beyond death, in God. So it is possible to continue to wish a person well and to pray for them. Sider and Taylor define their concept of love in terms of giving the person opportunity to repent on this earth. Some of us, however, would not care to limit God's action and our opportunity to repent, to this life. Bringing in the concept of everlasting life is dangerous. It could make us less sensitive to the deaths of others. Nevertheless, on a Christian view, it is difficult to see how it can be entirely left out of account. For if to love someone is to desire their good, their good in a Christian sense is not simply their good in community on this earth but eternal happiness in the communion of saints. Indeed, is it not true that to deny the possibility of shooting at someone and loving them at the same time is to deny the possibility of redemption? Someone becomes deranged and picks up a hand grenade to throw into a school playground full of children. Before he can throw it a policeman shoots at him, severely disabling but not killing him. In prison afterwards the person comes to his senses and is glad that he was shot at, glad that he was prevented from killing the children.

He is glad too for his own sake. He would not like to live forever with the thought of having murdered innocent young lives. Although it is foolish to speculate on what might happen after death it must, on a Christian view, at least be a place where people come to their senses and see things as they are. Ultimate reconciliation depends, for example, on the soldiers in Hitler's armies, who were killed in battle, coming to see that it was good they were stopped, even though it meant their own death. Of course, in the heat of the battle these considerations are unlikely to be present. But the principle holds. To deny that it is possible to love and shoot at the same time is to deny the possibility of ultimate reconciliation.[11]

According to Niebuhr, Jesus taught total non-resistance. But is the term 'non-resustance' an accurate one to describe the impact of the Kingdom of God and what it asks of us? Every line of the Gospels witnesses to God's resistance to evil in all its forms, a resistance expressed through casting out devils, healing the sick and exposing hypocrisy. Indeed, total non-resistance would be non-existence. To exist at all is to exist with a life of one's own; a life which partly defines itself in opposition to its surroundings.

A different terminology is needed to describe the character of Jesus' actions and I prefer the phrase 'non-coercive resistance'. The term 'non-resistance' originally had a fairly clear meaning—it meant not resisting physically, particularly not taking up arms against the sacred person of the monarch. But as a phrase it has now become confused and confusing. The New Testament puts before us a figure who resisted with all the power of his person, his words and his prayers. For the sake of clarity therefore, we need more distinctions than Sider and Taylor allow and a different terminology from that of Niebuhr. In addition to total non-resistance, which was not taught by Jesus, there are these categories of resistance:

1. Non-coercive resistance that relies only on persuasion.
2. Resistance that uses direct force, or the threat of force.
3. Resistance that uses indirect coercion, through such means as strikes and boycotts.

There are significant differences between all three but the fundamental distinction must be between a resistance that relies on persuasion alone and that which makes use of either direct or indirect coercion. It is clearly confusing, if not hypocritical, as Niebuhr pointed out, to claim the moral aura that might be held to belong to non-coercive resistance whilst in fact making use of indirect coercion.[12]

As is well known, Niebuhr criticized pacifists for an over-optimistic view of man and for failing to take the presence of sin seriously enough. This was part of this wider critique of liberalism and his exposure of hidden liberal assumptions in avowedly Christian claims. In his book, *The Relevance of the Impossible: A Reply to Reinhold Niebuhr*,[13] first published in 1941, G. H. C. MacGregor made a point, which he repeated in 1953, and which has been followed by the many pacifists since then who have acknowledged their debt to this book. MacGregor argued that the Gospels do indeed see an essential, hidden goodness in the heart of man. Yet Niebuhr never denied man's capacity for justice. He simply urged that his inclination to injustice must *also* be taken into account. However much we may appeal to the hidden goodness in man, there is one inescapable fact. Christ was crucified. 'Though Christ is the true norm for every man, every man is also in some sense a crucifier of Christ.'[14] Sider and Taylor, in response to the criticism that pacifism reflects non-Christian liberal assumptions, point out that Mennonites hold mainstream, orthodox beliefs on the incarnation, and the atonement; that there is no necessary connection between pacifism and liberalism and that though humanity is indeed sinful a new age has dawned and the spirit-filled Church has come into being. The same points are made by MacGregor and others. They argue that Niebuhr had no real sense of the Church, an inadequate grasp of the Holy Spirit and an undue emphasis on pardoning as opposed to enabling grace. They believe that within the spirit-filled Church, which is universal, there is grace and power to overcome the sin of man and to enable us to live out the commands of Christ.[15]

Suppose however, this criticism is admitted—what are its implications? We have a fellowship, a spirit-filled community, universal in scope, capable of raising the standard of individual behaviour and of obeying the most severe requirements of Jesus; capable of living out his spirit-filled life of love both within the community and the world. Suppose we grant all this: what follows? Must not a Christian withdraw, in some significant sense, from public office: and the Church decisively separate itself from national life? John Yoder, after analysing some of the twenty-five types of pacifism which he identifies, comes to his own form, which he calls 'the pacifism of the messianic community'.[16] This pacifism is messianic because it depends upon the confession that Jesus is Christ and Lord and it is Christocentric in that it is based on the assumption that God has been revealed in Christ. It is also a pacifism of the community. It is not simply for heroic individuals but for a community that experiences in its life a foretaste of God's Kingdom. It is a community dedicated to a deviant value system and empowered by the Spirit which is changing the world.

This is a magnificent vision of the Church. But how does it bear on those of its members who are serving in public life? For those in office have a duty to preserve, and make to flourish, the body for which they have a responsibility. We do not commend deans of science faculties who give away their science equipment to needier universities or bank managers who give away their bank funds. Public policy is based upon the assumption that there is a legitimate self-interest to be protected. It is difficult to see how a Christian, on Yoder's view, can have any part in it. Older forms of pacifism of the Mennonite type surmounted this difficulty by frank acknowledgement of the need to withdraw from society. The new pacifism does not wish to follow this path. Yoder believes that Christ's uncompromising demands are directed to all men.[17] Sider and Taylor, too, explicly reject all forms of dualism. They write:

> We do not believe God has a double ethic. We do not believe God ordains a higher ethic for especially devout folk and a lower ethic for the masses. We do not believe that God intends Christians to wait until the millennium to obey the Sermon on the Mount. We do not believe God commands one thing for the individual and another for that same person as a public official.[18]

There is not space to reflect on all these different expressions of dualism. There is one fundamental point, however, upon which all forms of ethical dualism rest, which is crucial to Niebuhr and to the Christian faith. At the Eucharist Christians acclaim, 'Christ has died, Christ is risen, Christ will come again'. The Christian Church lives between the times, between Christ risen and Christ coming again. This tension is part of its life and any attempt to collapse it by denying one of the poles inevitably gives rise to distortions.

Niebuhr argued that you cannot understand the ethical teaching of Christ without taking into account the eschatological dimension:

> The ethical demands made by Jesus are incapable of fulfilment in the present existence of man. They proceed from a trascendent and divine unity of essential reality, and their final fulfilment is possible only when God transmutes the present chaos of this world into its final unity.[19]

In other words, in this world morally right action does not guarantee a happy outcome. On the contrary, good people often suffer for their goodness. It is only in the Kingdom that the universe will be totally transparent to value.

Niebuhr rejected the idea that we have to wait for Kingdom come before experiencing the claims of its ethic. On the contrary it bears upon us now and it bears upon *every* aspect of our life, public as well as private. Nevertheless, there is a fundamental contrast between what is possible in the fullness of the Kingdom and what is possible now. There is a difference between the ethic of the Kingdom of God, 'in which no concession is made to human sin, and all relative political strategies which, assuming human sinfulness, seek to secure the highest measure of peace and justice among selfish and sinful men'.[20] There is then a tension that is basic to the Christian life because the Church lives between Christ risen and Christ coming again. The denial by pacifists of all forms of dualism is in effect a repudiation of this tension. As MacGregor writes:

> Christian pacifists have often been warned by self-styled 'realists' that we shall never bring in the Kingdom of God by acting in an evil world as if it were already here. Yet this is, I suggest, exactly what Jesus *did* teach: if only men were prepared to take God at his word and to order their lives here and now by the laws of a transcendent Kingdom, then the power of God would answer the cry of faith, and the Kingdom would break in upon them unawares.[21]

This is well said and it places the claims of Jesus squarely before us. Moreover, as Niebuhr's critics rightly urge, the presence of sin in human life in no way lessens the claim of Jesus' ethical teaching upon us. Sin or no we are called to respond as best we can. However, if we do act in an evil world as if the Kingdom of God were here, we must reckon with the possibility of failure. Christ was crucified and the disciple is not above his master. This point, which is not always grasped, has crucial implications. First, the way of self-sacrifice has to be personally chosen. It cannot be imposed. The individual Christian can choose this path and so can the Church: but can a nation? MacGregor quoted Dean Inge with approval, 'The notion of a martyr-nation, giving itself up to injustice and spoilation for the most sacred of all causes, cannot be dismissed with contempt'.[22] Sider and Taylor make the same point:

We can imagine America's leaders saying to the aggressor: 'You can create scorched earth and dead cities, but you cannot make us give in to tyranny. You can kill the innocent, but their blood will cry out against you; and God will hear.'[23]

In these assertions there is an illegitimate comparison between a Church, which might be called upon to choose martyrdom rather than defend itself and a nation handed over to tyranny by leaders elected to office precisely in order not to get the nation into a situation where the only choice was one of submission to tyranny or mutual annihilation. This is not to deny that many nations now and in the past have had to suffer silently rather than resist by force because that has been the least destructive course of action open to them. But that is very different from leaders, responsible for the safety of their people, letting them slip into that position when other alternatives are open to them.

Yet Christ is risen. The cross is only half the story. Perhaps we should ask a nation to walk the way of martyrdom in the hope that God will validate those who obey his commands? But we cannot predict when or how resurrection victory will be shown. Christ died with a mixture of despair, trust and hope. He did not go to the cross in the certainty that this was a tunnel through to resurrection on the third day. Christian hope gives rise to policies but is not itself a policy. Politics, on the other hand, works by calculation. Luther said he would rather have as ruler a bad man who was prudent than a good man who was imprudent. Prudence, that is, trying carefully to assess the consequences of our actions and to weigh them in the light of all the factors, is what politics is about. Christian hope is not a form of prudence.

The implications of this must not be avoided. The way of the cross can be chosen by an individual or by a Christian community. It can hardly be chosen by rulers for a nation as a whole. It is difficult to see how Christian pacifists of this ilk can in conscience hold public office.

Does God will, or not will, human communities to continue? There are three points to be made. First, 'mind', as Austin Farrer used to say, 'is a social reality'. There cannot be such a thing as a totally isolated individual. We were all once talked into talking and thinking by others. There can be no human personality without human community. Second, human communities more advanced than that of the Stone Age require a political centre. They are political communities. Third, although it is natural, as Aquinas said, for human beings to come together, because we are social beings, we can only stay together in a fallen world with a degree of coercion.

The conclusion must be that so long as God wills human life to continue he wills political communities and the means without which they cannot exist. It is therefore our responsibility to operate those mechanisms without which there can be no community. To think that human community can exist without some coercion is again to think that the Kingdom has come in its fullness.

Some modern pacifists allow coercion up to a point; they also allow justice as an independent norm up to a point but only within the state, not in the states system as a whole. Niebuhr was more consistent. He came at his consideration of justice through the social struggle and it was the same justice he was concerned to see implemented in the International order. The power of the strong over the weak, the tendency of the mighty to tyrannize the powerless, had to be checked both within the state and between states. The difficulty of looking for justice in the states system is obvious. There is no central authority with power to enforce its own decisions. Each nation has to act as advocate, judge and law enforcement officer in its own cause. The likelihood for self-interest here, the boundless capacity of people to deceive themselves and the scope with modern propaganda methods for governments to deceive their people, makes us highly sceptical about any government's claim to be on the side of justice. It was argued in the 1930s, as now, that the issues were so confused, the unrighteousness so evenly distributed, that we cannot choose. One of the issues about which Niebuhr felt most strongly was that despite this we still do have to choose. In the light of the absolute value of love we can and must make discriminate judgements. He was particularly scathing about those Americans who were hesitant to come into World War II because of the record of imperialism by the Allies.

Despite the apparent relativity of every conflict there are certain issues in which we can and must choose the lesser evil. This is so in the social struggle where we must choose for the powerless against those who enjoy inordinate privilege: but it is also true in the international sphere. The alternative is total relativity: 'If it is not possible to express a moral preference for the justice achieved in democratic societies, in comparison with tyrannical societies, no historical preference has any meaning.'[24]

Which is the lesser of the two evils, however? Yoder accused Niebuhr of having a sentimental depreciation of the horrors of war.[25] Even *a priori* it is unlikely that a man of his generation would be unaware of the horrors of World War I. In fact the entries in

113

Leaves from the Notebook of a Tamed Cynic, his chairmanship, for a time, of the Fellowship of Reconciliation and other explicit statements belie this.[26] Niebuhr, on the other hand, accused pacifists of always preferring tyranny to resistance. The horror of modern war is such that even without nuclear weapons there is a *prima facie* case for pacifism. Indeed, the modern debate between the pacifist and the Niebuhrian can legitimately begin with the assumption that war must be ruled out as the greatest conceivable evil. The burden of proof is on the non-pacifist to show that there is an even greater evil than modern war. The pacifist can point to the ability of occupied nations to keep their culture and values intact, to the inevitability of change, to the resources of love and prayer and to the hope that God will eventually bring release to the captive. The realist will be against these two rather bleak considerations. First, will any group that has achieved absolute power willingly give it up? What examples can be pointed to? People relinquish power when they are forced to do so and it is a strange assumption that bloody civil war is less horrific than other kinds of conflict. Second, what kind of tyranny is it? All societies have been characterized by spasmodic oppression, cruelty, corruption and injustice. This is very different from long standing tyrannies in the grip of an ideology that reinforces absolute control. In George Orwell's *1984* Winston Smith and his girlfriend believe they can defeat the society around them. Although they know they will be caught and killed they think they can win by dying hating the system. The pathos of the novel is that as a result of ruthless brainwashing they die loving big brother. We would have to say that such a society, if it ever came into being, would be the worst evil we could imagine because the possibility of being human no longer existed. This is not to assume that any society now or in the future would become like that, but *1984* acts as a salutary warning. It also questions the assumption that war, however terrible, is the worst evil we can conceive. There may be something to defend which is not simply material well-being, or a way of life, or particular cultural values, but the very possibility of being human.

The horror of modern war cannot be underestimated. Nevertheless, against this we have to set the following considerations. First, most pacifists accept the need to achieve some kind of rough and ready justice, if necessary with the use of minimal coercion, within the state. Is it anything but arbitrary to draw a line between the state and the states-system? Is the international scene to be dominated by those who are prepared to use power in the most ruthless and unprincipled way?

Second, we accept the necessity of law within the state. Is the international order to be handed over to total disorder, to complete lawlessness? For the UN being at present so weak, that is what the refusal to resist involves.

Our attempts to achieve justice and to impose law on the international scene are flawed: but so they are within the state. The attempt to procure justice always reflects class or group interest. Nevertheless, we do not abolish the police because they are more likely to protect the interests of the property owners than the dispossessed. More positively, and theologically: are we to refuse to co-operate with God in his work of creating *pax—ordo—iustitia*, that ordered and just peace without which there can be no human life?

Niebuhr believed that pacifism had a legitimate place within the Church: that it helped to symbolize and keep alive the perfectionist strand within Christianity. If everyone took the vow of celibacy life would cease. But the vows made by religious witness to a life lived for God alone and similarly with the vows of poverty and obedience.

Few pacifists are content to see their stance in purely vocational terms, something for them but not for others. They are conscious of claims laid on all Christians and potentially on all men as part of their response to, and new life in, Christ. There may here be an irreconcilable difference. For I have argued that we have to live with tension between this age and the life of the age to come and that so long as God wills earthly life to continue he asks us to co-operate with him in upholding both civil and international order. Consistent pacifism means withdrawal from key areas of public life. There are real differences in assessing the place of pacifism within the Church, yet perhaps this also is part of the tension we are meant to feel. For it is the legitimate desire of the pacifist to universalize the moral claims he experiences that troubles the non-pacifist, and rightly troubles him, for it brings to bear that absolute standard in the light of which our compromises are seen for what they are and to which we are called to conform so far as we can under the conditions of sinful finite existence.

TEN

Power, coercion and morality*

Deterrence works on the minds of potential adversaries. Its purpose is to convince them that the cost of any aggressive action would be unacceptably high. Within the NATO alliance this purpose is achieved by retaining the option to use nuclear weapons. Missiles in position, with men trained to use them, force a possible enemy to stop before taking a step that might be construed as hostile; and to conclude, on any rational assessment, that the destruction that could be unleashed would be out of proportion to any conceivable gain. The ethical aspect of a policy of nuclear deterrence has many dimensions, some ancient and a well considered part of the 'just war' tradition, others new. One perennial problem that has received far too little attention in recent discussion is the fact that all human relationships have a power factor. The neglect of this in the 1983 Church of England Board for Social Responsibility Report *The Church and the Bomb* was particularly serious and resulted in a distorted view of the dilemma.

The power element is an inescapable feature of all human relationships at both an individual and, more particularly, at a group level. The struggle to dominate or avoid domination goes on ceaselessly and takes many forms from the simple power of one personality over another, to underlying economic realities. The writer Philip Toynbee decided to allow a commune to use his house. Eventually the commune got into a state of disarray and Philip Toynbee decided to repossess his home, despite the opposition of its inhabitants. In the journal he was keeping at the time Toynbee wrote this:

> I delivered a violent harangue, to which nobody spoke a single word in answer. It was Them and Us with a vengeance now; the sweet freaks and children of nature up against the angry proprietor whose only thought was to drive them all away and sell the empty house for a fat sum. A melancholy change. Or, as some would say, no change at all, but simply the true situation no longer disguised by kindly pretences from both sides.[1]

Not all kindly, liberal-minded people are as aware as this. Living

---

* From *The Cross and the Bomb*, edited by Francis Bridger (Mowbray 1983)

in a benign haze they often fail to see the harsh structures around which much social life is constructed. Or if they are aware of it at a theoretical level they, mercifully, do not often have the chance to experience the reality. In Nadine Gordimer's novel *July's People*,[2] Johannesburg has been taken over by forces of black liberation. A liberal white family have been rescued by their houseboy, July, and taken by him to his home village. The novel explores the feelings of the white couple who now suddenly find themselves dependent on a person who has been totally dependent on them for the previous fifteen years. The predicament they find themselves in is focused in a series of small details, for example, who keeps the keys of the Land-rover in which they have escaped? Or, for that matter, who now owns it, the white couple or their houseboy to whom they owe their lives and on whom they are now totally reliant for food and safety? The novel brings out well, in an undogmatic way, how the most altruistic people still share in the fruits of domination of the class or group to which they belong. Those who preached a social gospel in the 1920s and those who urged pacifism in the 1930s had to be taught the realities of power by Reinhold Niebuhr.[3] It appears that today the Church has almost totally failed to assimilate his message.

The word 'power' is vague and this reflects the fact that there are so many different forms of power. No definition can completely escape assumptions but the word will be defined here in as neutral a way as possible. *Power is the capacity to achieve a desired goal.* This leaves the question of the means whereby the desired goal is achieved open. Max Weber's definition also leaves the question of means open, though it stresses that the goal will be achieved even if there is opposition. ' "Power" is the probability that one actor within a social relationship will be in a position to carry out his own will despite resistance, regardless of the basis on which this probability rests.'[4]

The possession of power, being in a position to carry out our will, having the capacity to achieve a desired goal, is not evil in itself. As human beings we all possess power to some degree, or we would not be here. Even a baby has the power to take in food and as it grows it develops power to walk and generally to obtain what it wants (always restricted of course by the power of others to get what they want). Our existence, our being, is inseparable from power of some kind and in some degree. The same is true of God.

Divine power

In recent decades there has been a tendency to underplay the notion of God's power. Within process theology there has been a healthy emphasis on God's persuasive love as opposed to his force. In W. H. Vanstone's *Love's Endeavour, Love's Expense*[5] there was a powerful attempt to see God's creation, as well as the incarnation, as a *kenosis*, or self-emptying. God, it was argued, does not have reserves of power over and above what he expends in creation; in that creation he totally drains or empties himself. The book is a moving attempt to make the moral element paramount in our understanding of God. This is absolutely right. Power by itself availeth nothing. As Simone Weil once put it, Christ could die and rise again three times in front of her and it would do nothing to win her allegiance as a moral being. Our response to God is, first and last, a moral response; that is, we see in him the source and standard of all that is good, true and beautiful.

Nevertheless, a powerless God is a logical nonsense. If God exists at all he has the power that is appropriate to his being as God. It belongs to God, and to God alone, to create *ex nihilo*. It belongs to God to transmute matter into the very stuff of eternity at the end of time. It belongs to God to raise Christ Jesus from the dead. The resurrection cannot be considered apart from the moral worth of the life and death of Jesus. It does not seek to impress by a display of naked power. But nor on the other hand is the resurrection simply the register of a change of outlook on behalf of the disciples. It is God doing what it is proper for God to do, bringing life from death. This is a power that belongs to his being, as it belongs to our being to understand and manipulate the forces of nature in order to build a civilization. Furthermore, it could be argued that without this power and a willingness to use it, God would not have been morally justified in creating the universe in the first place. It must be part of our moral evaluation of God that in bringing into existence sentient beings he had the power to bring about an ultimate state of affairs in which they would bless their creator for their existence.

Power is the capacity to achieve a desired goal. God has the capacity, it belongs to him as God, first to create the world and then to redeem it. But what means does God use? Persuasion or coercion? There is nothing wrong with force in itself. The morality of its use is determined by the object. Where the object is material, force is the appropriate means to employ. We use force to wield a cricket bat or a paint brush, a spade or a saw. So God creates the universe by the direct and unhindered operation of his will and in the case of material objects his will for them directly coincides with the operation of their being.

Where creatures have a mind and will, however, it is persuasion rather than coercion that is morally proper. This is true without qualification in God's dealings with his creatures in relation to himself. A forced love would be a contradiction in terms. It would not be love, for love by definition is a freely chosen delight in a person for their own sake. We deem it totally inappropriate and morally reprehensible for a parent to try to compel a child to love them. They might be able to force some response from an unwilling child but what they forced would not be love. The same is equally true in our relationship with God. Nevertheless the use of force for other purposes cannot be ruled out altogether on moral grounds. We deem it appropriate for example, and morally proper, if a parent insists that his child wear a luminous strap when cycling and that he back up this insistence with the threat of penalties. Out of love for the child and a concern for his safety the parent may have to use sanctions. For it may be only in this way that the life of the child is preserved. Or again, in a family with a number of children, it may only be possible to maintain the order that is necessary for communal living through the use of penalties. It may be essential, for example, that the family sit down to a meal together. The mother has a job and the ordered structure of the household demands it, even apart from questions of family fellowship. So the children have to drop their tasks, even worthy ones like homework, in order to come to a meal. It may on occasion prove necessary to use sanctions to achieve this.

Penalties, or the threat of penalties, are not incompatible with love. They may be necessary both for our safety and in order to harmonize the often conflicting desires and wills of persons in community. But what is the true nature of these penalties? Sometimes the impression is given both in the case of human beings and of God that they are the arbitrary infliction of pain by someone who has been offended or outraged. This picture is a travesty. The moral justification of penalties arises from the fact that all actions have consequences. A person in a pique, for example, takes it out on another member of the family. This other person drives off in a car and because they are upset they have an accident. This accident has all kinds of consequences and so it goes on in an endless series of causal connections. The fact that all our actions have consequences is sometimes unpleasant but it provides the basis of all our planning, thinking and attempts to act responsibly. Because, within limits, we can predict what the consequences of our actions will be, we can plan for the future and make rational decisions about it. God's justice, seen apart from his love, consists simply in letting events take their course; in letting human beings suffer the natural consequences of their deeds. Sometimes, perhaps more often than not, it is other people rather than we ourselves who suffer the ill consequences of our ill deeds.

This fact brings to the fore two other features of our existence which need to be taken into account. The first is that we are so made by God that loving behaviour is designed to lead to our fulfilment and flourishing. He has created us not so much that virtue will be its own reward, though in a sense it is, but that virtue will lead to the well-being and eternal blessedness of our nature.[6] The second feature is the solidarity of mankind both in sin and in Christ. Although at the moment we only grasp this through the use of a loving imagination it is ontologically true that if one suffers all suffer.

Taking into account these considerations therefore, the essence of punishment is letting people suffer the consequences of their actions. But the loving mind does not want this to happen to the beloved. A loving parent does not want a child to suffer the consequences of his carelessness by being run over. Nor does a loving mother want her family to suffer the consequences of total anarchy. This means that if a child fails to wear a luminous strap for safety, or if children fail to turn up to the planned family meal, there are penalties. These may be minor or severe, though usually they take the form of loss of pocket money or being made to do extra washing up or being forbidden the use of the bicycle for a period. But in essence their nature is the same. They are an anticipation, a foretaste, of the unpleasantness of the predicted consequences of the action in order to bring it home and to prevent it coming about. Punishment, whether it is in the home, or in prison or in purgatory, may serve a number of functions including deterring other people or safeguarding others. But these functions are only justified on the basis of the central fact about punishment. It is, *for love's sake*, an anticipation of the harmful consequences of a harmful action, in order to avert the full consequences.

Coercion and love

It can now be seen that properly understood coercion has a place in divine love. For coercion is simply letting people see something of the consequences of their actions. When a parent says to a child, 'If you don't wear your luminous safety strap, you won't be allowed to ride your bike in the dark', this could be called a threat. It could be objected to on the grounds that the child is being forced by the threat of something unpleasant to do something against his will.

Nevertheless what that parent says is a perfectly proper expression of love; and this form of expression has a place in God.

Martin Luther pictured God ruling the world in two ways. With one hand he offered people the love of Christ and by winning a free response to this love brought people into the Church. With the other hand he maintained the fabric of society through coercion. So, according to Luther, society was held together in two ways; by Christians who did what had to be done out of love; and by coercion, so that society kept going with some degree of order whether people willed it or not. Modern Lutheran theology has tended towards modifications of Luther's 'Two Kingdoms' but it highlights an essential distinction. On the one hand, as was discussed earlier, love to be love must be freely chosen. A person, of their own volition, comes to delight in someone else, whether that person is another human being or God. This love cannot be forced or it loses its essential character. It can only be won and the only way it can be won is through the persuasive power of love itself. On the other hand whether people are loving or not society has somehow to be held together. If life is to go on at all the fabric of society has to be maintained, human communities have to be ordered.

What the preceeding paragraphs have tried to show is that the coercive power which is necessary for this ordering is not a denial of love but the appropriate expression of love under certain conditions. This coercive power is wielded by human beings but if ultimately it is God who rules the universe, if God is responsible for this side of life as well as for the more intimate tender side, then it is necessary to show that such coercion is compatible with love. Martin Luther said that if he was attacked when he was going about his business as a minister of the gospel he would follow the injunction of the Sermon on the Mount and not resist. This seems perfectly proper. The gospel can be neither propagated nor defended by force. There is something utterly out of character about missionaries defending themselves with guns. On the other hand Luther said that if he was attacked as a citizen he might very well defend himself for then he would be doing his part in maintaining the order of society. In practice the distinction might be hard to make but at the theoretical level it is both clear and legitimate.

It is for this reason and on the basis of this distinction that Christians should reject the 'crusade' mentality. People sometimes talk about defending Christian civilization or Christian values against atheistic communism. But though civilizations of all kinds can and should be defended against forces which seek to destroy them, what is distinctively Christian cannot and should not be so defended. This sounds a hard doctrine. What is most precious to us we most want to defend. Nevertheless what is Christian can only be championed on the basis of persuasive love. What has to be defended are the conditions which make human life of any kind possible.[7] The good has to be freely chosen but the conditions which make it possible for the good to be chosen have to be maintained. These conditions cannot be upheld simply on the basis of good will; coercion is necessary both within states and between them.

Further exploration is necessary as to why coercion is needed not simply on an occasional basis but as an essential, continuing constituent of human society. In classical Christian realism its necessity is attributed to the fall. Man is a fallen creature, a sinner, who is always likely to wreck every new constellation of good. Nevertheless the necessity of coercion for the organization of human community does not arise simply out of this aspect of human nature. Three other features are enough to account for it. First, human beings pursue their own interests. Second, they have only a limited capacity to take into account the interests of others. Third, when human beings are organized into groups, both these tendencies are accentuated and made into a cardinal principle. All these features belong to human life as such and are not in themselves the result of any fall.

Thus, it is necessary for the survival of both the individual and the species that creatures pursue their own interests; indeed it is a mark of vitality, of the will to struggle and survive, that they do so. If a baby did not have enough self-interest to reach for the bottle, it would die. If the schoolboy, or girl, does not have enough self-interest to stand up for himself or herself, he or she is likely to become psychologically squashed. That we have only a limited capacity to take into account the interests of others is not the sign of some dramatic fall from grace but an indication of our immaturity. We have been made, by God, part of the animal kingdom, with enough self-interest to survive, yet with a dawning capacity to be aware of the needs and claims of others. It is the heart of the challenge of life that this capacity grows. But the picture is an Irenaean rather than an Augustinian one. We are infants struggling through to maturity rather than perfect beings thrown out of paradise. Then, when it comes to group life, the willingness to strive for the interest of the group becomes a virtue; the unwillingness to take into account the needs of other groups not necessarily a vice. For example a university that seeks to engage the most able research students is not acting in a reprehensible manner. The fact that it does not let them go to a minor college struggling for survival is not necessarily a vice.

A number of modern novelists, as well as most of human history including most modern history, indicate all too clearly the truth that man is 'fallen'. Nevertheless, although this makes the necessity of coercion in human affairs more insistent, this necessity can be accounted for in other terms as well. It may be useful to do this, if only for the reason that some modern people find it impossible to make sense of assertions such as 'man is fallen' or else they are alienated by such language. Coercion is necessary because human beings pursue their own interests, they have only a limited capacity to transcend those interests for a greater good, and in organized group life these tendencies become normative.

It is, for example, all too easy to understand how, if one was born on a kibbutz one would be fighting pasionately for Israel, and if one was born in a Palestinian refugee camp one would be fighting with equal conviction for the PLO. Both sides are imbued with a will to survive; for both sides the individual will to survive is invested with the status of a virtue when it is put at the service of the cause; on neither side is sympathy towards the other side's point of view prized or encouraged. Both sides no doubt share the general lot of fallen mankind. Yet less mysterious than that is the simple fact that both sides have very different perceptions, in particular very different perceptions about where right lies. In this situation goodwill is desperately necessary but a solution is not going to be achieved by goodwill alone. When a political solution is found, it will be one that will have to be enforced; enforced perhaps by outside powers on the parties to the dispute and by the leaders of each side on their own extremists.

According to Marxist analysis economic forces are the determinants of human history. Each class inevitably pursues its own econmic interests. Yet it can be questioned whether the economic factor is always the pre-eminent one. In early feudal society it was a combination of military and priestly power that was usually successful. The economic power of these castes was a consequence not a cause of their dominance.

According to some people, (e.g. Nietzsche), human beings are characterized by a basic will-to-power so that through every means at our disposal we are engaged in a ceaseless struggle to dominate or avoid being dominated. There is clearly much truth in this analysis, as there is in the Marxist one, but again it does not

123

cover all the constituents of a conflict situation. There is for example the element of insecurity. Israel desires, apparently, to retain the West Bank. She has been extremely reluctant to give up territory captured in recent wars. Outsiders often see this in terms of her expansionist ambitions. She herself sees it in terms of a need to be secure. The fact is that the defensive/aggressive mentality, the desire to be secure and the need to expand a little in order to remain secure, are so closely interwined it is often impossible to separate them.

Group self-interest

The fact remains that however we account for it, whether in terms of economic determinism, a will-to-power, or a legitimate desire for security, human groupings tend to pursue their own interests whilst only partially taking into account the perceptions and interests of other groupings. The failure to realize this was one of the most notable weaknesses in *The Church and the Bomb*. The authors of the Report argued that Soviet defence policy was not aggressive and that it only looked as though it was because of their intention to strike hard and quickly if a war did break out. Yet this fact, even if true, should not lead to less vigilance in relation to them any more than a comparable conclusion in relation to the USA should lead to less vigilance in relation to them. For all major powers have an incipient imperialist tendency.[8] The defensive/aggressive mentality in which we all share leads them to strive for the maximum rather than the minimum security. So the Soviet Union seeks to retain control over her satellite states, Poland, East Germany, Hungary and so on. She seeks to gain control in other states on her borders, as in Afghanistan and she generally seeks to win friends and influence people throughout the world. None of this is in the least surprising, particularly, as the Report rightly shows, as the Soviet Union has the longest border in the world to secure and she has been both invaded and harassed by other powers during the last sixty years.

What is true of the Soviet Union is true in one way or another of America. One of the major ways in which the two superpowers seek power and influence in the modern world is through arms transfers. America and the Soviet Union, who between them have over eighty per cent of the market, pursue their rivalry in the developing world by exporting enormous quantities of arms. Arms transfers have doubled in the last decade and three-quarters of the trade goes to the developing world. In a number of regions, such as the Middle East, American and Soviet arms transfers are a mirror image of one another. In the modern world invasion of another territory is highly dangerous (it might precipitate a nuclear war) and it is more difficult to retain bases in foreign countries. So super power rivalry takes a different form. Each seeks client states, countries dependent upon it, who can be relied on to maintain and pursue its interests.[9]

Major powers pursue their own political interests. They seek to secure their borders and this includes having states on the borders. They tend to move in if there is a power vacuum. Similarly if there is instability in a particular region each major power will have a particular concern about it, the Soviet Union to aid 'forces of liberation', America to strengthen forces of stability. Given this ceaseless struggle for power and influence, this endless hard-nosed jostling for position, how can the twin goals of justice and peace be best achieved in the world?

First, it must be acknowledged that there are legitimate security needs of all states, even traditional enemies and potential adversaries. From the foregoing analysis it is clear that the world in which we live is one in which all states have, and will continue to have for the foreseeable future, security needs. How these needs are met will vary. At the moment they take the form of a defence capability or membership of an alliance which has promised support in the event of being attacked. In some parts of the world there are signs of an approach to security on a regional basis. One day, pray God, it will be possible to achieve security on a world-wide basis in a way which avoids the endless warring of sovereign and suspicious states on the one hand, and the potential tyranny of a world government on the other. But until that time comes all states have to take steps, either on their own or in company with others, to safeguard their security. This must be affirmed, without qualification, even about one's most dire adversary.

Second, attempts must be made to achieve a rough parity of power between adversaries.[10] Power was earlier defined as the capacity to achieve a desired goal. The goal in this case is security from external attack. The means by which this is obtained is through convincing potential aggressors that the cost of any aggression would be out of proportion to any conceivable good that could be obtained by it. There are a number of forms of power that can be utilized in the world to ensure peace and justice, such as economic coercion and persuasion, particularly when linked to traditional diplomatic skills. These skills tend to be underrated in relation to military strength but they are vital for international stability. The world contains innumerable political problems,

125

often overlapping with one another. Above all these need political and diplomatic skills through which alone the many conflicting requirements of the international order can be brought together into an acceptable compromise. Nevertheless force and diplomacy go hand in hand. Coercion, including military coercion, remains an essential constituent of world order.

The purpose of a military capability is to convince a potential aggressor that aggression would unleash unacceptable damage. It forces other states to stop and count the cost before undertaking any action that might be construed as hostile. There are many types of coercion, most of them morally repugnant. It was earlier suggested, however, that not all coercion has this character.[11] All actions have consequences and it is not necessarily morally wrong to bring home to people what the consequences of their actions might be. For the Christian believer this truth is grounded in an ultimate state of affairs where the full consequences of our actions as human beings are known and suffered. When a state makes it clear through its possession of a defence capability that it will resist attack it is simply spelling out the fact that actions have consequences and that it is part of the moral character of the universe that they should.

There is often talk of a nuclear or military 'threat'. The use of the word 'threat' in this context is misleading. A threat is something we abhor on moral grounds. But a military capability, including a nuclear one, is only a threat to states contemplating aggression. Otherwise it is simply in existence as a reminder that events have consequences. The law of the land, with its penalties, is not a threat to those who keep the law. But it stands as a reminder that, for example, drunken driving can lead to death and those caught drunk in charge will suffer, through imprisonment, something of the suffering they inflicted or might have inflicted on other people.

The analogy with the law of the land is of course in some ways a simplistic one. On the whole within a country people know what the law is. Within the international order there are endless disputes with very different perceptions about what is the right and the wrong. Within a country the law makes an attempt to be impartial and it is administered by an authority that stands above the parties in a dispute. In the international order the parties take the law into their own hands for the only higher authority, the United Nations, has no power at the moment to enforce its authority. Nevertheless, what is at stake in the international order, as much as within a country, is the moral law; not simply international law, but moral law grounded finally in the being of

God himself. However mistaken nations may have been in their understanding of the rights and wrongs of a particular issue, however often deceived in self-righteously abrogating to themselves the role of law-enforcers when they were in fact law breakers, the international order no less than the national order is based upon moral law. This means both that actions have consequences and that it is part of the moral character of the universe that they should. Any state with a military capability that is genuinely defensive is a standing reminder of this. Potential adversaries are aware that any act of aggression would lead to unacceptable damage being inflicted upon them. This is pre-eminently true of relationships between nuclear powers but it is also true of all military forces. For it is the primary purpose of all military force, not just nuclear force, to deter.

It was earlier argued that power, understood as the capacity to achieve a desired goal, was not in itself an evil. On the contrary it belongs both to divine and human nature that we are able to obtain something of what we want. If we did not have this capacity we would not exist. There is a positive aspect even to military power and the situation of a balance of power. This can be seen most easily at an individual level. When two people are roughly equal in wealth or status or mental ability there is more likely to be a basic respect for one another than when there is gross disparity. Human beings have a tendency to dominate or patronize one another. Where there is a rough equality—in the goods or qualities which both parties respect—this tendency will be less likely to assert itself; the parties will be more likely to take one another's needs and interests seriously. What is true at the individual level applies in relationships between groups. There is a proper pride and status that belongs to every nation. This cannot be purchased by military might and the attempt to do this is always disastrous, as was the case with Iran under the Shah. Nevertheless, a defensive capability is a necessary and proper component of nationhood. There is a popular inclination to think that non-aggressive nations like Switzerland or Sweden have no forces at all. This is not true: Sweden spends more per capita on defence than France, Great Britain or West Germany.

Christian element

Even amongst those who have followed the argument with some degree of sympathy there will remain some unease. The line of thought has been very secular, it seems; where is the distinctively Christian element? Jesus told his followers not to follow the

127

example of pagan rulers who make others feel the weight of their authority. 'It shall not be so among you.' Rather, his followers are to be like him, servants of others. This service led him to death on the cross although, according to one Gospel account, he could have summoned legions of angels to his assistance. This moving and distinctive attitude of Jesus took theological form after his death. Paul affirms that the weakness of God is stronger than the power of men. He praises Christ as the eternal son of God who emptied himself to come amongst us as a man. As the Dean of King's College, Cambridge, put it to me:

> Don't you think that renunciation of wordly power and force is a major and substantive Christian thing, integral to NT Christology whether in the Mt/Lk temptation stories or Paul *passim*? It seems to be so to me, and to be a treasure in the Church's keeping which is now urgently needed as something more than a theological ornament, renunciation being a thing so difficult and so necessary that people need all the help they can get. I don't think there can be love (including political love) without renunciation. I don't think there can be salvation without it and fear that without it there is destruction—or so my Bible seems to say.

This is elegantly put, and coming from a distinguished scholar represents a considered and not just a popular view of what the New Testament contains. Clearly John Drury is right about the connection between love and renunciation of power at the individual level. In personal relationships if another person tries to 'pull rank' or makes threats based on superior force or wealth; if he tries to be 'one up' through the assertion of superior mental abilities or culture; if in any way he tries to make the other person feel small or inferior—then we regard this as a failure of love. Indeed we have been so influenced by this understanding of love that we would also regard it as a failure of manners or elementary courtesy.

The crucial question is how far this is either possible or appropriate in dealings between groups. If we say that it is not appropriate then we seem to allow for a double ethical standard, one for our dealings with others when we meet them on a personal level and one for our dealings with them when they are part of a group, whether that group is a rival business, a trade union or a hostile country. Nevertheless there are real difficulties, not only in discovering exactly what Jesus meant, but in applying what he said in the contemporary world. The main difficulty has to do with the fact that his teaching was given in the light of his expectation about the imminence of the Kingdom of God. Some scholars deny that this was part of the teaching of Jesus himself and they attribute it to the early Church. Others so understand the nearness of the Kingdom that they imply Jesus would have taught the same truths in the same way, even if he had thought that the world would continue on the same course for several thousand years.

The position taken here is that Jesus did think that the Kingdom, the decisive rule of God in human affairs, was near and that his ethical teaching has to be seen in integral relationship to that conviction. In other words if he had believed that human society would continue in its old way for thousands of years he would have balanced his teaching by more emphasis on what he took for granted, namely the law of the Old Testament.

The law of the Old Testament is applicable to the management of human society. Jesus assumes this. He does not so much overthrow it as call people to live in a way that transcends it, a way that will be vindicated very shortly, when God is clearly seen to reign on earth. When Jesus was asked to solve a dispute and said, 'Who made me a divider and judge among you?' he then called people to look at their basic motivation. This was his particular prophetic task. He did not imply that the law had no role. On the contrary the law clearly does have a role and it is precisely that of divider and judge in the case of disputes.

It cannot be denied that a Christian is called to live without dominating others and that if he finds himself in a position of dominance he has to find a way of meeting others on terms that are not a threat. Furthermore, it may very well be the witness of a particular Christian to assert the primacy of this approach in the political realm and not only in the sphere of personal relationships, for example, by being a conscientious objector. But this latter stand must be seen first and last as a witness to the ultimate rule of God in human affairs. It cannot, on Christian grounds, be regarded as a way of achieving desirable results in this world. Christ's death on the cross was not a way of bringing about the resurrection. The resurrection was a supernatural act of validation by God. The early Christian martyrs did not see their deaths as a way of hastening the Kingdom. They cried 'How long O Lord?' but they did not think that there was a causal connection between their martyrdom and the coming of the end. Their deaths were primarily an act of witness. And this is how in the modern world renunciation of power or rights, in particular instances, should be viewed.

What has occurred in some quarters is a blend of pure Christian pacifism (the extreme form of renunciation of power) with Gandhi's concept of non-violent resistance. His technique was highly effective in India and also when used by Martin Luther King. It may also prove useful in other situations. Clearly also from a moral point of view it has much to recommend it. Nevertheless, for all its spiritual claims, it is still a technique (combining both coercive and non-coercive elements). Jesus believed that his heavenly Father would bring in the Kingdom, indeed was already bringing it in. He himself lived in that light and called others to do so. But it is God who brings in the Kingdom. So it is that when Christians renounce power or rights this should be seen like martyrdom as an act of witness. There is no necessary causal connection between the renunciation and other events that follow. It could be that there is a favourable response. Sometimes at an individual level someone who comes across as 'all gift, no threat' disarms us; our barriers go down, our own tendency to dominate or impress is put aside and we try to relate to the other person as a person. But in relationships between groups such an outcome is much less likely. On the whole groups exploit weakness shown by others. This is not to deny that statesmen should seek to build up trust between nations by every means at their disposal. There are many ways in which this can and should be done and unilateral gestures of renunciation may have a place. But dramatic and wholesale unilateral renunciation of power would be both dangerous and immoral.

Foolish and immoral

One of the prime functions of government is to defend its people. Those who are elected to office in it are expected, rightly, to fulfil this function. A government that neglects this function is being not just foolish but immoral. The proper consideration in relation to any defence decision is whether it will genuinely help to preserve the security of the realm. It would be immoral, for example, for a Christian stateman to renounce a particular weapon if he genuinely believed that the weapon enhanced the defence of the realm or if he thought that holding onto the weapon would enable an agreement to be made with an adversary power which would bring real reductions in their weapons. That politician, as a Christian individual, might be tempted to make a moral gesture by renouncing the weapon. He might believe that by doing so he was witnessing to the truth of God's Kingdom which is based on trust and not on force. Nevertheless, as a politician in government it would be immoral, a betrayal of trust, to renounced the weapon for those reasons. He must take only those steps which truly contribute to the security of the nation. His main concern therefore will always be with the practical consequences of suggested decisions. Will it or will it not have the desired effect? And this, despite all eschewing of moral gestures (unless they are calculated to serve a specific and predicted purpose) is a highly moral endeavour.[12]

In the fourth century the Christian Church ceased to be a small persecuted sect. Instead it became allied with government. The Roman army, once held at arm's length by Christians, became a Christian closed shop. Christians have always been divided in their attitude to this change in status under the Emperor Constantine. Many Christians regard this as the great betrayal, the time when the rot set in. For others it is the point at which the Church grew up and took its share with others in maintaining the fabric of ordered society. Doing this means getting the hands dirty, taking responsibility in and for a coercive order. Augustine was not only a bishop. He served as a magistrate meting out punishment.

There is no way national or international society can be maintained with some degree of justice, order and peace without coercion. It is possible for some Christians to renounce this totally. But this must be understood as a witness to an ultimate order that one day, under God, will be. It should not be seen as a means of bringing that order closer. *Some* renunciation in *some* situations may serve an important purpose. But such decisions must be made only on political grounds on the calculation that they will enhance the genuine security of the nation. Multilateral weapons reduction, for example, is a bargaining process. Even given a genuine desire to achieve real reductions it is the nature of this process that each participant seeks to obtain the maximum concessions from the other side whilst conceding as little as possible itself. If one side thinks the other will concede something without anything being asked in return it is likely not to give anything in return. The difficulty is well illustrated in Kissinger's remark about trying to exact concessions from Israel: 'When I ask Rabin to make concessions, he says he can't because he is weak. So I give him more arms, and then he says he doesn't need to make concessions because Israel is strong.' A statesman, *qua* statesman, has to take this tendency into account. If the statesman is a Christian he has to take it into account no less than anyone else.

Luther made a distinction between the Christian ruled by God's persuasive love disclosed in Christ and the citizen ruled by God's coercive love working through the structures of society. Reinhold Niebuhr too made a distinction. In his case a distinction between what was possible between individuals motivated by love, where one person might give up what was rightfully due to him, and society made up of groups all pursuing their own interests. Niebuhr's analysis still retains much of its validity. Nevertheless, as he later acknowledged, and as Luther admitted, the true distinction is not between the individual and society or between the Christian and others. The source of the distinction is within oneself and within everyone, and it is between the capacity to transcend one's own interests in the interests of others and one's habitual reluctance to do so.

The simplest example of this problem is provided by taxation. Even if it were clearly explained to every citizen what taxes were being spent on, and an education programme was mounted to show how indispensable taxes are, how many people would pay the full amount they were assessed for if the collection was done on a voluntary basis with no penalties for those who defaulted? Not much tax would be collected in this way, even from avowed Christians. So tax, like everything else that is essential to the maintenance of society, is made the subject of laws. Laws, with the penalties for breaking them, exist to ensure that most people do most of the time what some people would do some of the time on a voluntary basis. Laws exist to close the gap between what in our better moment we choose to do and what for most of the time we are likely to do. And what is true at a national level applies equally at the international. Coercion is necessary for the existence of an ordered human society and it is necessary for society as a whole at both a national and an international level because it is necessary for each one of us as individuals, whether or not we are Christian believers.

This essay has argued that although power has become a dirty word, it is an essential constituent of the being both of God and man. But if power is defined as the capacity to achieve a desired goal the crucial question concerns the method by which this goal is to be achieved. The only properly moral method of winning the free love of free creatures is the persuasive example of love itself. This is revealed in Christ and preached in the gospel. Nevertheless, coercion, although it too has an ugly sound, implying immoral threats by immoral people, is not in itself always immoral. It belongs to the universe that actions have consequences and to the moral nature of the universe that ultimately we suffer the consequences of our own actions. 'God's coercive love' consists in allowing this to happen or making us aware that this will happen. It is primarily through this coercive love that God maintains the fabric of ordered society. In this way he establishes and upholds the conditions which make any kind of properly human life possible.

This coercive love is necessary for the just ordering of society because human beings pursue their own interests and have only a limited capacity to transcend them on behalf of the interests of others. Both these tendencies are deeply engrained in the working of human groups, not least in relationships between states. The fact that man is a 'fallen' creature is not the cause of this state of affairs but it accentuates its worst features. Within this kind of world the most likely way of reaching and retaining some degree of international stability is through a parity of power between potential adversaries. This power, the capacity to inflict un-acceptable damage if attacked, forces nations to be careful and to avoid actions that could be construed as overtly hostile.

Balances of power are often precarious. Where the threat of destruction is almost total, as it is between the nuclear powers there is *some* hope that war can be averted. Where the threat of devastion is not total, as in the Middle East, a strong defensive capacity deters but peace is always fragile. Nevertheless in the world in which we live, the failure to deter is often a cause of war, as it was in the case of the Falklands, where the Argentinians were allowed to think that Britain had neither the capacity nor the will to resist. Balances of power as a way of keeping the peace have always been volatile. They must be accompanied by ceaseless political effort and sensitivity by all parties not simply to keep war at bay but to resolve the dispute which has given rise to the adversarial stance.

But power vacuums are even more dangerous. In a world where states are always seeking to extend their sphere of influence they are a standing temptation. Furthermore, a nuclear balance of power contains a feature that has never been present before. No side could win a nuclear war and it could never be in the interest of any power to fight a war against another power possessing nuclear weapons. This brings an element of stability into the balance that is totally new. Finally, utterly horrifying though nuclear weapons are, they act as a terrible warning to everyone involved, not just potential enemies, about the terrible consequences of going to war. Reflection on the reasons for which men have gone to war in the past, many of which now seem so trivial, can make us grateful for the horrifying reminder provided by the existence of nuclear weapons of the effects of human sin and folly. Never again will men be able to shrug off the thought of going to war; and in this there must be divine mercy as well as divine severity.[13]

ELEVEN

Human rights in theological perspective*

Human dignity

The concept of human rights is usually assumed to be a secular notion; and the emergence of human rights in the philosophies of the late seventeenth century, culminating in the French Revolution in the late eighteenth century, a secular movement. This needs qualifying. The American Declaration of Independence in 1776 declared, 'All men are created equal, (and) are endowed *by their creator*, with certain unalienable rights'. Indeed, as we know, the founding fathers of the United States and of the constitution were devoutly, fiercely Christian. We note too that the French made their declaration in 1789 'in the presence and under the auspices of the Supreme Being'. No less important is the fact that the truths inherent in and safeguarded by the concept of human rights were, before the eighteenth century, expressed in other ways and guarded by other means: the accountability of sovereigns to God; the divine law; and the position of the Church, at least before the Reformation, as a countervailing power to the unbridled tyranny of the state.

From a consciously Christian point of view rights are grounded, first of all, in the value of the created order. I say rights, rather than human rights at this stage, because it may be that others besides humans, animals for example, have rights. One of the features of our time is the movement to conserve species of animals and plants and to preserve the environment from pollution. There are millions of birds in the world and hundreds of species. Why should some men and women devote a great deal of time and trouble, say, to preserving a species of wild guinea-fowl in the tropical forests of South America? They recognize and value the richness and variety of creation; the inherent worth of every form of life.

So the question of rights is wider than human rights. Nevertheless, it is on human rights that we now focus. All talk about human rights presupposes a recognition of the dignity and worth of the

* From *Human Rights for the 1990s*, edited by Robert Blackburn and John Taylor (Mansell 1991)

human person. On the whole moral philosophers are shy of saying anything as basic as that. But Christian theologians are not, or ought not to be, ashamed of being counted with the babes and sucklings out of whose mouths unadorned simplicities can come. And even moral philosophers will on occasion admit to what, of course, they believe. So Ronald Dworkin writes: 'Anyone who professes to take rights seriously . . . must accept, at the minimum . . . the vague but powerful idea of human dignity'.[1]

'This idea is associated with Kant', continues Dworkin. One wonders why Kant is singled out rather than the framers of the legal codes in the Old Testament, or Jesus, or Aquinas, to suggest just a few of the thousands of pre-Kantian alternatives. For the worth and dignity of the human person is basic to the Judaeo – Christian–Islamic tradition. This could be illustrated by countless writers from all three religions and talked about in a variety of ways. I will focus on some fundamental Christian doctrines as a way of highlighting the point. First, human beings are created by God; and, moreover, created in his likeness. We are not the chance by-product of a random and ultimately meaningless splurge of life on a small cooling star. We are the delibrate creation of an eternal and loving spiritual reality. He who is the source of all value has chosen, as it were, to break bits off himself. But that metaphor, though deliberately chosen, is wrong. For when God broke bits off himself he brought into existence creatures with a real independence. As the old Jewish metaphor puts it, God picked up the skirts of his clothing to create a tiny space where he was not, in order that there might be a space where free creatures could live. All creatures, because they come from God, share in something of his value. But human beings, who are able to choose, think, pray, and love, are said, because of these special qualities, to have been created in his image.

Here a protest must be entered against one assumption that lurks around in the religious unconscious. It is that the creator can do what he likes with his creatures: that they have no rights against God. I am sorry to say that this view is found even in Paul. Using a picture derived from Jeremiah that God is the potter and human beings his pots. Paul argues that we have no right to complain if some are selected for salvation and others are not.

> Man, who art thou that repliest against God? Shall the thing formed say to him that formed it, Why hast thou made me thus? Hath not the potter power over the clay, of the same lump to make one vessel into honour, and another dishonour?[2]

But even staying with this analogy, the conclusion is not what Paul would have us believe. For the potter has not just tossed off the pot. He has worked at it for day after day, indeed for aeon after aeon. He has literally sweated blood over it. He has, literally, put his heart and his soul into it. The pot that is produced, flawed though it may still be, is infinitely precious to the creator. Or we can put it another way. God creates and at once recognizes the value of what he has created. Here is the foundation for a consciously Christian approach to human rights: *God makes man in his own image and respects the worth and dignity of what he has created.* With this affirmation both Jew and Muslim would agree. But the Christian wants to go even further. Such is the value of human persons in the eye of their maker that he himself becomes a human person; he takes to himself human nature that we might share his divine nature. The Good Shepherd goes out for the one sheep that is lost, hunts high and low for it until he brings it home to eternal life, rejoicing. Human beings are that precious in the eyes of God.

The violation of human dignity

In a family governed by harmony there would be no need for either parents or children to talk about rights. The value of each person would be fully recognized and respected. The language of human rights is necessary because in the world as a whole that is not the case. Human beings are tortured, imprisoned without trial, discriminated against, kept in permanent poverty and so on. It is necessary to assert rights in order to protect human persons from this cruel and degrading treatment. In short *the basis of human rights is not simply human dignity as such but the fact that this human dignity is so often denied in practice.* This second aspect is likewise fundamental to the Christian view, which has always insisted that human life as we know it is fatally flawed. As Reinhold Niebuhr put it: 'Though Christ is the true norm of every man, every man is also in some sense a crucifier of Christ.'[3]

It is from this two-sided truth that the Christian Church seeks to construct a Christian policy. It is because of this that it has both affirmed the state as an expression of the essentially social nature of human persons and argued for the tragic necessity of a coercive power in the state, without which human social life would not be possible.

The state, in Christian theology, is in principle a divinely sanctioned institution. But states are ruled by sinful human beings. As sinful human beings need the power of the state to curb their lawlessness, no less do the rulers of the state need a curb on their potential for oppressing their citizens. From this follow all the classical checks and balances of liberal democracies, the separation of powers, elected governments for a fixed term and so on. These classical democratic arrangements are an expression of a belief in the freedom and dignity of citizens: but no less, and perhaps more importantly, they express the fear of tyranny that is incipient in every human government. It follows then that from one point of view human rights legislation belongs to the emergence and refining of the democratic tradition. For human rights express the dignity of human beings, and also seek to protect that dignity against arbitrary powers of government.

Utilitarianism

A theological perspective on human rights will therefore respond positively to Dworkin's distinction, in his discussion of utilitarianism, between personal and external preferences, a distinction he believes that has not been properly taken into account in other discussions on human rights. Utilitarianism is based on preferences. But these preferences may be personal, for example a white student may prefer segregation because it improves his chances of getting into law school. Or his choice may be external, that is, he dislikes black people and disapproves of social situations when the races mix. The problem, according to Dworkin, is that in practice—that is in a democratic society which is based on the preferences of its citizens—it is not possible to differentiate between personal and external preference. There is therefore the likelihood of inequality being built into the system. For the system will inevitably reflect not just what citizens want for themselves but their attitudes to others. For this and other reasons Dworkin champions what he calls a strong sense of right:

> The concept of an individual political right . . . is a response to the philosophical defects of a utilitarianism that counts preferences and the practical impossibility of a utilitarianism that does not. It allows us to enjoy the institutions of political democracy which enforce overall an unrefined utilitarianism, and yet protect the fundamental right of citizens to equal concern and respect by prohibiting decisions that seem, antecedently, likely to have been reached by virtue of the external components of the preferences democracy reveals.[4]

Utilitarianism is the underlying assumption of liberal democracy, but all societies depend on some collective goal or idea. Human rights, in Dworkin's view, are a safeguard for the individual against any such idea of the common good. In his famous phrase they are political trumps: 'Individual rights are political trumps held by individuals. Individuals have rights when, for some reason, a collective good is not a sufficient justification for denying them what they wish, as individuals to have or do, or not a sufficient justification for imposing some loss or injury upon them.'[5] 'If someone has a right to something, then it is wrong for the government to deny it to him even though it would be in the general interest to do so.'[6]

To take a contemporary example, in a society of limited resources there might be a widespread distaste of homosexuality in general and those with AIDS in particular. A democratic government, responsive to the popular mood, might deny those with AIDS adequate medical care. It could mount an argument that this was in the common interest, in the sense that it reflected the preference of the majority of the citizens. Or, in an undemocratic country, the government might just decide that it was in the common interest that AIDS victims should die untreated, as a deterrent to others. In either society there needs to be a right to equal medical care; a right that belongs to every citizen whatever a government might or might not decide was in the common interest.

In a perfect society human beings would be able to make personal preferences, and at the same time both sympathize with and respect the personal preferences of others. But we lack that imaginative sympathy and respect. Even if we have it in some degree we are inclined to let our personal preferences ride roughshod over other claims. In short, the distinction that Dworkin makes, and which is inherent in the democratic societies we know, corresponds to the twin insights of Christian theology: our capacity for love and our denial of love: our ability to recognize human dignity in theory while denying it in practice.

Human rights are *natural* rights. By that is first of all meant the fact that these rights can be recognized by all people, whatever their religion or lack of it, whatever their politics or their ideology. Hitherto I have discussed the consciously Christian basis of human rights, about human beings being made in the image of God and yet crucifying that image of God. Yet it is equally part of Catholic tradition that human beings have value, and that this value can be recognized as such, without any conscious religious belief. There is, according to Catholic tradition, a natural law and, corresponding to this there are natural rights.

Natural law and natural rights

Natural law has been subjected to attacks from three quarters. First, there have been those Protestant thinkers who, emphasizing the corruption of the human race, have denied the capacity of natural, unredeemed man to respond to moral law. This is manifestly absurd, and in fact has the effect of undermining the Christian faith. For how can Christians come to recognize Jesus to be 'the way, the truth and the life', without some inkling of what is the way, the truth and the life? Secondly, there are legal positivists who deny the existence of any laws or rights that are not already present in legal form. But a theistic view of the world will always want to insist that human laws ultimately derive their validity from, and are subject to correction by, a higher moral law. The moral obligation to obey the law is not derived from the law itself, and law is, rightly, in a constant process of flux. Unjust laws, such as the Group Areas Act in South Africa, are not morally binding (though it may be deemed prudent on occasions to adhere to them). Thirdly, moral philosophers have sometimes doubted whether the concept of natural law has any meaning. Certainly few today would want to defend the thesis that what occurs naturally, that is, in unimpeded nature, is *ipso facto*, a design carrying moral obligation. However, what is protected by the concept of natural law is the conviction that human beings are moral beings; that irrespective of any religious beliefs they have the capacity to recognize moral truths; and that whatever differences of culture or religion may divide us it is possible for people of differing backgrounds to engage in moral discourse with one another on the basis of at least some common assumptions. Indeed the development of modern human rights law is a remarkable tribute to natural law in this sense. From the United Nations Charter in 1945 to the latest Instrument of the International Labour Organization people of the most diverse backgrounds have agreed on a long series of laws and rights. This agreement and the discussion that produced it presupposes capacity for moral, and not just legal, discourse that belongs to human beings as such: that is *natural*.

Some, in the natural law tradition, see natural law and natural rights as being closely bound up. Jacques Maritain, for example, after arguing that human beings, as such, have a destiny and that destiny is natural and therefore obligatory for us, wrote: 'If man is morally bound to the things which are necessary to the fulfilment of his destiny, obviously, then he has the right to fulfil his destiny; and if he has the right to fulfil his destiny he has the right to the things necessary for this purpose.'[7]

Whatever reservations moral philosophers may have about natural law there appears to be less reluctance to use the phrase *natural* rights. There are, of course, still those who say, like Bentham, that it is a nonsensical notion and that talk of them as 'natural and inprescriptible' (that is, inalienable) is just 'nonsense upon stilts'. But, from a Christian perspective, they exist; not just as legal rights but as moral rights which undergird and subject to improvement all legal rights. These rights are *natural*; that is, they belong to all human beings *qua* human beings and they can be recognized as such by everyone whatever their religious convictions.

Christian suspicions of rights

Although, as we suggested earlier, Christians were active in the formulation of rights in the American Declaration of Independence, and though the concept of natural law contains an implicit recognition of human rights, there is nevertheless a niggling doubt in some quarters about whether talk about rights is really compatible with Christianity. This doubt must be examined. First, there is the idea that a creator can do as he likes with his creatures. Creatures, it is said, have no rights: and this, if true, seems to undermine any idea that creatures have rights even between themselves at the creaturely level. But, as we argued earlier, God has created man in his own image: and *God himself recognizes and respects the supreme worth of what he has created.*

Second, there is the notion that Christian ethics is an ethic of duty, rather than rights. Even if this is true, duties presuppose rights. My duty not to murder presupposes the right of other human beings to life. But it is not certain that the Christian faith is committed to a duty-based, rather than a goal-based, right-based, or value-based moral philosophy. It is true that the common starting point for Christian action is doing the will of our heavenly father. But this will is for the well-being and flourishing of his creatures. How we decide what will make for their well-being and flourishing is illuminated by the bibical revelation. But in moral reflection on this, the notions of right, good and value, as well as duty, all have a place. Indeed, if Christianity is committed to the idea of the worth of each individual person (as opposed to any collective goal) it would seem to favour the move being made in some quarters towards a right-based moral philosophy.

Third, there is the idea, derived in particular from the Sermon on the Mount, that Christians should be in the business of waiving their rights rather than asserting them. This raises very complex and disputed questions of how we are to interpret and apply the perfectionist strand in Christian ethics. My own position is that this element, focused on the Sermon on the Mount, acts as an absolute standard which judges all our human compromises, but that it does not, under the conditions of sinful finite existence, take away our civic duties and rights. We have both duties to the state and rights under it. Luther was quite wrong to tell those taking part in the Peasants' Revolt of 1525 – 'Suffering! Suffering! Cross! Cross! This and nothing else is the Christian law.'[8] As he emphasized our duties to the state, so he should have urged, no less strongly, our rights under it. Those rights exist whether or not individual Christians choose in certain circumstances to waive particular rights. For, of course, there is the world of difference between choosing to waive one's own rights—the right to sue, for example, as mentioned in Matthew 5.40—and urging others to waive theirs. Rather, in the world in which we live, a world in which there are so many powerless, Christian love is best shown by championing the rights of the weak, and expanding the areas in which their rights are respected, against the vested interests of the powerful.

Unfolding rights

Human rights are rooted in moral values. Because of this legal recognition of rights is a dynamic historical process. It is as the result of a gradual—too gradual—process that rights have become enshrined in declarations, conventions and covenants that go to make up International Human Rights Law. First it was the barons who obtained recognition of their legal rights in the Magna Carta of 1215, and not only their own rights but the rights of all freemen. Then came the Charter of 1354 when Edward III introduced the important concept of 'due process of law'. In the eighteenth century the process was speeded up and the bourgeoisie obtained some of the political and economic liberties that we take for granted in the West today. In our own century we have seen those political and economic rights being claimed by the great mass of human beings.

The fact that the legal recognition of rights has been the result of a long, slow historical process need not lead us back into a legal positivism or make us think that the concept of a natural right has no meaning apart from its legal expression. Dworkin draws a distinction between a concept and a conception. For example, the American Constitution lays down the concepts of 'due process of law' and the equal protection of the law for all citizens, but it did not tie future citizens to the particular conceptions of due process and equal protection in force in the late eighteenth century. Yet guided by these fundamental concepts they were to express conceptions of them in varying circumstances. As a father, who tells his children to act fairly, does not tie them to his own notions of fairness, but urges them to work out differing conceptions for different circumstances, so we might say, that there is a natural right of every human being to equal respect and concern; but the unfolding of the implications of this is the result of a long series of political and legal decisions. A natural human right is, in Kantian terminology, the combination of a transcendent ideal with a categorical imperative: a combination about which some philosophers are sceptical but one to which Christian theologians, for whom both fact and value are ultimately grounded in the being of God, are sympathetic.

Nor does the idea of truth being revealed by a long historical process embarrass theologians (though some would reject the possibility). As the doctrinal truths of the Bible were only spelt out as the result of a process of development so also ethical truths have taken time to be seen in their fullness. In the early Christian Church there was a new equality before God. Rich and poor, bonded and free—all shared the common meal and knew they were equally subject to the just judgment of a loving God. As Paul wrote:

> There is neither Jew nor Greek, there is neither bond nor free, there is neither male nor female: for ye are all one in Christ Jesus.[9]

The full implication of that epoch-making text has not even now been fully secured legally, politically, economically, or even ecclesiastically. Yet the history of the West over the last 1,000 years can be seen, in part, as a grasping of its implications.

One of the disadvantages of the old natural law concept was that it blinded people to the dynamic, developmental possibilities inherent in ethical insight. The ruling picture, taken from the political structures of the time, is hierarchical, submissive and static. The super-sovereign, God, gives his eternal law. Human beings through the use of their reason reflecting on nature, grasp this as natural law. In addition, God reveals his divine positive law. The two are brought together by secular rulers and the Church to provide laws, both secular and ecclesiastical, for Christendom. All is revealed, and all is enforced through a hierarchy from God to the lowest magistrate. The human duty is to listen, submit and obey. Some basic rights are, of course, preserved in this system. From time to time prophetic voices, like that of Francisco de Vitoria in the sixteenth century, pointed out ways in which basic rights were being denied. But this magisterial, architectonic system hardly encouraged the drawing out of insights that challenged and called for change in the received wisdom.

By contrast, modern theologians who are concerned with human rights asociate them closely with liberation theology. As the phrase suggests, the central emphasis of this theology is that God is ceaselessly active in history, liberating human beings from all that enslaves and oppresses them. From the Exodus to the liberation struggles of today God is freeing people, not just from sin and death but from oppressive systems and structures. This involves Christians today in a new commitment to the poor, in line with God's bias to the poor revealed in the Bible. As Jose Bonino has put it:

> For the vast majority of the population of the world today the basic 'human right' is 'the right to a human life'. The deeper meaning of the violation of formal human rights is the struggle to vindicate these larger masses who claim their right to the means of life . . . the drive towards universality in the quests of the American and French revolutions, the aspirations in the *UN Declaration*, finds its historical focus today for us in the struggle of the poor, the economically and socially oppressed, for their liberation.[10]

Again, Moltmann, who has written a number of essays on human rights, has said: 'I think that only with this concrete starting point in the theology of liberation can universal theories and declarations about the freedom of man be protected from their misuse.'[11]

The modern context

Since World War II the main sources for Christian reflection and comment on human matters have been not so much the works of individual theologians as the Vatican in the form of various papal encyclicals[12] and the World Council of Churches (WCC) through the pronouncements of the General Assemblies. I do not wish to comment on these in detail: suffice it to say that they have played their part in forming the general commitment to human rights that has produced the current body of human rights law. I want to look rather at a few of the major intellectual issues that have emerged, to see how these appear in a theological perspective.

The modern human rights movement began immediately after the end of World War II as part of the determination to build a better world, a world in which what had happened in Germany could never happen again. Some of the pressure for human rights has continued to grow from the desire to protect individuals from brutal governments, whether in South America, Africa, or the Middle East. But the human rights movement, not least in its Christian form, has also been shaped by two other major factors. First communism in the Soviet Union. For here is not just one more example of an oppressive government from whom the individual needs to be protected: here is an ideology which offers a particular challenge, both intellectual and practical, to the whole liberal notion of human rights. We may summarize that challenge under three heads. First, liberal notions appear, from a Marxist standpoint, too individualistic. Second, they are therefore too much concerned with individual freedoms and too little with the basic necessities of life; those necessities which are a basic right for all people and which must be a priority for governments to obtain them. Third, from the liberal standpoint, the USSR has seemed gravely to violate certain fundamental freedoms.

The World Council of Churches, of which the Russian Orthodox Church is a member, has tried to maintain a delicate balance between affirming the fundamental freedoms that are dear to liberals, including Christian liberals, while not jeopardizing the precarious position of the Orthodox, who are required to be loyal to policies of their government.

The other major factor, besides Soviet Communism, that has shaped the Christian debate on human rights is the concern, particularly by Roman Catholics in South America, for the basic necessities of life at present being denied millions of poor by oligarchies working in conjunction with world capitalism. From this is derived the close connection between human rights and liberation theology that has just been mentioned. From this point of view human rights as a championing of the individual against the power of the state has seemed very much a European concern. What is wanted, on this perspective, is intervention by the state on behalf of the poor against the tyranny of unrestrained capitalism.

Intervention for the most vulnerable

These different contexts and needs highlight the fact that human rights are not a static once-for-all achievement, but rather a moral imperative that requires constant appraisal and application. Nevertheless, these rather different emphases can be held together by Christian theology.

First there is the supreme value of each individual, as has already been discussed. But in Christian theology man is a social being. Mind itself is social reality. Man is made in the likeness of God not as a solitary individual but as a person in relationship, reflecting the relationship within the Trinitarian Godhead. The end of man is the communion of saints—a fellowship of persons knit together by love.

This has important implications for human rights. For it means that free-booting individualism is a denial of the essential nature of human personhood. We are persons only in relation to other persons. The other person's welfare is my welfare. It means too that the state, which expresses and builds up man as a social being, has a particular responsibility for the well-being of all its citizens. The function of the state is not simply to mark out the pitch or mow the grass so that free individuals can compete with one another. The state has a duty to intervene to safeguard the interest of the more vulnerable, for they too are members of the whole and it is the welfare of all people as part of the whole that is at stake. If the Christian emphasis upon the dignity of each individual acts as a check on all views in which a collective goal is regarded as supreme (not least the communist vision) the Christian emphasis on the social nature of man rules out a merely minimal concept of the state. This is reinforced by Christian insight into the sinfulness of man. For if the presence of sin necessitates checks and balances on the potential tyranny of rulers, it no less leads to the necessity of state intervention against the unrestrained pursuit of gain by the strong, and the need for a protective cloak around the most vulnerable.

This debate about the nature of political society is reflected among moral philosophers in the debate between freedom and equality. In the Western liberal tradition the freedom of the individual has long been regarded as the most fundamental of human rights. H. L. A. Hart has written: 'If there are any moral rights at all it follows that there is at least one natural right, the equal right of all men to be free.'[13]

More recently Ronald Dworkin has argued that, on the contrary, the most fundamental of rights 'is a distinct concept of the right to equality, what I call the right to equal concern and respect'.[14] Dworkin argues that this is in fact the deep theory underlying our notions of fairness, including the well-known account of John Rawls.[15] Dworkin does not sit lightly to freedom. On the contrary, he has argued that the just requirements of a system based on equal concern and respect is to take seriously the choices of each individual.[16] How better to treat them equally than to give them equal choice. Nevertheless, it is equality that is fundamental for Dworkin and his formula of equal concern and respect has distinct theological reverberations. It immediately calls to mind a God who, it is said, values every hair of our head; a God who mixes with the rejected and invites them into his Kingdom of Eternal Life. In Dworkin's view the concept of equality leads to the legitimacy of positive discrimination in favour of the deprived. Positive discrimination is also to be found in the Bible. The biblical God is a God of the poor, the rejected, the despised: and he intervenes on their behalf so that the last shall be first. In the person of Jesus, who is the poor person *par excellence*, who sums up the theme of outraged and innocent suffering that runs through the Bible, in Jesus the crucified , God intervenes on behalf of the powerless. Jesus is raised from the dead: the last is made first, and in him all those who are last will be first. The Bible is a book about positive discrimination. Its theme song is an imperative to discriminate in favour of the marginalized: and its triumph song is an affirmation of God's vindication of the powerless. It is the right of those whom Franz Fanon called 'The wrretched of the earth'—to life, to the basic necessities of life, to the human dignity we all share—that is the most pressing of human rights problems in theological perspective today.

The idea that the state is founded on a contract is a fiction that some have found useful and it goes back earlier than the seventeenth and eighteenth centuries, when the idea came into prominence. But there is an older idea still, that of a covenant: a solemn, binding agreement between God and man. On his side God promises loving kindness and faithfulness. In return he asks of man—what? To share in his work; to share in the risk of creation. Creation is a risk: some of the time it seems a risk that was not justified. But God invites us to share in his great work, his work for the well-being and flourishing of all his children. In particular he invites us to share his commitment to the most vulnerable, to ensure their rights as human beings.

TWELVE

World population and birth control[*]

Why there is a problem

I do not intend to deal in detail with the predicted figures for world population growth. Nevertheless, I need to set them out again very briefly in order to indicate the challenge with which we are faced. The figures suggest that over the next 10 years there could be an annual increase in world population of up to 97 million. This is the equivalent of one United Kingdom every 7 months or two whole Europes, East and West, over the 10 years or a school class of thirty every 10 seconds. Global population which today stands at about 5.6 billion could, on these predictions, be at least 10 billion by the year 2050 and on the worst case scenario 12.5 billion, more than double the population today. Ninety-seven per cent of this growth will take place in the developing world. By the year 2025 the population of the developed world will form only 18% of total world population, well down from the 30% it once was. These figures also reflect dramatic age differences. In the United Kingdom before long pensioners will outnumber young people. The developing world however will be predominantly young. As has been written:

> Imagine a Europe that feels like Bournemouth—a lot of older people, most quite comfortably off, with inevitably, the attitudes and values of that age and income group. Imagine an Africa that feels like the outskirts of Cairo—one that has become much more urban, and younger, sadly perhaps even poorer, and able to watch a soap opera version of the rich world through satellite television on every street corner.[1]

Clearly there are factors which would reduce those figures. AIDS is one feature of the future for example. It has been estimated that in some countries as many as one-third of pregnant mothers are infected with the HIV virus.[2] There is also the relative success of some countries in bringing down their rate of population growth. India now has a fertility rate of about 4, a fall of about a third in the last two decades. China, after its ferocious policy of curbing family size has a rate of about 2.4. Policies there and in other countries

[*] One of the 1994 Linacre Lectures printed in *Population and the Environment*, edited by B. Carledge (OUP 1995)

could become even more effective, making the present dire predictions look too pessimistic.

This rate of world population growth is seen as a major problem for a number of different reasons, which I will not go into. Stress has been laid recently upon the mass migrations which will result from it. Some emphasize the potential political instability. The two most often cited reasons however are the utilization of limited resources and damage to the environment. But on both these concerns we need to look first at the beam in our own eye before we focus on the mote in the eye of the developing world. For, as we know, it is the developed world, forming only a minority of the world's population, that uses up most resources per head. A Bangladeshi for example consumes energy equivalent to 3 barrels of oil a year, a US citizen the equivalent of 55 barrels. The average person in Britain eats 12,000–14,000 calories of food equivalent a day, once animal feedstuffs are taken into account. The average food equivalent in India is only 3,000 calories per day, less than a quarter.

Until now the developed, industrial world has certainly been the biggest culprit as far as the pollution of the environment and damage to the atmosphere is concerned. A family in the United States with only two children will consume more of the world's resources and produce more global pollution than a family in sub-Saharan Africa with over thirty children, were such a family to exist.

So it goes without saying that creating sustainable patterns of consumption in the North, which do minimal damage to the environment and atmosphere and which use up the minimum of resources is the first challenge with which we are faced. If the major problems caused by world population growth are using up the world's resources and damaging the environment, then we in the developed world are very much part of those problems. That said, however, and that challenge faced, there are still good reasons why we should be concerned about population growth in the developing world. The first and most important reason is that countries with slower population growth rates saw annual incomes rise by an average of 1.23% a year in the 1980s compared with a fall of 1.25% in countries where population grew faster. Food production fell behind population growth in 67 out of 102 developing countries between 1978 and 1987. Population growth is integrally related to taking people out of poverty. And, with one billion people in the world living at or below starvation level, we do not need to be reminded of the urgency of this.

QUESTIONING BELIEF

Second, as far as the environment and atmosphere are concerned, whereas the developed countries probably possess the capital and scientific resources to become environmentally clean by early next century, the atmospheric effects of such virtue are likely to be eclipsed by the continued increase in pollutants from China, India, Mexico and other fast industrializing countries now unable to afford sophisticated emission controls. The greenhouse effect, pollution of the seas and the destruction of the forests affect us all, wherever the damage is being done.

So anxiety about the rate of world population growth is not just a selfish concern of the developed world. It vitally affects the living standards of the poorest countries themselves and it affects the quality of life of the whole globe.

Economic development or family planning?

Not everyone accepts this conclusion. There is a fundamental challenge both to the prophets of gloom and to those who emphasize the necessity of national birth control programmes. This challenge comes, in different ways, from both the political right and the political left. An editorial in the *Far Eastern Economic Review*, was, for example, headed 'The more the merrier – reject the dismal prophets of population control'.[3] This article drew a distinction between population and population density in Asia. It argued that population density is more significant than total population and that, interestingly, the places at the high end of the population density list are among the wealthiest in Asia, Hong Kong, Singapore, Taiwan, South Korea and Japan. Nor is this relationship confined to Asia. The Netherlands is one of the most crowded places on earth but, it said, 'we don't hear the World Bank warning of too many Dutchmen'. Indeed, the article suggested that there is often a racial caste behind the warnings of impending doom: .'The problem it seems, is always brown or yellow babies, never white ones.' More positively it went on to argue that the best answer for those worried about population growth is economic prosperity. As people grow more wealthy, they tend to defer marriage and children. Lower population rates follow rather than precede development. Their solution, not surprisingly, was on opening markets and bringing about a more effective capitalism.

From the left and also the Roman Catholic Church a similar message comes: concentrate on development – though there is less emphasis here upon the benign effects of capitalism. Development agencies have for decades now urged that the fundamental

150

problem is lack of development, exacerbated by the burden of Third World debt, unfair terms of trade, and so on. They too have argued that if only people can be given adequate food, housing, health and education the rise in population will inevitably fall, for a variety of reasons, not least because infant mortality will fall and it will not be necessary to have a dozen children in order to ensure that two of them stay alive to keep their parents in their old age. In short, what we have here is a justice problem and an undue emphasis upon family planning, can detract from this. Not surprisingly, it is the developmental, justice aspect of world population growth which is emphasized by the Roman Catholic Church. It is a view with which the Anglican Church has much sympathy. This is, of course, a disputed area but the evidence suggests that however much we quite properly stress the necessity of economic development, family planning still has an important role to play. Bangladesh is one of the world's poorest and most densely populated countries yet fertility rates declined by 21% between 1970 and 1991, to 5.5 children per woman from 7. In that period contraception use among married women of reproductive age rose from 3% to 40%. Evidence from the world fertility survey suggests that if all women in the developing world who do not wish to become pregnant were empowered to exercise that choice, then the rate of population growth would fall by about 30%. By the year 2025 it could translate into three billion fewer people. It seems clear that economic growth and the availability of family planning need to go together. As has been written:

> At times there has been controversy as to whether socio-economic development or family planning is more important. We believe that this has become a largely academic question, as research has shown over and over again that both contribute to declining fertility, and that the more of each is present the faster fertility will decline. Socio-economic development is clearly the more important factor because it sets the parameters within which programmes function; however, no matter how rapid socio-economic development is, the transition from high to low fertility is greatly aided by well organised family planning programmes, as the last decade has clearly demonstrated.[4]

No organization could be more committed to social justice and sustainable development than Oxfam. Yet they fully support the availability of birth planning services because there is an expressed and unmet need for them, especially among women; they contribute to improving the health of women especially in the reduction

151

of maternal mortality, for example 150,000 women a year die through illegal abortions; they help to improve the well-being of children and they increase opportunities for women's personal and social development.

Some recent evidence shows that the traditional assumption that family size falls with economic progress does not always hold true. Sri Lanka, Thailand, Bulgaria and Kerala in India have all shown sharp falls in family size despite relatively low prosperity, while the Gulf States have maintained fertility rates of more than three during a period of sharply rising wealth. As has been said, 'The things that really bring down family size are more complex, to do with culture and education.'[5] Kerala is a good example. Unlike the rest of India there is a 90% literacy rate, a high percentage of Christians and the Communist party has been in power for good periods.

The reasons that Oxfam puts forward to support the availability of family planning services as part of its total commitment to development, point to the heart of the matter. This is the availability of choice for parents, particularly women. The opportunity to exercise responsible parenthood, of choosing the number of children to have and when to have them in order that the possibilities for their well-being and development might be maximized, is the key consideration. It is the key consideration in both the developed and the developing world. It is the crucial factor whether or not there is a challenge posed by predictions of dramatic growth in the world's population.

The Anglican acceptance of contraception

Before I go on to say something more specific about Anglican approaches I should stress that I will be dealing simply with the issue of contraception. I will not be discussing sterilization directly, nor abortion, to which the Church of England is strongly opposed except in the most carefully defined circumstances.

From an Anglican perspective birth *control* is unacceptable. It smacks too much of coercion and the developed world telling the developing one what to do. Birth control is out but birth *choice* is in. Indeed, as has been argued elsewhere: 'demographic targets that governments set can in most cases be met or exceeded simply by responding to the *expressed reproductive goals* of individuals. Family planning objectives should be expressed in terms of satisfying '*unmet need*'[6] (for contraceptive provision).

The availability of contraception enlarges the area of our choice and offers greater opportunity for us to take responsibility for our own lives and those of our offspring, with a view to their well-being and growth under God. From this standpoint the Anglican Church fully supports making the information and technology as widely available as possible. Understandably, however, the Church of England had to move from an inherited position of opposition. The Church of England as such has made no independent contribution to this subject. Rather it has played its part in the formulations of successive Lambeth Conferences, the decanal gathering of Anglican Bishops from throughout the world. Resolution 41 of the 1908 Lambeth Conference said:

> The Conference regards with alarm the growing practice of the artificial restriction of the family, and earnestly calls upon all Christian people to discountenance the use of all artificial means of restriction as demoralising to character and hostile to national welfare.[7]

Resolution 68 of the 1920 Lambeth Conference revealed a shift away from absolutism. 'The Conference, while declining to lay down rules which will meet the needs of every abnormal case', it began. However, it continued:

> Regards with grave concern the spread in modern society of theories and practices hostile to the family. We utter an emphatic warning against the use of unnatural means for the avoidance of conception, together with the grave dangers – physical, moral and religious – thereby incurred, and against the evils with which the extension of such use threatens the race.

It went on to urge the importance of self-control and to assert that the primary purpose of marriage is the continuation of the race through the gift and heritage of children and that the sexual union was not to be regarded as an end in itself.

Resolution 9 of the 1930 Conference showed a much more positive attitude: 'The functions of sex as a God-given factor in human life are essentially noble and creative.' And Resolution 13 began: 'The Conference emphasises the truth that the sexual instinct is a holy thing implanted by God in human nature.' In contrast to the 1920 Resolution it said: 'It acknowledges that intercourse between husband and wife as the consummation of marriage has a value of its own within that sacrament, and that thereby married love is enhanced and its character strengthened.' Resolution 15, voted on with 193 in favour and 67 against, said:

> Where there is a clearly felt moral obligation to limit or avoid

parenthood, the method must be decided on Christian principles. The primary and obvious method is complete abstinence from intercourse (as far as may be necessary) in a life of discipline and self-control lived in the power of the Holy Spirit. Nevertheless in those cases where there is such a clearly felt moral obligation to limit or avoid parenthood, and where there is a morally sound reason for avoiding complete abstinence, the Conference agrees that other methods may be used, providing that this is done in the light of the same Christian principles.

The 1958 Lambeth Conference was less qualified:

The Conference believes that the responsibility for deciding upon the number and frequency of children has been laid by God upon the consciences of parents everywhere: that this planning, in such ways as are mutually acceptable to husband and wife in Christian conscience, is a right and important factor in Christian family life and should be the result of positive choice before God. (Resolution 115)

In 1968 Resolution 22 noted the publication of the papal encyclical, *Humanae Vitae* and whilst expressing its appreciation of the Pope's deep concern for the institution of marriage and the integrity of married life went on:

Nevertheless, the Conference finds itself unable to agree with the Pope's conclusion that all methods of conception control other than abstinence from sexual intercourse or its confinement to the periods of infecundity are contrary to the 'order established by God.' It affirms the resolutions of the 1958 Conference of 113 and 115.

These resolutions show clearly how the Lambeth Conference moved from total opposition, to qualified acceptance and then full acceptance. My predecessor, Kenneth Kirk, who was Bishop of Oxford from 1937 to 1955 was previously Regius Professor of Moral and Pastoral Theology in Oxford. In a book first published in 1927 but revised for a new edition in 1936 he suggested that the main two reasons for a change in the attitude of the Anglican Church were first, enhanced appreciation of the value of children, with the implied assumption that it might be easier to express this value if there are fewer rather than more. Secondly, and this is the main reason he gives, the change in the position of women. This, he wrote, 'has led to a natural, proper and wholly Christian demand that the wife should not be forced, by the exigencies of married life, to abandon all the activities in which she found her interests and occupation before marriage'.[8]

All the recent Anglican statements on this subject have set contraception firmly within the context of a loving, stable and life-long marriage union. It is the importance of this above all that has been stressed. As part of this, as was seen from the changing emphasis in the Lambeth Conference resolutions, there has been a growing appreciation of the value of the marital sexual union in itself, for itself. This change can be particularly clearly seen in the introduction to the marriage service. The 1662 Book of Common Prayer stated that the causes for which matrimony was ordained were:

> First, it was ordained for the procreation of children, to be brought up in the fear and nurture of the Lord, and to the praise of his holy Name.
>
> Secondly, it was ordained for a remedy against sin, and to avoid fornication: that such persons as have not the gift of continency might marry, and keep themselves undefiled members of Christ's body.
>
> Thirdly, it was ordained for the mutual society, help, and comfort, that the one ought to have of the other, both in prosperity and adversity.

The 1928 Book kept the first reason, though in slightly different language. The language of the second reason however was changed radically:

> Marriage was ordained that the natural instincts and affections, implanted by God, should be hallowed and directed aright; that those who are called of God to this holy estate, should continue therein in pureness of living.

The Alternative Service Book of 1980 has a totally re-written introduction. It gives the reasons for marriage in these words:

> Marriage is given, that husband and wife may comfort and help each other, living faithfully together in need and in plenty, in sorrow and in joy. It is given, that with delight and tenderness they may know each other in love, and, through the joy of their bodily union, may strengthen the union of their hearts and lives. It is given, that they may have children and be blessed in caring for them and bringing them up in accordance with God's will, to his praise and glory.

Here we see that what was traditionally the third reason, mutual society, help and comfort has become the first reason. The second reason, relating to the sexual instinct has become very positive, its purpose is 'that with delight and tenderness they may know each other in love', whilst the traditional first reason, the procreation of children, has become the third one.

Professor Gordon Dunstan, one of Anglicanism's foremost ethicists in recent years, reflecting on the process whereby the Anglican Church changed its mind on this issue has written that the resolutions did no more than reflect 'a moral development already made, tested and acted upon by Christian husbands and wives, episcopal and clerical as well as lay, for years before'.[9] He went on to say:

> It exemplifies an instance in which the *magisterium* of the Church formulated and ratified a moral judgement made by a sort of *Consensus Fidelium*, for which a good theological justification was worked out *ex post facto*. That *Consensus* which, in the history of doctrine, has been claimed as the forerunner of dogmatic formulation, is here claimed as a source of moral insight which a church may, indeed must after testing, properly make its own.

This is a crucial indication of the nature of Anglican moral judgements. They are not simply laid down from on high. The official pronouncements of the Church reflect the tested experience of the wider Christian community, particularly that of lay people. Another good example, though one which was rather slower to take effect, would be the way the church after more than a thousand years' condemnation of usury, accepted that lending money on interest for the purposes of trade was morally legitimate.

Roman Catholic arguments

For several decades now there has been no Anglican voice arguing against contraception. The main arguments against have come from the official pronouncements of the Roman Catholic Church. With some temerity I must now consider these. I hesitate to do so because we are so used these days to working together in mutual charity and forebearance, refraining from criticism of one another. Nevertheless there is a clear difference here, which must be honestly stated.

Perhaps it is legitimate to do so because, as is well known, there is fierce disagreement within the Roman Catholic Church itself. The Papal Commission set up by Pope John XXIII on this issue produced a majority report which allowed for the moral legitimacy of artificial means of contraception. Much to the shock of many of the faithful, Pope Paul VI took a different line in *Humanae Vitae*, firmly upholding the traditional prohibition. Since then however, debate has continued unabated, with many reputable Roman Catholic theologians opposing the papal line. However, it has its defenders. A major work by an American Professor of Philosophy, Janet Smith, published in 1991 surveys *Humanae Vitae*, a generation later and in some 425 pages defends both its conclusions and reasoning.[10] I will focus on only one kind of argument, that from natural law.

The first key phrase of *Humanae Vitae* appears in paragraph 11: 'The Church . . . in urging men to the observance of the precepts of the natural law . . . teaches as absolutely required that in *any use whatever of marriage* there must be no impairment of its natural capacity to procreate human life.' The second key phrase occurs in paragraph 12: 'This particular doctrine, . . . is based on the inseparable connection, established by God, which man on his own initiative may not break, between the unitive significance and the procreative significance which are both inherent in the marriage act.'

The key phrase in paragraph 11 reads in the Italian, the language in which *Humanae Vitae* was written:[11] 'Che qualsiasi atto matrimoniale dev e rimanere aperto alla trasmissione della vita.' The Latin (the official language of the Church) substitutes the words *Per se destinatus* (in itself ordered) for the Italian 'aperto' (open) although the Latin *apertus* would apparently easily have worked here. The phrase *Per se destinatus*, though, is philosophically more precise. One version of the Catholic Truth Society translation reads, 'It is absolutely required that any use whatever of marriage must *retain its natural potential* to procreate human life'. Another version renders this phrase rather freely but faithfully, 'In any use whatever of marriage there must be *no impairment of its natural capacity* to procreate human life'.

Earlier criticisms of papal teaching had often pointed out that we continuously interfere in nature for human well-being. Every medical operation is in some sense contrary to nature. Roman Catholic critics had therefore described the traditional natural law teaching, which suggested that the biological function gave the theological meaning, as biologism or physicalism. Janet Smith argues that a rational defence of the natural law objection to contraception does not depend on purely biological or physiological arguments. She thinks that contraception is wrong not simply because an act of sexual intercourse has its physiological end violated but because it is a *human* act of sexual intercourse and

157

thus a violation of man not only in his physiological dimension but in his psychological and spiritual dimension as well.[12] However, this said, she does nevertheless hold that this understanding of a human act is in some sense dependent upon the physiological significance of the act. This is how she states what she calls Version C of the natural law argument, which she finds to be fundamentally sound:

1. It is wrong to impede a procreative power of actions that are ordained by their nature to the generation of new human life.

2. Contraception impedes the procreative power of actions that are ordained by their nature to the generation of new human life.

3. Therefore, contraception is wrong.

When we look further at her argument her emphasis is on the fact that human life is a great good. Furthermore, 'human life is such a great good that not only should life itself be respected but so too should the actions that lead to the coming to be of human life'.[13] She then gives the example of how we transfer respect from one thing to something else, for example, we extend the respect that we have for an individual to members of his or her family. But a couple may very well argue that they have the highest respect for human life and just because they have this respect they intend to plan carefully how many children they are going to have and when they are going to have them, in the most careful and scientific way possible. Or, we might argue, we have the highest respect for human life as a gift from God, and are quite willing to transfer this respect to the means by which this life is generated. But it by no means follows that this respect precludes limiting, by technical means, the times when that life can be procreated.

Let me approach the matter from a different angle. The evolutionary significance of the act of intercourse is no doubt that children might be produced and the species flourish. But that may only rarely be the conscious motive of those who engage in the act. Similarly, experience shows that physical intercourse can nourish and bond the union between a man and his wife. But it is doubtful whether the couple engage in intercourse specifically for that purpose. Rather, they make love because they want to, it feels natural, it is a way of giving and receiving pleasure and a way of drawing close to the other person. If we are talking about the human meaning of the act, which it is surely right to do, then the human meaning transcends, though it can include, any of these three ways of looking at it. A couple can consciously hope to conceive. They can consciously hope that their union will be deepened. They can consciously hope that they will give and receive pleasure. But the conscious, human, meaning is not to be identified with any biological reason why the couple come together.

Paragraph 12 of *Humanae Vitae*, already quoted, says that there is an inseparable connection, which man may not break, 'between the unitive significance and the procreative significance which are both inherent to the marriage act.' Janet Smith seems weak on arguments to support this, maybe because there are none that really stand up. I would say: A kitchen table may be designed for eating. But writing letters on it is a perfectly acceptable and proper use. Or, to take an analogy she sometimes uses, that of the eye. The purpose of the act of intercourse is to produce children as the purpose of the eye is to see, she suggests. But the eye itself is a means whereby impressions are registered on the brain. The human act of seeing goes way beyond the recording of impressions. It includes reflection, association and imagination. It produces great works of art and can lead into delight and praise. No doubt evolution produced the eye in order to help us survive. But survival is rarely to the forefront of our seeing. The act of seeing becomes a human act of seeing involving the mind and heart and soul. Whilst it is true that the human act remains dependent upon a physiological process, the meaning of that act is certainly not so dependent. Similarly, the act of intercourse remains dependent upon certain physiological happenings. But the meaning is a human meaning that is not circumscribed by those physiological processes.

Anglicans would argue that one of the purposes of marriage, as indicated in all our prayer books, is the procreation of children. But this is a purpose that belongs to the whole marriage, and is not tied to every particular sexual act. Janet Smith considers this view under what she calls the 'principle of totality'.[14] She argues that from a moral point of view each act must be considered individually and that acts cannot receive their moral specification as part of the totality. She gives the following example:

Restaurant owners may be open on occasion to serving blacks, but on occasion not. Could they argue that the 'totality' of their acts are open to inegration? They may also argue that the good of the restaurant requires such occasional discrimination, otherwise they would not get enough business to stay open.

Moreover, staying open is in the best interests of the blacks whom they would like to integrate into the clientele of the restaurant. Some would argue that each act of discrimination is wrong, but the principle of totality, as understood by many theologians, would seem to justify acts of discrimination designed to serve the purpose of integration.

This, however, is a totally misleading analogy. Acts of discrimination are wrong in themselves. They cannot be made right by being seen as part of a total programme of integration. Acts of sexual intercourse which use contraceptive methods, however, are not wrong in themselves. They are, or can and ought to be, human acts expressive of love, nourishing the marriage bond. As already argued, this purpose can stand independently of the purpose of procreation.

Professor Gordon Dunstan points out that Resolution 115 of the 1958 Lambeth Conference: 'Affirms a duty – to subordinate procreation to responsible decision – and a liberty to choose such means to this end as conscience, in view of the particular circumstances of the marriage, shall decide.'[15] That well sums up the Anglican view, the duty to make a responsible decision and a liberty to choose appropriate means to this end.

I come back to a point made earlier, namely that earlier Lambeth Conferences did in fact reflect the experience of Christian people, bishops, priests and lay women and men. I believe that this will in the end be the case in the Roman Catholic Church. At an intellectual level, the debate shows no signs of diminishing.[16] The opposition continues despite repeated papal reiterations of the traditional teaching. Meanwhile lay people have made their decision. Fertility rates in Western Europe now average only about 1.7 children per woman – the UK rate is 1.8, Italy and Spain have rates of only 1.2, below the level of former West Germany of 1.4. The figures of predominantly Catholic countries such as Italy and Spain speak for themselves. It is unlikely that this low rate of fertility is simply the result of the rhythm method. I believe that in due course Roman Catholic lay experience will be reflected in official Catholic teaching as, in the 1930s, Anglican lay experience began to influence declarations of successive Lambeth Conferences.

THIRTEEN

Is there a role for charity in a modern state?*

Professor A. J. P. Taylor began his history of England in the twentieth century with the words:

> Until August 1914, a sensible law-abiding Englishman could pass through life and hardly notice the existence of the State, beyond the post office and policeman. All this was changed by the impact of the Great War.

All this was changed. The state has shaped more and more of our lives. However, since 1987, as we know, there has been a radical attempt to roll back the frontiers of the state and to encourage people to accept greater responsibility for their lives. Most recently in his lecture 'Ethics and Public Finance', Michael Portillo has said:

> The Christian message is not about taxation, public spending and collectivised charity . . . It is about individual responsibility . . . Taxation, by reducing people's disposable income, removes choices which are rightly theirs. By taking money from people in order to provide for their wants, we deny them the right to provide for themselves and their families and to make the moral choice of assisting others . . . The call to do good that lies at the heart of Christianity demands an individual response. You can't do good by proxy.

I believe that this polemical contrast is misconceived and its understanding of Christian faith partial. So the first point I want to make is that the state does have a proper continuing responsibility. Some worry that an emphasis on the state for welfare undermines a sense of personal responsibility: there is also the other worry, that an emphasis on the role of charities will obscure the state's proper role and prevent people from acknowledging it. The responsibility of the state is for the 'common good', the good of the whole. In

* The Joint Annual Lecture on Philanthropy of the Association of Charitable Foundations and the Allen Lane Foundation, delivered in London on 10 November 1993

practice this means an especial care for the weakest and most vulnerable members of society. For in a liberal democracy economic forces are nearly all-powerful. You do not have to be a Marxist to recognize the power of financial interests; their ability to dominate the media and therefore their capacity to persuade people through advertising and changing fashions, to buy the goods they manufacture and market. You do not have to be a cynic to recognize the power of business in politics, very obviously in countries like Japan but no less significantly here. I am not anti-business. On the contrary, I am rather pro-business. But the essence of a liberal democracy is a system of dispersed and counter availing powers. Liberty, as Thomas Hobbes said, is power split up into little pieces. Parliament needs eternal vigilance to prevent it being at the mercy of major economic interests; to safeguard its historic role on behalf of society as a whole, not least to act as a balancing power on behalf of those least able to work the system to their own advantage against those who can and do.

Furthermore, in contrast to Michael Portillo, I believe taxes are a good thing. Of course, we must always be watchful that public money is not wasted, that it is used in a way that is as effective as possible, so the attempts of radical governments of the right to disturb complacent self-serving bureaucracies is to be welcomed. But in principle taxes are not just a necessary evil, as popular wisdom suggests. They are a positive good.

There is an obvious sense in which we all benefit from our membership of society through national defence, public transport, state schooling, public hygiene and so on, including, we might add, Parliament. For all these benefits we pay, including paying the salaries of MPs. But there is a profounder dimension to taxes in the modern state. Taxes enable our fleeting fluctuating charitable impulses to be both consistent and effective. In our better moments we all have charitable impulses. We would like old people to be well looked after, the mentally ill to receive proper treatment, the handicapped to be given all possible help to live active lives and so on. But if it was left simply to us or to the charitable sector alone, there would be no guarantee that such needs would be met. Taxes enable what we wish in our charitable moments to be given sustainable expression. The resources needed will not depend upon whim, upon passing moods, they can be allowed for whatever our personal feelings. To support taxes in this way is an act of personal responsibility. To acknowledge, for example, that the babies of single parents, in a society with over three million unemployed need state support, is a mature decision; to recognize that such babies require support whatever our feelings might be about feckless fathers or struggling mothers, is a similarly wise expression of personal responsibility. Talk about responsibility cuts both ways. Quite properly we want to encourage responsible and caring parenting. But we all have responsibilities, including responsibility for the ordering of society for the benefit of all.

It is also worth challenging Michael Portillo's assumption that we have an absolute right to our income and that what we do with it is a matter of largesse or charity. The great Christian Fathers of the fourth century, Chrysostom, Ambrose, Gregory of Nazianzen and so on argued that God had given the good things of the earth to humanity as a whole. All had a claim on them as a matter of justice. Any surplus was owed to the needy, it was an obligation of justice not simply an option of charity. As Ambrose put it: 'Not from your own do you bestow upon the poor man, if you make return from what is his. For what has been given is common for the use of all . . . therefore you are paying a debt.' Or Chrysostom, even more strongly: 'This is robbery – not to share one's resources.' Chrysostom harried the wealthy ladies of Constantinople to strip off their jewels and cast them into a trunk to be sold for the maintenance of the poor in the great institutions he founded. We pay taxes because in that way those in need can rely on help whether or not we feel like stripping off our jewels.

There is a role for charity in a modern state, as I will go on to argue. But there is also a proper role for the state itself. To affirm this is in no way to down play the necessity of personal responsibility. On the contrary it is a mature expression of personal responsibility to want to ensure that those in real need in our society can be helped whatever the whims or moods of particular givers. It is the charitable impulse expressing itself in a mature, responsible manner. So now to the role of the charities.

Although the role of the state is now indispensable, the State is in fact a Johnny come lately to the scene of social welfare. It was only late in the nineteenth century that it moved into education and it is only in the twentieth century, as Taylor pointed out, that it has really become the major player. Before then it was the great charitable institutions upon which the poor, the needy and the sick relied. The Centris Report *Voluntary Action*, about which I will be saying more later, focuses on the nineteenth century as the great period of voluntary action. But of course voluntary action goes back right to the origins of European civilization. It was usually the Church which encouraged the foundation of hospitals, poor houses and such welfare as there was. It was the Church that had a virtual monopoly of education. In recent years the Church has sometimes been criticized for being political. But although many of the traditional spheres of operation of the Church have been taken over by the state, the Church has seen no reason to give up its concern for human well-being in these areas.

So, as Dr Edward Norman, the scourge of left-wing clerics has put it: 'These incursions make it very difficult for the Church not to be politically involved, for politics has actually moved into its own sphere.' My point in mentioning this is not to highlight the role of the Church but to point to the long tradition of charitable activity in this country, one which was by no means all of the Lady Bountiful type, before the state moved in on the scene. We sometimes forget how strong and in many ways effective these charitable institutions were. David Green's book *Re-inventing Civil Society* shows for example how strong the Friendly Societies were and how much health provision there was before the advent of the NHS. In 1920 there were 6.6 million registered members of Friendly Societies, 2.5 million members of registered Trade Unions and 2.5 million members of co-operative societies. I do not share David Green's assumption about the absolute desirability of a minimal state. But I do share his positive emphasis upon the role of charitable insitutions of various kinds. In the last decade there has been a tendency to polarize the debate between state action and personal responsibility. What has been neglected is what Edmund Burke called 'the little platoons of society', the inter-mediate human communities and organizations which in fact mean so much to us. They are not a substitute for the role of the state, but they are an essential aspect of every human society, the one through which most people find their identity and meaning, from the family through to the Church, Mosque or Synagogue, the Co-operative Society, the Community Action Group or the campaign to meet some special need.

Charities, in the technical sense, belong amongst these intermediate communities and they have, I believe, a vital, indispensable role to play.

First, charities can innovate. A group of people or an inspired individual discerns a need that is not being met. They pioneer ways of meeting it, which influences a much wider group of people. Of the many examples one could take, I focus on the modern hospice movement. It was only some thirty or so years ago that the first hospice was founded, offering care for the terminally ill which both kept them out of pain and enabled them to approach their death with ease of mind and soul. Since then hospices have sprung up all over the country. Even more important, the whole standard of terminal care in ordinary hospitals has been given new higher standards to which doctors and nurses aspire. Charities can often meet needs that present legislation prevents other bodies from responding to. For example the Children's Society set up the first safe house in London because this was work that could not be done by local authorities who were bound by statutes which limited their responsibilities to children in their own area. Furthermore 40% of runaways were people who had run away from local authority care. Similar examples from other areas could be found a hundred times over.

Second, often springing out of this, charities can campaign on behalf of a particular group of people. Again, of the innumerable examples one could take, I focus on the development agencies. They know from their work for the most vulnerable people in the world that particular projects by themselves are not enough. They know that issues like terms of trade and the burden of debt on the poorest countries in the world have to be tackled. They know the importance of long-term development aid. Here, of course, we approach that dangerous borderland into the political. But one of the reasons why it is so vital for the development agencies to campaign on these issues is because they have so little political glamour for politicians. They say there are no votes in them and we all know how hard it is to get issues of overseas development or Third World debt on the agenda at the time of a general election. If it was ever possible to separate the purely charitable from the overtly political, it is probably not possible now. For the state affects so much of our life. Political decisions, for good and ill, shape our society. It is sheer sentimentality to think that you can be concerned for human well-being whilst not being concerned about those political decisions which radically affect whether people live or die. So for many charities there is an inescapable campaigning element.

Third, charities are able to channel local energy to meet local need in an appropriate and sensitive manner. Of the many examples I could choose, again I simply focus on one, the role of housing associations over the last two or three decades. When I was in Fulham, I had the privilege of chairing two small housing associations. I found that the combination of local people from the community and locally elected politicians as trustees was a very effective one. There was real energy and goodwill directed towards, in this case, elderly people who needed housing. The trustees knew the locality intimately and what was needed. The politicians knew how to work the system to obtain the necessary housing association grants. The other trustees had access to other kinds of information and help.

Fourth, charities provide an opportunity for people to offer some form of service to other people. It has not been fashionable to say this in recent years and it can smack of patronizing do-gooding. It is certainly not popular on the hard left. But as human beings, whatever our religion or lack of it, we have as an essential aspect of our nature the desire to give and to receive. Communities are built up by relationships of mutual giving and receiving and it is through membership of such communities that we find and develop our own identity.

These are, I believe, the four fundamental activities of the charitable sector: pioneering work to meet freshly perceived needs, campaigning on behalf of people in need, channelling local energy to meet local need in sensitive and appropriate ways and helping to create those communities in which we have the opportunity to give as well as to receive.

Everyone here will now be familiar with the main recommendations of the Centris Report, *Voluntary Action*. It wishes to make a sharp distinction between service providers and campaigners. It believes that tax concessions should be withdrawn from both types of charity and any financial support must depend on the performance of service providers. Service providers should compete for contracts in a market in which independent profit-orientated businesses will also be operating. Campaigning charities will be funded entirely by private donations and be freed from all regulation.

There is much in the Centris Report of value, particularly the way it puts modern charity in the historical context of nineteenth and twentieth century developments. The conclusions also have that kind of clear, challenging logic about them which forces us to think. I mean no disrespect either to Centris, or to Enoch Powell or to Tony Benn when I suggest that the Centris Report has the same effect on me that the compelling speeches of Enoch Powell and Tony Benn do. They seem to have a clear, consistent line and persuasive emotion. Yet there seems something not quite right about them, they seem slightly off-centre, the basic assumptions wrong or the rough complexity of human existence not fully comprehended. Everyone in the charitable sector needs to be forced to think, even radically, from time to time about what we are doing, and we can be grateful for the furore created by the Centris Report. But, whatever truth there may be in some of its criticisms of some charities as dinosaurs, bureaucratic and inefficient (and I leave that for others to judge), I will argue that the main conclusions of the Report should be rejected. First, we cannot draw such a tidy distinction between providing a service and campaigning on behalf of those for whom the service is provided. It is in the process of providing a service, say for needy children, that the need is perceived to do more for them or to do what is done differently. Out of the experience and expertise arises a campaign. Or, starting the other way round, of what credibility has a campaign if it is not rooted in some real experience of those for whom the campaign is being waged. Real experience does not necessarily mean providing a service, but there is no better way of getting real experience than such day by day contact. A charity, for example, which is providing housing and facilities for single mothers and their children is in a good position to know how such people can best be helped in the sphere of public policy and social provision. Campaigners without some real experience are likely to have an air of unreality about what they propose or lack of credibility. Of course some charities will be mainly service providers and others will be mainly campaigners but to divorce the two functions in the way that the Centris Report suggests would be disastrous. As someone once said, to every complex question there is an answer which is simple, clear – and wrong.

Secondly, I worry about the effects on service providing charities, if their only source of funding was contracts; if they had to compete for contracts with independent, profit-making organizations. I should stress that I am not against competition, on the contrary, the creation of markets, genuine markets or internal markets can be a salutary way of eliminating waste and achieving more for limited resources. But what would the effect be on a service provider of competing for contracts, particularly if the other competitors in the field were profit-orientated? This is of course an imponderable but I suspect that there would be a rapid draining away of voluntary effort and voluntary spirit. People would wonder quite what they were doing simply providing cut-price services to save government money. I suspect the heart would go out of the matter. And this is more important than we think.

Charities, that is bodies which encourage and channel good will and voluntary action provide an essential role model in our society. I am not one of those who think that people in business only work for a higher salary and profits. On the contrary, I think that everyone who works does so with a variety of motives, partly out of perfectly proper self-interest, partly to provide for a family, partly because of the fulfilment of the work and the place it provides in the community and partly because most businesses do in fact provide goods or services that other people need. If they didn't, they would rapidly go out of business. So there is an element of altruism in most work. However, it is by having models of less adulterated altruism, of a purer charity if you like, that the ideal is set forth and maintained. It is because we have literally thousands of charities in which people freely give of their time and energy and money for the service of other people that the ideal is kept alive and the ideal is recognized to have some role to play even in companies which are quite properly directed towards profit. Andrew Phillips, in his introduction to a book on new charity legislation, warns against the wrong kind of professionalism which discourages volunteers. The voluntary sector, he writes: 'must also encourage those citizens who lack confidence, and those who may not by some be thought particularly "capable" to be volunteers. Often those self-same people possess more than their fair share of that goodwill, compassionate insight without which charity is not charity.'

The Centris Report recommends that service providing charities should be funded by the contracts they can obtain and not by direct grants and by tax concessions (for only then is there proper value for money). There is the implication that there is something unhealthy about direct grants and tax concessions. On the contrary, such funding, with all the appropriate qualifications about openness, proper accountability and elimination of inefficiency, is a very proper way for government to express its responsibility for a particular class of people. Let me take the example here of voluntary-aided schools, which still provide such a significant section of our education. The churches have a good bargain through their voluntary aided schools because they only have to provide 15% of certain costs. The government also has a good deal, for such schools encourage local responsibility and support and commitment by the church or whatever body it is running the voluntary aided schools. But they also retain a perfectly proper, indeed the major stake in it, through providing most of the finance. Government has a responsibility for education, which it chooses to exercise in this particular way, partly through delegation and partly through retaining a financial stake. It leads neither to inefficiency nor complacency. A similar point could be made in relation to housing associations where again, the state is the major provider of finance. There is nothing reprehensible about either the government making major grants or charities receiving them. It is the kind of partnership which is appropriate in a liberal democracy. Furthermore, it is in fact a policy of which the present government has stated it is firmly in favour. As the Prime Minister said in his speech to the Per Cent Club on 19 October 1993: 'I stand foursquare behind the tax concessions we have made to the voluntary sector . . . I want to make it clear that tax relief and charitable giving is here to stay.'

The Centris Report argues for a divorce and that is their term, between what they regard as genuinely voluntary organizations, their so-called first force and contract funded service providers, their third force. The Report says:

> An organisation must be either a first force organisation or a third force organisation. It cannot be both. It is similar to the choice Herman Hesse put in his journal called Wandering. You can be a seeker or a farmer, but not both. In opting for the first force you become a seeker; in opting for the third a farmer.

All good existentialist stuff. But when a farmer discovers that some of his land is unproductive he seeks ways of making it more productive or looks for land in another part of the country. When he finds that land he farms it. Many charities quite properly are both seekers and farmers. The seeking improves the farming and the farming engenders the seeking.

The Report admits that one of its fundamental assumptions is to get back to a genuine voluntary spirit in a truly voluntary sector. It involves they think a radical change of mind set: 'A different world view, one that appears out of step with the dominant materialism of our age.' There is in fact a strong element of dualism running right through the Report, in which the large traditional charities tend to be demonized and the small black or Irish mutual help and solidarity groups tend to be idealized. It brought to mind Troeltch's distinction between church-type institutions and sects. The Centris Report in its spirit and its recommendations is essentially sectarian. There is nothing wrong in that provided we recognize it for what it is. It emerges quite clearly for example in the idealization of the true, pure volunteer groups. It writes:

> The organisations will interlink and could form a movement based on the principle of social solidarity. This implies a one world view where everyone, regardless of skin colour, belief, gender and other characteristics or life circumstances has a role to play. Differences between people are accepted, individual ego is down played and the main guiding principle is empowerment

169

within a frame of justice and mutual respect for people, other life forms, and the environment.

Amen and Amen again. But the fact is that the ego is present in all organizations, however small and idealistic and unless this is recognized the ship will be wrecked. No one saw this more clearly than Philip Toynbee in the 1960s in his experience with an idealistic commune and his own reaction to that commune on his premises.

The obverse of this idealization is the very sharp criticism of large traditional charities. The Report writes that:

> Charity is a medieval concept that has no place in the modern world. It can reinforce the boundaries between 'haves' and 'have nots' finding itself on the cusp between greed and guilt. Advertisements make the public feel guilty, are successful in enlisting donations for handicapped people but tend to demean sufferers ... The very existence of charities reinforces the perception of the person with disabilities as an object of pity dependent on the charity of others.

The Report quotes Katharine Whitehorn's uncharitable thoughts about charity directors living 'high on the hog' and Germaine Greer, who has written that charity offers an opportunity to people who themselves are not in need to have 'an obscene ego trip', and so on.

Charity is not a medieval concept. Behind it lies Caritas, which is the essential, defining characteristic of what it is to be a human being. It is interesting that Krzysztof Kieslowski, generally regarded as the greatest film maker of the late twentieth century climaxes his film, *Three Colours Blue*, with a great paean of praise based on the words of 1 Corinthians 13 which of course underlies the whole European concept of Caritas. Far from being medieval it is utterly modern, rooted in the New Testament and drawing its sap from the Hebrew Scriptures.

The New Testament concept of Caritas or Agape to use the word they used knows nothing of largesse from on high. It is about a mutual giving and receiving in a community in which the poor have pride of place. The emphasis was upon *Koinonia*, in which we always have as much to receive as to give, if not more. This again was a central theme of the fourth-century Fathers. If wrong images have sometimes in the past been projected by the large traditional charities, and I make no judgement about this, then the way forward is not by abolishing them but by a change of perspective. A priest in the Diocese of Oxford who worked as a chaplain with the mentally handicapped said that the experience has decisively changed and shaped his approach to ministry. They brought home to him how much more we have to receive from others. On a world-wide scale the point has been made most vividly by Henri Nouwen, a Canadian Roman Catholic priest who lives and works with the mentally handicapped, who whenever he travels around the world to lecture always goes with some of those with whom he lives. There is I think an essential connection between this and the fact that he has become one of the most highly regarded spiritual writers of our time for both Protestants and Catholics. People much better qualified than I am will know what changes need to be made by the larger charities both to make them as cost-effective as possible and to be engendered still by a sense of compassion. They too will know in what ways perceptions need to be changed to bring about this sense of genuine human solidarity between people who in various ways help one another. Sectarianism is I believe mistaken in many ways, not least because sooner rather than later it leads to massive disillusionment as it is once again dashed on the rock of human egotism. Moreover, in focusing on a visionary ideal it can distract people from the changes which can and should be made in more traditional organizations. First force organizations, the genuine charities according to the Centris Report, do need as much help as we can give them. The large foundations in particular need to be as sympathetic as possible to small, highly motivated and perhaps radically challenging groups. But this need not imply the abolition of service-providing charities or their transformation into a so-called third sector. Nor should this be allowed to divert charities from continuing to evaluate what they do in the light of their highest ideals. Ideals are for all of us, not just new challenging groups.

In the best defence yet written of liberal democracy, the American thinker, Reinhold Niebuhr stated: 'Man's capacity for justice makes democracy possible. Man's inclination to injustice makes democracy necessary'. It is a view of democracy that springs directly from a Christian understanding of human nature. We have an altruistic side, a capacity for justice, that is an essential aspect of our human nature which cannot and should not be stifled. At the same time, we have an inclination to injustice, to pursue our own interests at the expense of others. From this twin perception there springs the vision of a society which makes maximum provision for people to express generosity and compassion for others and, at the same time, which is so organized as to prevent overweening power in any one section. The point about democracy is that it not only enables us to express free choice but it sets up a structure to prevent potential tyranny. Charities are an essential part of this system in two ways. First of all they provide opportunities for people to be generous and compassionate, unstinting in their service of other people. This is not just an optional extra to human society, a gloss on brutal self-interest. On the contrary, it gets to the very heart of what it is to be a human being in society. Without it society would not just be the poorer, it would cease to be society. Secondly, the charitable sector, which is vast, provides one of those essential countervailing powers to state monopoly and the juggernaut of market-driven policies and organizations. In 1990 there were 171,434 charities registered with the Charity Commissioners. Charities' total income in that year was £16.18 billion – equivalent to 3.4% of gross domestic product. Up to 483,000 people undertake paid work in Britain's charity sector – equivalent to 2.2% of all those employed. In terms of employment figures, the sector is up to 80% bigger than Britain's motor industry. It is comparable in size with the energy and water supply industries. The exact number of people who volunteer is difficult to guess at.

Figures vary between 23% of the population who take part in at least one voluntary activity in a period of 12 months and 44% of the population. On either percentage the figure runs into millions. There are for example 50,000 volunteers alone helping to run charity shops. Charities are not just a relic of the past, they are not just a way of government getting service on the cheap. They provide another perspective, another centre of power and influence, thereby helping to maintain the delicate balance of power which characterizes a truly democratic society.

I began by arguing that the state has a proper role to safeguard the common good, particularly the weakest and most vulnerable members. In stressing a role for charities, this point must not be lost sight of. But that said, charity has a crucial role to play both now and in the future. Charities pioneer new work, campaign on behalf of those in particular need, focus local energy and enable people to give of themselves to others. The present system whereby the Government gives grants and tax concessions to charities is a proper exercise of responsibility by the Government, whereby it both retains a stake in a particular area and delegates to people best qualified to work in it. Charities for their part are an essential feature of a democratic society enabling people to give to others and helping to safeguard liberty, by ensuring that no one group has a monopoly of power or perspective or care.

FOURTEEN

The morality of good business*

The Church has been severely criticized in recent years for its alleged failure to support the mechanisms of wealth creation. In fact, a negative attitude to business has been one aspect of our culture for a long time. In Trollope's novel *Dr Thorne*, the author writes:

> Merchants as such are not the first men among us; though it perhaps be open, barely open, to a merchant to become one of them. Buying and selling is good and necessary; it is very necessary, and may, possibly, be very good; but it cannot be the noblest work of man; and let us hope that it may not in our time be esteemed the noblest work of an Englishman.

This passage, written in 1858, reflects the importance of trading in a trading nation but its aspiration, the noblest work referred to, is still directed towards the great landed estates of the countryside. It is an attitude that owes more to the Romantic Movement of the early nineteenth century with its idealization of nature and plain old-fashioned snobbery than it does to Christianity.

From a Christian point of view the values inherent in a market economy: the stress on consumer choice, the inevitability of risk-taking, the attempt to meet stated wants, are congruous with our understanding of what it is to be a human being in society, made in the image of God. Of course, not everything that goes on under the heading of the market is equally desirable but unless the system itself is worthwhile, there is little point in worrying about the morality of its separate components. It is fruitless to get worked up about a stench in a particular cupboard unless we believe that the house itself is good to live in and worth making something of. If on the other hand the structure of the house, for all its faults, is sound, if we think that the business of financing, manufacturing, marketing, buying and selling is fundamentally worthwhile then there is every reason to try to ensure that it has integrity in all its aspects. Three books by Christian theologians were published in 1992, in addition to my own, taking a positive attitude to the market and

* The Stockton Lecture for 1993, delivered at the London Business School, from *Business Strategy Review*, Spring 1993

the enterprise culture: one sign, that whatever the popular perception, the Christian Church is not adopting a lofty attitude to that on which we all depend. I agree with Kenneth Adams when he writes:

> A society which does not deeply believe in the worthwhileness of the activity by which it lives, and therefore does not hold that activity in reasonably high esteem, faces a major moral dilemma which will prevent it having a hopeful and positive attitude towards its whole future.

Lord Hailsham once remarked that it is important for all politicians to have something in their lives that is more important to them than politics. For the more intelligent of my friends, he went on, it is religion, for the less, hunting. It is no less important for us to see that business has a purpose beyond itself. This is not the pious platitude of a Churchman. For example, the Constitution of Dayton Hudson, the American retailing group has these words: 'The business of business is serving society, not just making money. Profit is our reward for serving society well. Indeed, profit is the means and measure of our service – not an end in itself.'

The bottom line has an essential place as an indicator: but it is not an end in itself. The business of business is serving society.

The first point about the morality of good business then is that we actually believe in what we're doing. As humans we are inescapably moral and spiritual beings. We cannot live for ever in a schizophrenic state, confining our value system to our personal and domestic lives, whilst blocking out all wider considerations in our working life. Nor is this necessary. Business properly understood and properly managed is a place where we can feel good and do good.

Given this basic conviction, we can then go on to reflect on the morality of different aspects of the enterprise. Nothing in life is value free, nothing is morally neutral. Every institution, every enterprise, the law, universities, including the arts and business, reflect and express certain values. It is not in the first instance a question of measuring the morality of business by standards external to it: rather of looking to see what values are inherent in the company itself, and amongst the people who work for it and reflecting on them. It is an unhelpful polarization when those outside business are seen only as critics and those within appear on the defensive. The plain fact of the matter is that no business would survive unless it operated on the basis of certain moral truths. The two previous Stockton Lectures in this series have made it abundantly clear, from people at the heart of the financial world, that morality is a major consideration. In recent years more and more European companies have introduced mission statements and codes of conduct, although Europe still lags behind the United States in this regard. In America about 75% of companies have codes of conduct. It was estimated that in the UK, France and Germany about 40% had them by 1988, a rise compared with the 14% estimated to have them in 1984. However, a survey conducted amongst the 400 leading companies in Britain by the Institute of Business Ethics in 1991 indicates that that figure is too high as far as the United Kingdom is concerned. Only 28% of the total sample indicated that they had a written code. But this is a rise from the 18% who had them in a similar survey conducted in 1987. So there is clear evidence of an increase, an increase which will almost certainly continue. The basis of these company codes is the recognition that it is not just the shareholder to whom the company is accountable. There are a number of groups who have a stake in the company. The claims of each of these stakeholders, the employees, the suppliers, the customers, the wider community and the environment need to be recognized.

Some remain cynical or unconvinced about the value of such codes. They look good in the annual report but what is their reality? Yet, even at its lowest, as the Duc de la Rochefoucauld (1613–80) put it, 'Hypocrisy is the homage paid by vice to virtue.' Can we go beyond homage, beyond proper recognition, in order to ensure proper implementation? There are, first, questions to be asked about who has drawn up the company code. Has it been drawn up by a small group at the top or as a result of a process of consultation in which all those affected have had an input. Consultation can be a long drawn-out process. In the Diocese of Oxford we have drawn up a Vision, Priorities and Targets paper. This came about as a result of a two-year process. There was dicussion in every parochial church council and the results of their deliberations were taken into account in the production of our final document. Our hope, of course, is that because more people have contributed to it, more people will be able to own it and make it a reality.

There is the further question, about how a code of conduct can be communicated and kept effective in every aspect of its business. It will need reviewing, it will need monitoring. The next stage for those companies which have pioneered the way in this field is the setting up of adequate mechanisms for testing the effectiveness, the reality of what exists on paper. Company codes, mission statements which include values, are of growing importance. But they are expressions of, not substitutes for, a deeply imbued sense of corporate values. Company codes, like laws, have a crucial role to play. Otherwise vague generalities about goodwill can remain vague generalities. But codes can simply be there to look good or they can be applied in a minimalist legalistic way. They are effective when they are seen as part of, but only part of, a corporate culture, a corporate ethos, with a strong sense of moral purpose both about what it is doing and the way it is doing it.

For many centuries the professions have had codes of professional conduct. But in addition to this they have assumed certain values. Similarly the medieval guilds, the predecessors of present day livery companies, set standards which they felt a responsibility for maintaining. The professions and the guilds have been crucial to the transmission of values in our society. Their role in preserving and handing down not only ways of doing things but ethical ways of doing things is an under-researched but highly significant feature of our history. Their influence can be compared to that of schools and churches as shapers and handers on of values. I suspect that in modern society companies, particularly the large companies, whether they relish the prospect or not, have a similar role. For through their membership of such companies people are educated into a certain ethos. This means that the personal values of the key people in a company are of crucial importance. One of the issues of most concern today is the environment, indeed it is in danger of becoming over fashionable. Business has a key role to play, not only in a negative sense of avoiding direct pollution of the environment but in developing new markets which do not use up non renewable sources and which do not damage the environment. Business is not simply passive, waiting for customers to choose. Business is dynamic and actively educating customer choice. Through the influence of key individuals, that choice can be educated into areas of what has been called green growth.

Rogues arise in every walk of life, including of course the Church, but we know they are rogues because of widely accepted standards partly expressed in codes and partly because of the presuppositions, assumptions, the very air that is breathed in the corporate culture. But what I'm suggesting goes way beyond the exposure and flushing out of the occasional criminal. I wish to indicate a much more positive approach, a sense of the worthwhileness of what is being undertaken and because of this belief in its worthwhileness, proper attention being given to serving the needs of society in all its aspects.

Those mostly closely involved in this field seem to agree that there is some way to go. A report on a major conference of industrialists, academics and politicians from Europe and the United States said that those present 'saw the new emphasis on ethics in business schools as a necessary but insufficient move in the right direction. Scepticism about the effectiveness of self-regulation was also marked.' In the eyes of many self regulation is simply not working. As one report puts it:

> What the Government, and for that matter the SIB (the Securities and Investments Board) has failed to appreciate is the fact that many senior members of the financial community have long taken the view that self regulation has become synonymous with self interest.

At another conference on 'Ethics and the City' one participant argued that, 'legislation could never be as effective as a standard of conduct so firmly ingrained in corporate identity that it becomes almost unthinkable for any employee of that company to break it'. Others stress the importance of monitoring and communication. As one put it: 'Once a company, like any other social group has reached a certain size, complexity, and turnover of personnel, there must be ways and means of transmitting that culture.' For this to be effective, like the lager whose name I will not mention, it needs to reach the parts that other beers do not reach. This is clearly linked to issues of decentralization, delegation of responsibility and empowerment to people at the lowest level. One example of the way this has worked to bring about a sensitive response to one particular aspect of human need, is the way that British Gas, through a combination of direction and delegation, have enabled the disabled to be better served with appropriate fittings and service.

I know that for some time now the threat of short-termism has been on the minds of a good number of people: the pressure exerted by shareholders who at the Annual General Meeting will be looking for as good a return on capital as they can get this year rather than sometime in the future. This, as we know, can lead to less investment and less being spent on research and development and training, which are essential in many industries if they are to retain a share in future markets. It can also lead to an excessive number of takeovers. During the ten years 1972–82 one-third of the biggest 730 floated companies in Britain changed ownership. The comparable figure for Japan was under 8%. In response to this Charles Handy has called for the development of the 'existential corporation'. Linked to this others call for a change in the Companies Act which, designed to give shareholders limited liability, may perhaps have given them also too limited a responsibility for the future of the company. So some explore alternate models in Germany or Japan, which seem to offer the possibility of greater continuity for long-term development. A variety of ideas have been offered. One is that voting rights could be restricted to shares which have been held for at least twelve months. Another is that there should be a punitive tax on all short term capital gains and no tax at all on longer term ones.

I am not competent to contribute to this debate in a detailed way though I would like to learn from it. What interests me is the contribution that religion and morality might possibly make to the formation of a culture capable of taking a longer view. We live in the age of immediate gratification and the quick fix. What might be done to counteract this pressure for instant realization and immediate results?

In the Hebrew Scriptures there are two fundamental presuppositions. First, God wants the whole earth to flourish. His purpose is that the whole of humanity should find their proper fulfilment in an environment that prospers. He wants our corn and wine and oil to increase. The prime focus is on this world rather than the next. Indeed most authors would have had some sympathy with the reply of Sir Winston Churchill when he was asked whether he believed in an afterlife, 'There may very well be two worlds, but I prefer to take them one at a time.' Nor are the Hebrew Scriptures concerned primarily for an inner subjective sphere at the expense of the public domain. On the contrary, it is life in all its aspects, social, economic and political, with which the books are concerned.

The second fundamental assumption is that if we live mindful of God, in accord with his purpose, all things will indeed prosper. If on the other hand we seek to displace God, disaster will ensue. If we live in harmony with the divine law for the universe, things will work out well, if we don't they won't. We see this conviction expressed most vividly and consistently in the Wisdom Literature, books like Proverbs and the Psalms and the sadly neglected Books of the Apocrypha, like Ecclesiasticus.

It soon became apparent to the people of Israel that the easy equation of well doing and well-being simply did not work out. People who do the right thing sometimes suffer for their integrity. The unscrupulous too often prosper. The Book of Job is the classic, impassioned critique of the claimed connection between goodness

179

and flourishing. Christianity reinforced this scepticism, for Christ was crucified and Christianity soon developed a cult of the martyrs. It was assumed that the good *would* suffer in this world and that their glory was in the next one, not this. Now whatever the truth in this, and of course there is truth in it, it has to be seen against the background of the Hebrew Scriptures, that God wants his children to flourish and that to do right is to go with the grain of the universe. In the long-run rectitude will bring its own proper reward. This is a truth that the Jewish community have retained rather more strongly than the Christian.

I am not, I must emphasize, advocating the so called American Gospel of prosperity, the vulgar and dangerous doctrine that if only we put our trust in the Lord we will automatically prosper in material terms. Some of the most shining lights of the Christian faith this century are those who have stood against the forces that rule this world, the economic and political powers that be, and have been tortured and shot for it. It must also be quite clear in the world of business that sometimes, at least in the short term, the most ruthless, those most willing to break or bend the rules, to cut corners in various ways, will gain a short term advantage. But this uncomfortable experience should not detract from the fundamental insight of Judaism, Christianity and Islam, that the universe is on the side of value; the good will 'out' and this good will be revealed not just in peace of mind but in the way things are. In the long run, to put it crudely, right dealing will pay off. The question, of course is how long is the long run. The pressure of shareholders cannot be resisted for ever.

This is true but there is no simple answer to the question. It remains a fact, however, that God's purpose is first of all for this world; that a moral purpose is expressed in and through it; and that to live at one with that moral purpose, through recognizing and responding to the range of claims upon us and acting rightly, though no guarantee of success in the short term, will certainly lead to flourishing in the longer one. And this is in fact the basis on which many companies operate today. They know full well that fair treatment of employees, integrity in dealing with business associates, and a recognition of the proper claims of the wider community and the environment are indispensable to the future success of a business. The most controversial claims of course are those of the wider community and the environment. Nevertheless, a good number of major companies now see their involvement in the wider community in commercial terms. As the chairman of one company puts it:

THE MORALITY OF GOOD BUSINESS

Business is the wealth creator in society, but to do it needs a healthy and flourishing environment in which to operate. To assist in the creation of a prosperous and balanced society is not only good for society, it is good for the long term future of industry and commerce . . . There are very sound commercial reasons for the exercise of social responsibility.

Business in the City makes this theme part of their approach to companies. Lending expertise, setting up training programmes for Inner City young people, seconding experienced people—all this helps to create a community more likely to produce potential customers in the future. They also point out that there has never been a reported scandal from any company that has actively, as opposed to just financially, involved itself in the regeneration of the wider community. It seems that if the corporate values include a recognition of wider claims, those values will be pervasive in every aspect of the company's dealings.

Now I also happen to believe that goodness is worth pursuing for its own sake and that *fiat iustitia, et pereat mundus*, holds true. Let justice be done, though the world perish. I do not think that Christian ethics can be seen in purely prudential or commercial terms. Nevertheless, as I have stressed, for the reasons given, the convictions that well doing and well-being are integrally connected, is one to hold on to.

I mentioned the limitation of company codes, as at present instituted. They are not always effectively communicated or monitored. One way in which they are being kept up to the mark however, is through customer and community pressure. There are now a good number of interest groups, lobbies focusing on the environment, animal products, trade with oppressive regimes, harm done to the developing world and so on. I can well understand that from the point of view of an already harassed Managing Director such groups are a great nuisance. But they are increasingly effective. In the end they force a company, for the best commercial reasons, to pay attention. Nestlé, for example, have had to devote large resources to campaign against the world-wide campaign to stop them hooking mothers in the developing world on artificial milk products. When the General Synod of the Church of England voted to support this campaign and in particular to boycott Nescafé, letters went from Nestlé by first-class post to every vicar in the British Isles.

Actually, it was slightly counter-productive as the last thing vicars in Wales and Scotland wants is to be thought subservient to resolutions of the General Synod of the Church of England. But apart from the effect of particular boycotts there is a growing interest amongst the public in companies that have a sound ethical basis both in the product they sell and the way they operate. One aspect of this is the growing share of the market taken by ethical investment trusts. An organization like EIRIS, Ethical Investment Research and Information Service, is now able to monitor every company in the country, by a whole range of indicators, to do with its employment practices, its products, its dealings with the developing world and so on. As more big pension funds and other investment institutions make use of such information, either from EIRIS or their own research, this kind of consideration will come increasingly to the fore. I recently received an information sheet from Scudders, the American stockbroking firm. It offered to supply me with a fact sheet on every listed company detailing their record on every aspect of ethical concern. In America the New York City Pensions Fund, one of the largest in the United States, worth $45 billion in all, is extremely active in pressing companies in which it invests. Led by Elizabeth Holtzman, described as a Joan of Arc with a hatchet, the primary aim is as she says, profit and then she goes on: 'Because of the long term investors, my concern is to make sure our investments are sound. I don't want companies to take actions that will adversely affect shares. If this approach also helps to advance social responsible concerns that is well and good.'

They take credit for moving some of the major American companies from South Africa, for making other companies much more sensitive to environmental issues and so on. They invest in local housing projects, run down shops and small business loans, nearly all in poor areas of New York. They have put down a series of motions at company meetings this year on a range of issues. Ellen Schneider-Lenné, was surely right when she said: 'I am convinced that ethical considerations will increasingly spread among companies, thus giving the "Ethical avant-garde" a competitive edge.' It is clear that the big funds have a particular opportunity here. A quarter of the UK market is in the hands of only twelve fund management groups and the top fifty hold over half the equity. A few dozen individuals make decisions in respect of many millions of shares. The Christian Church for most of its history has been violently opposed to usury. Of course trading went on and this trading required financing. The Church justified this financing if certain conditions were met, one of which was that the lender had a real stake in the enterprise, took a real risk, such as losing a whole cargo. Today, as we know, ownership and management seem totally detached. Perhaps a common concern for ethical considerations will bring them together, fund managers reflecting an increasing concern for the ethical dimension in the public and the company gaining by helping those responsible for the investment see that a longer term view is necessary. It is often pointed out by those sceptical of this movement, that people vary enormously on what they feel strongly about. Some are primarily concerned with the effect on the environment, others with animals, others with the employment of women, others with oppressive regimes and so on. But the logical conclusion of this is not that none of them need to be taken seriously but all of them at least have to be considered even if they are not given equal weight.

I noted at the beginning that there is a congruity between certain values basic to the market economy and values central to the Christian faith. But the Christian approach to institutions in this world can never be unambiguously 'Yes'. There will be an inevitable ambivalence, a 'No' as well as 'Yes' because of the Christian awareness of the dark side of human nature. This dark side will always take the form of flawed structures as well as personal failings. We saw this most obviously in the communist system. But, in a lesser degree, it is present in our own. Adam Smith the great champion of the market economy was first a moral philosopher and saw the market integrally related to moral considerations. Part of his concern was protecting the public. As he wrote, any proposal that came from the business community should always be looked at sceptically: 'It comes from an order of men, whose interest is never exactly the same with that of the public, who have generally an interest to deceive and even to oppress the public, and who accordingly have, upon many occasions, both deceived and oppressed.'

Capitalism as we have it too often works against the interests of the powerless, those least able to stand up for themselves, those least able to work the system to their own advantage. Those with economic strength are able to pull the levers of political power. They are also able to buy the advertising and acquire dominant positions in the media. Thomas Hobbes said that liberty is always power split up into little pieces. In any political system, including a liberal democracy, there is always the danger of concentrations of power which have the seed within them of potential tyranny. That, of course is why we have the checks and balances of a democratic system. But political ideals do not stop the accumulation of money, power and influence in the hands of a relatively few, which may be used benevolently but which can often be used without a proper degree of imaginative sympathy for those at the bottom of the pile. And as we know, those at the bottom of the pile are relatively worse off than they were. In the last decade or so, the poorest 10% of the population, for a variety of reasons, have become poorer. They have no stake in the economy, in every way they are losing out.

The usual approach to this problem is to say that the worst excesses of a free market must be corrected by political action. And no doubt this is partly true. We will continue to need political policies which will pick up the pieces and engage in a measure of redistribution. Professor Galbraith has said that 'the modern mixed economy depends on the functional underclass'. He goes on:

> It must be part of our purpose to speak for this underclass. And to accept that much of the support and help that it needs can come only from the State. Job creation, welfare payments, education, job training, drug counselling, housing – all urgent needs of the underclass – are at public cost.

Part of this is undoubtedly true. But few can be totally happy with a system simply designed to let the market economy rip in this most ruthless way, with St John's Ambulance men around to revive those who faint. I am not happy with this scenario for two reasons. First, one of the major qualities of those successful in business is drive. Quite simply, they are able to make things happen. There is a loss to the nation as a whole if these qualities are only channelled into company affairs. Second, on a Christian view of human existence, indeed a properly human one, ends and means need to be seen together. The words of a poem are not simply means to convey a thought. The words are an integral part of the whole, which is of a piece. A good end cannot be produced by means whose methods totally contradict the values enshrined in the goal. People working in a business know this. If a worthwhile product or service is the goal, this cannot be achieved by means which ignore all values. So in our national life we cannot simply see the market as a morally neutral realm desirable for producing a good end, prosperity. The market and those who work within it have a relation to that end in all that they do.

In practical terms, I think this means those in business playing a larger role in the social and political life of our country with a view, as John Major put it in his very first statement when he became Prime Minister, to improving the quality of life for the whole of our society. More and more companies are now bringing their particular gifts and expertise to bear on the development of local communities. This is in microcosm what could happen on a larger scale. Until now business has thought of its connection with the political realm in terms of substantial donations to political parties which they think are most likely to further the interests of business in general and their business in particular. This is understandable but rather limited. If companies are now recognizing the valid claims of all stakeholders then their approach to the wider political realm also needs to reflect this. In short, the motivation for wider influence in that political sphere will not be simply to further the interests of business, though that will remain a part, but to make a distinctive contribution to the regeneration of our life as a whole. Some of us are by trade mere talkers. Those in business are of necessity, those who have to make things happen.

For the Christian Churches, the developing world remains a matter of prime concern. Here of course transnational corporations (TNCs) have a particular opportunity and responsibility. Their sheer size is staggering. Between 80% and 90% of the exports to the United States and the United Kingdom are associated with TNCs. The combined sales of the top 200 TNCs in 1986 were equivalent to around 31% of the non-socialist world's gross national products. Between three and six TNCs account for 90% of world exports of wheat, corn, coffee, fresh pineapples, forest products, cotton, tobacco, jute and iron ore. Many of these vast TNCs are getting larger still.

I believe it is wrong to demonize TNCs, as some tend to. But their economic muscle, which is often vast in relation to the poor countries in which they operate, needs to have the same checks and balances as any power anywhere. Because these companies are transnational, capable of moving their paper assets swiftly from one country to another, they are that much more difficult to regulate. They are so vast they provide a culture in themselves. I would like to stress the positive side, the opportunity and the responsibility of TNCs for sharing in the development process, in all its aspects. Two concerns in particular must be uppermost. First, the terrible burden of debt crushing so many poor and middle income countries. Second, the terms of trade with the developed world.

In the current round of GATT negotiations we have heard a great deal about the interests of French and American farmers. We have heard little about West Indian banana producers and other

Third World economies dependent upon a single crop. In the latest world commodities report it is reported that from 1980–1991 prices for commodities exported by developing countries slumped 36% in real terms whilst those for the industrial nations fell by 20%. Farm subsidies in the developing world continue to increase, so that in Western Europe, North America and Japan farmers on average receive 64% more than they would have done without protection from international trade. Industrialized nations have also protected their own agricultural markets from imports from the developing world. To many developing countries the GATT is a rich man's club which ignores their needs. Indeed one specialist argues that a GATT deal will result in a 5% increase in average food prices amongst the 110 of the 155 developing countries who are food importers. This is especially serious for Africa where 80% are importers.

I do not believe that these kinds of considerations can be left solely to politicians, nor that the only contribution that business ought to make is to pursue the interests of their own companies in a narrow and short-sighted way. The claims of those with least economic power need also to be taken into consideration. Of course all companies have to continue to operate competitively, or they would go out of business. But to act competitively in the modern world is to look beyond the present horizon and take a longer view; to see a world of which our children and our children's children are a part, together with the children and the children's children of those banana producers, ore extractors and cotton growers and in which, if we act justly and do right our company will also be present, making a profit and serving the wider community.

EPILOGUE

Has religion a future?*

When Bishop Butler was asked to be Archbishop of Canterbury in 1747, he declined on the grounds that 'it is too late to try and support a failing Church'. A hundred years later Thomas Arnold was no less gloomy: 'The Church as it now stands', he stated, 'no human power can save.'

So the theme of a Church in decline is an old one. It is nevertheless still the familiar dirge of many who comment on the role of religion in our times. The assumption behind most reports in the secular press is that Christianity in general and the Church of England in particular, are already being lowered into the grave. For example, a large picture of the inside of a ruined church appeared in one paper with the caption that it 'lies derelict like many others around Britain which have closed as fewer people attend'. Yet in 1990 the Church of England opened as many new churches as it closed redundant ones. Since 1969 430 new churches have been opened.

In a general election campaign a few years ago, a constituency organization invited a cabinet minister to address the general public. Four people turned up. Since the widespread addiction to television, it has not been easy to attract people to attend events in person. Weekly attendance at football league matches is now considerably less than 500,000 in the United Kingdom. This is despite the fact that football receives huge converage in the media, with perhaps two or three pages in many daily newspapers devoted to it, and that vast resources are poured into the game. Against this background it is significant that weekly attendance at Church of England services is one and a half million, three times the number of those who watch football, whilst weekly attendance at churches of all denominations is some 5 million. Church membership in the United Kingdom is bigger than trade union membership and of course much bigger than that of any political party. Although religious coverage on television and radio is much less than politics or sport, in response to public interest there is more religious broadcasting from the BBC now than at any time in its history.

During the 1960s it was argued by a number of sociologists of religion and assumed by a wider public, that we were seeing an inevitable process of secularization. Then other scholars began to

* W. H. Smith Contemporary Paper 13, 1993

probe a little bit more carefully into what the indicators of such secularization might be. It soon became clear that in many ways the society in which we are living is far from secular. The majority of our newspapers, including some reputedly serious ones, carry horoscopes. In France it is reported that there are now 40,000 professional astrologers, more than there are priests, and many companies employ their services when making business decisions. We may not have reached that state in Great Britain yet and no doubt a good number of people who read their horoscope do so lightheartedly, nevertheless the widesperad interest in such matters and in the occult suggests paganism rather than secularism. The growth of cults and new religious movements has been a feature of our time. Whilst numerically they are not very significant, the centre at King's College, London, which specializes in research on this subject, has dossiers on more than 500 of them operating in this country. This can hardly be of comfort to the Christian Churches, but it does indicate a continuing concern with the ultimate mystery and meaning of human existence.

One clear change, and, if you like, indication of secularization, is the decline in the power, wealth and public position of the established Church in England. It is a process that goes back a long way, at least to the dissolution of the monasteries. But the most dramatic shift has taken place in recent decades. By the 1850s nearly every village had not only its own church but its own parson. Often that parson had private means and lived in an elegant eighteenth century or vast nineteenth-century rectory. The village still has its church, usually immaculately maintained, but it will share a priest with other villages. The old rectories will be occupied by bankers and stockbrokers, whilst the vicar will live in a small modern house. Yet there is a positive side even to this, in the increasing role played by lay people in Church life. In the Church of England, for example, there are more than 9,000 readers (unpaid lay ministers), often gifted men and women, who have done three years training, and who serve the Church in various ways.

The Church of England has shared in the general decline of some of our ancient institutions, notably the aristocracy, and is more modest both in its own understanding of itself and as it is viewed by others: which is no bad thing for a religion committed to the values of humility and vulnerability.

The English have rarely worn their religion on their sleeve. Apart from the last quarter of Queen Victoria's reign, we have not really been a churchgoing nation since the Restoration. The one thorough religious census before modern times, that of 1851, is as revealing in the number of those who did not attend a place of worship as it is of those who did. In 1930, over sixty years ago, Easter communicants in the Church of England stood at about 2 million, considerably less than 5% of the population. Professor Robin Gill has recently shown that the Victorians built far more churches than were needed and it is this fact, as much as any other, that has fueled what he called 'The myth of the empty church'. Overbuilding of churches in the Victorian period led directly to small congregations, declining morale and a widespread perception of failure. The fact that 100 people are now worshipping in a church that can seat 500 makes people think that there must have been a time when that number of people worshipped in it. But the church might very well have been surplus to requirements in the first place. The English may have their virtues but the public observance of religion is not amongst them. 'We must have a religion that is cool and indifferent', remarked one of Queen Victoria's ministers, 'And such a one as we have got.' The Celts of course show more enthusiasm. John Ruskin, comparing portrait painting in Venice with that in England, wrote that the English gentleman might wish to be portrayed on his horse or in his study, but never at prayer. If Venetians desired a 'noble and complete portrait', they nearly all chose to be painted on their knees.

Nevertheless in 1990, 71% in Britain claimed to believe in God and the surprisingly high figure of 54% thought of themselves as religious. Although the ability of the Churches to give adequate answers to help with ethical and family matters had, in the opinion of many, declined in recent years, the number of those who thought it important to find time to pray or meditate had gone up from 50% to 53% in Europe as a whole. What is also interesting about all these figures is that even when there has been a slight decline in recent years, it is still from a surprisingly high base. Gordon Heald of Gallup has drawn the conclusion that the values surveyed are deep-seated and stable.

All predictions about the future, apart from the certainty of death and taxes, need to be treated with extreme scepticism. As Augustine lay dying in 430, even though Hippo was beseiged by the Vandals, he could never have believed that North African Christianity, the glory of the Western world, would, after short periods of Vandal and Byzantine rule, give place to a new religion. Those under seige in Istanbul in 1453, hard-pressed though they had been for centuries, could not have brought themselves to believe that the Byzantine world, the most brilliant Christian civilization we have known, which stood for more than a thousand years, would be taken over and converted into a no less rich Islamic civilization. Or, to put it from an Islamic point of view, following the capture of Rhodes in 1521, of Cyprus in 1570 and of Crete in 1669, Muslims could have been forgiven for thinking that the advance of Islam was inexorable. But it was not; at least in that century. The only prediction it is safe to make is that history produces the unpredictable, as we keep finding when wars break out and take us by surprise. It was astonishing that the glittering, sophisticated Byzantine world should collapse and Christianity shift its centre of gravity to the less couth West and North. It now shows signs of shifting from Europe to Africa and certain Asian countries. There are, for example, more Anglicans in Nigeria than the whole of the Church of England and the Episcopal Church in the United States put together.

From the standpoint of religion, the times might be propitious or unpropitious; all might be swept away or all might flourish in a new-found fervour. We simply do not know. When asked to define his outlook, William Golding replied that he was 'a universal pessimist but a cosmic optimist'. This is the Christian stance on existence. There is no automatic progress to a better future, whether considered in material or spiritual terms. Every achievement has within it the seeds of its own destruction. But, from the standpoint of faith, there is an ultimate optimism about the whole creative process.

This cosmic optimism, which unites Christianity, Judaism and Islam (as well as others) has the following fundamental tenets. First, behind this strange existence of ours, at once painful and beautiful, there is a wise and loving power. Second, we are inescapably spiritual beings. Third, the divine purpose expressed in this universe will, despite all setbacks and frustrations, finally prevail.

In Islam, religion is very much a public matter, embracing the whole of human existence. Every aspect of society, its drains and schools as much as its mosques and laws, are to be ordered according to divine revelation. This understanding of religion is bound to have an effect on Christianity's own understanding of itself. One religious essayist noted that, when he went to fill up his car with petrol, a Muslim also present on the forecourt, realizing it was time for prayer, took out his mat and said his prayers then and there. The Christian commentator said that it made him regret, for the first time, the decision he took in the 1960s no longer to say grace in a public restaurant. For years we have assumed that religion is a private, subjective matter. If Islam is increasingly forcing religion into the public sphere in so many countries of the world, including our own, it is doubtful if this purely inward emphasis can be sustained. When public policies are challenged in the name of a religion then other religions present in that society will in the end be called to make a public response.

One of the great myths of our time is that there can be certain spheres which are value-free or morally neutral. People sometimes think that the arts or business are worlds in which consideration of values or religious perspective do not apply. Nothing could be further from the truth. Every work of art expresses a certain feel for life, whether it is Francis Bacon's sense of 'exhilarated despair', Graham Greene's Christian obsession with the 'dangerous edge of things', or John Taverner's Orthodox faith.

The assumptions behind so much of our public life may be wise or foolish. But they are not value-free. They need to be exposed, examined and, from a Christian point of view, subjected to a Christian critique. Some of these are Englightenment assumptions which in a post-modernist world, no longer stand up to scrutiny.

It was obvious to Dostoevsky, as it is to most Russians, that religion is a passion or it is nothing. So it is to people in many other cultures. Yet in Britain, as one priest said to me, we have a context of 'benign neutrality'. This has historical roots, as we can see by contrasting our own religious culture with that of the United States.

Many visitors from Britain to the United States are struck by the strength and vitality of churches there. It is stimulating to worship in a packed church, see hundreds turning up for an hour's solid adult Christian education on a Sunday in addition to worship, and enjoy the ministry of a church with a large professional staff all paid for by a generous congregation; stimulating but at the same time depressing, for all the social forces which work in favour of religion there are absent in Britain.

First, from the beginning, the founding Fathers of the United States so prized their religion that they were prepared to emigrate to a new country where they could ensure its proper place. There they were determined to work for its survival and strength. In England, on the other hand, religion has been part of the scene for so long we simply take it for granted. Second, the United States is a vigorous, free-market economy, where everyone knows that if you want something you have to work for it and pay for it. In contrast, until recently the Church of England has been paid for mainly by

191

historic endowments and the idea that everything is provided has been encouraged by a welfare state mentality. As someone said, people expect the resurrection of the dead on the NHS these days. I fully support the National Health Service and proper state provision for social needs. But when it comes to religion, we need to assume more responsibility for our own financing. This is in fact happening and the Church of England is gradually being educated into both the practical necessity and the Christian liberation of this. But it is taking a long time. Third, as far as the Anglican Church is concerned, in the United States the Episcopal Church has a clear image. The majority of Episcopalians seem to have been something else first, Baptists, Presbyterians or one of the 200 different forms of Christianity that exist there. They have been drawn to the Episcopal Church, not purely out of snobbery, but because it teaches a distinctive form of Christianity, one bringing together tradition and innovation, reason and faith, the aesthetic and the spiritual. In this country, because the Church of England has been bound up with our national culture for so long, it is often difficult to discern what is special about it.

There is nothing to be gained by lamenting these facts, they are simply part of the cultural context in which the churches in Britain have to operate. But if they help to preclude fanaticism they also make it difficult to bring about real commitment, at any rate to the outward observance of religion. Yet Anglicans today are more 'committed'. There is very little nominal church attendance. Few, if any, go because it is the 'done thing'. So, while church attendance overall has fallen, the number of communicants has risen since the late 1970s.

The polls show that more than 70% of the population believe in some kind of God, in some form of wise and loving power behind the universe. Nevertheless, the number of regular churchgoers is only 16%. This gap is not difficult to account for.

First, in the modern world there is plenty else to do that is interesting, without going to church. People's lives are full. Second, the daily toll of human suffering that is brought to us via television, radio and the newspapers continually keeps before us the question of whether after all there can be a wise and loving power behind a universe that produces so much pain and cruelty. Third, there is the very mixed record of the churches themselves. On many issues in the past, not least religious intolerance, they have been to blame or been too slow in responding to human need. Nor today are we blameless: far from it. Then, fourth, some church life is unsatisfactory, both in its worship and its communal relationships. It seems to offer little that really satisfies the soul; nor is its quality of life always superior to other groups. Sometimes it can seem even worse.

This is to put the case somewhat bleakly, though no doubt not as darkly as it deserves. And clearly, at least 16% of the population have found that pearl of great price within the Christian community which enables them to live with or overcome these negative factors.

But the point is that for those who have not had an overriding Christian experience, or who have had an unfortunate brush with the institutional church, there are plenty of understandable reasons for staying away, whilst at the same time retaining the comfort of some belief. A BBC Audience Research survey in 1981 found that fewer than 10% of those who had abandoned regular church-going had done so because they 'no longer believed the Christian faith': many more cited pressure on time, family or other interests as influential factors. This does highlight one problem, endemic to modern life, the privatization of belief, with the growth of those aspects which are seen as individual and private rather than communal. This 'believing without belonging', as Dr Anthony Russell describes it, is a crucial challenge for the Church and all religions as they plan for the future.

Then there is the question of what kind of religion people have encountered. It is a tribute to religion that we assume it to be a good thing. Yet there are as many bad forms of religion as there are good. Most of us experience religion before we begin to weigh its claims. It goes into us to attract us or repel. It can come to us with sense and sensitivity or absurdity and oppressiveness. Faith, I believe, is natural to human beings. But as Austin Farrer once put it:

> The corruptions of faith herself are so many and so appalling as to allow atheism to pass for illumination. The evidence of faith is that it convincingly shows us things in their true colours; having once seen man in God, we know that we have seen man as he is; we can never again believe another picture of ourselves, our neighbours, or our destines. But superstition and bigotry can so darken and blind the eyes, that nothing is visible in its true colours, or, indeed, with any colours at all; superstition is a night in which everything is either black or else invisible; and atheism or so-called humanism, is the very break of day compared with it.[1]

As Karl Marx rightly assumed, the criticism of religion is the beginning of all criticism. In an open, healthy society, religion should always have its claims probed and its record examined. Nevertheless, in our society at the moment, there are two ways in which the churches suffer unfairly.

First there is the sheer ignorance of so many who, sometimes incidentally, cast aspersions on organized religion. Scholars who pride themselves on being sticklers for accuracy in their own field can write with astonishing inaccuracy when it comes to religion. People who are used to exacting intellectual disciplines in their own subject become lightheaded and intellectually irresponsible, when it comes to religion.

Second, there is the attitude of those whom the nineteenth-century German thinker, Schleiermacher called 'cultured despisers'. Christianity has nothing to fear from the truly cultured and, thank God, some of the most creative and intelligent people in our society profess the Christian faith. Others are observant Jews or practising Muslims. But there is a kind of colour supplement intellectual who thinks it is the smart thing to pass disparaging remarks about religion, usually Christianity; and in particular the Church of England. There has been one well-known television expositor in recent years, for example, who liked to begin his orations with the sentence, 'Modern philosophy has taught us that we cannot believe this . . . or that . . .', before he went on to outline his own radically reduced form of Christian understanding. The irony of this was that at the time he was telling us modern philosophy did not allow us to believe, five out of the six major Chairs in secular philosophy in this country were held either by traditional Christian believers or people sympathetic to Christian belief in a traditional form.

The late, lamented John Harriott put it well:

> As a heavy reader and radio listener I cannot count the times when writers and speakers seem to feel obliged to preface their remarks by announcing their disdain for religion. 'Of course, I'm not religious myself', 'Of course, I've no time for religion', 'I've no religious beliefs', 'I was brought up a Catholic . . . I had a convent education . . . but' But what? 'But I've grown out of all that rubbish, I've seen through it all. Now I breathe a larger air. Now you can be sure I'm bright and sensible, sound in mind and fully qualified to be heard here.'
>
> The idea that you have to be dumb to be religious, that religion is a, thankfully, lost cause, is the new intellectual slavery. Dissidents are at best strange zoological specimens.

Religion, God knows, has much to answer for; the crimes and absurdities committed in its name are many:

> But strangest of all is the curious assumption that to close the door on religion is to step into a wider world. Argue by all means that the believer's universe is all delusion, but not that a vision of human life stretching beyond time and space is smaller than one that sees it ending in a handful of dust. . . . And that to believe human beings are infinitely precious to God, reflecting his nature which they are born to share, and by grace can stretch their powers beyond their natural reach, is somehow less enriching and enlarging than to think them just animal slime. Delusion it may be, but at least a delusion of grandeur. Delusion it may be, but at least a dynamic delusion, adding point and energy and nobility to life. And to reject it, if rejected it must be, is hardly a matter for self-congratulation, but rather for mourning and the drawing down of blinds.[2]

It is true that some, like Sartre, have abandoned religion with a great shout of joy; rejoice, rejoice, there is no God. Or, like James Joyce, have felt enormously liberated by throwing off the effect of a strict religious upbringing. But the claim that there is a wise and loving power behind the universe, one who invites us to enter into an intimate relationship with himself, one who has a purpose for our individual lives as well as for the universe as a whole must, for anyone with any feeling, stir the heart that it might be true. And as for Christianity, nothing could be more sublime than the story that the infinite God has taken upon himself finitude, has humbled himself to come amongst us and reveal his eternal splendour in a human face. Difficult to believe certainly, impossible to believe perhaps, but wondrous and beautiful, as many of the greatest works of European and Byzantine art bear witness. In Paul's words:

> For it is the God who said, 'Let light shine out of darkness' who has shone in our hearts to give the light of the knowledge of the glory of God in the face of Christ. (2 Cor. 4.6)

This essay has concentrated on Christianity, mainly in its Anglican form, because that is what I know from the inside. Nevertheless, Islam is playing an increasingly important role in the modern world. Since the Arab invasion of Spain in the eighth century Europe has experienced Islam as a threat. In the eighteenth century this was overlain by a sense of the exotic East and in the nineteenth century Europeans assumed that Islam was in a state of degeneration and irreversible decline. Since the 1950s this combination of fear, arrogance and false romanticism has been severely shaken but it is still difficult for people, including self-styled liberals, to get Islam in proper perspective. Too often it is simply associated with fundamentalism and fanaticism. Islam is in fact as varied a phenomenon as Christianity. If there are dangerously intolerant elements in some Islamic societies, the historical record of Islam as far as tolerance is concerned is better than that of most churches. It has inspired compassion in millions of ordinary lives. European culture owes a huge amount to Islamic philosophy and science, whilst its cultural achievements still evoke admiration. The mosques of Sinan bear comparison with the churches of Wren. Sixteenth-century Iznik tiles were far superior to anything comparable produced in Christian Europe at the time. The elegance of Arab calligraphy is a sheer delight and so on.

The relationship of Christianity and Islam is a complex, painful one, different in Egypt from Nigeria, different in the Sudan from Pakistan or Britain. In Britain, at the local level, relationships are warm. Particularly during the Salman Rushdie affair and the Gulf War, churches made a conscious effort to make and sustain relationships, which still survive. Indeed, Islam in this country looks to the churches, rather than secular liberalism, as an ally, at least on the level of understanding and practical co-operation.

Since World War II there have been numerous statements by church bodies on Jewish-Christian relationships. The Holocaust has shamed the Church into trying to put its relationship with Judaism on a new footing. Significant progress has been made, yet, at a popular level, far too many stereotypes still linger. Too often Christianity is preached as the good guy in contrast to Judaism as the bad guy. There is a massive task of re-education amongst ordinary church members still to be undertaken so that Jews and Christians see themselves and feel themselves to be natural allies rather than opponents.

Judaism itself is in a most interesting situation. The Jewish community as a whole is full of the most extraordinary vitality, talent and dynamism. Yet the majority of Jews today are non-observant, even in a minimal sense, and a significant percentage are agnostic.

The way forward for religion is not through any lowest common denominator, or watered down version. Such ideas have very little appeal to mainstream believers. Interfaith dialogue encourages people to be true to their own religious tradition, whilst at the same time respectful of and open to those of others. The hope is that through contact with religions other than their own, people will have their own grasp of the truth broadened and deepened. But this requires a fundamental shift of attitude, from the arrogance of truth to the humility of truth. In the past, adherence to what is believed to be the truth has led to a sense of superiority towards other religious traditions. Without giving up our understanding of the truth, we are being called to enter into closer relationships with believers of other religions, in order that all might be enriched.

There is a basic, inescapable contradiction at the heart of religion. Like marriage, we cannot live with it and we cannot live without it. God is the supreme reality, from whom moment by moment our being flows. To live at one with him is life. To turn our backs on him, through indifference or rebellion, brings disaster. We are dependent upon God as we are upon the air we breathe or the ground we walk on. To live in radical dependence upon the ground of our being is simply to acknowledge reality. To fail to acknowledge reality skews the whole of human society. Saints are those who consciously and consistently live out this reality. Yet religion is a defining fact in some of the most brutal and insoluble conflicts on the earth.

This contradiction is inescapable and ineradicable. Because God is real and we are spiritual beings, there is a restlessness about us which will never be satisfied with a purely physical existence. We look for some great cause to give ourselves to, whether communism, nationalism, sport or the arts. And because we are flawed, we are always in danger of attributing infinite value to that which is less than infinite, of giving absolute loyalty to what is less than absolute; in short, of committing idolatry.

So religion is here to stay. It will not go away.

Millions and millions of people believe and believe passionately; and they believe in the particular religion which has shaped and nurtured them. It is this religion which, for all its faults, gives meaning and purpose to their lives, which inspires idealism and encourages compassion.

There is only one way to a better future and that is for the religions of the world to be more self-critical. The injunctions for this are built into the very structure of Christianity. For Jesus taught his followers to pray, 'Father, forgive us our sins as we forgive those who sin against us.' There is no automatic progress towards a redeemed humanity. The way lies through an awareness of sin and forgiveness. The goal is a community of people seeking the forgiveness of God and offering forgiveness to one another. This applies just as much to institutions as it does to individuals.

Seeking the forgiveness of God implies a willingness to look critically at our own tradition, to spot tendencies to arrogance before they become manifest. A willingness to recognize our own faults and to reach out in relationship to others despite any hurt we may feel, breaks down barriers. I cannot write on behalf of other religions but this I know to be true of Christianity; and I would be surprised if there were no resonances to this in the other great religions of the world.

Since the Enlightenment every possible argument has been deployed against the truth of religion—and failed. In the modern world a new tactic is being tried, which is to ignore or suppress the centrality of religious faith in the lives of so many. The really interesting question to ask someone who has been in solitary confinement, perhaps for years, is what helped them to keep going. This is also the interesting question to ask anyone about their ordinary life. 'What men live by', the title of one of Tolstoy's stories, which Solzhenitsyn took over as one of the chapter headings in *Cancer Ward*, is both fascinating and of supreme importance. Yet, in the obituaries which appear in our newspapers, there is little or no reference to this. Sometimes, when one has known the person and known that religion has been the mainspring of their life, you would never guess this from reading about them. What is even more disturbing is the way distinguished people in the past, for whom religion has been at the very core of their being, are having that religion rubbished. To take just one example already quoted in this book (p.73), Gerard Manley Hopkins wrote to Robert Bridges about religion in the words: 'It is long since such things had any significance for you. But what is strange and unpleasant is that you sometimes speak as if they had in reality none for me . . .' Sadly, the same accusation can be made against some recent biographers of Hopkins. Hopkins did indeed go through terrible anguish in his last years. But we need to see this in the perspective of his consciously accepted discipline as a Christian and a Jesuit. From this point of view the Sonnets, though terrible indeed, betray a mind that is totally sane and faithful.

Considered worldwide, religion is above all the hope and consolation of the poor. It is the poor, in their millions and millions, who are sustained and upheld by their faith. This was why Karl Marx was fundamentally sympathetic to religious belief, calling it: 'The sigh of the oppressed creature, the sentiment of a heartless world, and the soul of soulless conditions.' He believed, of course, that this hope was misplaced. It should have been directed towards the task of transforming this world rather than projected on to another world altogether. Since then, Marxism has been discredited both theoretically and in its practical working out. Moreover, religion has shown an uncanny persistence even under severe oppression in communist societies. Yet, it is important not to lose sight of the element of truth in Marxist analysis. The fact is that the economic and political system which now dominates the world does work against the poor, those least able to stand up for themselves. And religion does help the poor survive in this world. We see this particularly clearly in Latin America at the moment. There, both the Pentecostal churches and the Roman Catholic Church are active and successful amongst the poor. They bring real benefits. These Christian communities provide scope for social learning and personal liberation, especially among women. They create a space in which people can see themselves as actors. Yet they are not really able to dent the system. As David Martin puts it: 'The new priest may animate the small cultivators for a while, but ultimately they simply cannot pay the accelerating costs of opposing the landowners.' Among the Pentecostals, the poor devise their own worlds of cleanliness, discipline, aspiration and spiritual ecstasy. But these are 'quite sealed off from the injurious wider society'.

Today, no one ought to rest content with this disjunction between the juggernaut of capitalism on the one hand and the sphere of personal and small-scale communal liberation on the other. Nor does a lofty sociological analysis really help. To talk about Pentecostalism or Adventism or forms of popular Hinduism, as compensation for particularly depressed and deprived groups, fails to get to the living heart of the matter. For these faiths sustain, inspire, bringing real hope and courage. And any morally based religion is better than no real religion at all. The simplest minded literalist is closer to the truth than the detached, disdainful analyst who regards such beliefs as 'for them'.

It is some of the liberation theologians, such as Aloysius Pieris in Sri Lanka, who have grasped this. They take the religion of the poor seriously, recognizing that it does indeed provide personal liberation. They also take the myths of such religion seriously, as indicating the hope and possibility of a transformed world. So they look for and work for and encourage others to work for a changed economic and political structure.

The New Testament is quite clear that the Church belongs to the poor. We can choose to stand with the poor in their struggle or stand aside. To stand with the poor means struggling against the forces in our own society which work to depress further those least

199

able to stand up for themselves or work the system to their own advantage.

In Evelyn Waugh's novel *Helena*, Helena, the mother of the first Christian Emperor, Constantine, finds pieces of the cross on which Christ was crucified. When she has done so she reflects on the coming of the three kings to worship the Christ-Child. How laboriously the Wise Men came: 'How odd you looked on the road, attended by what outlandish liveries, laden with such preposterous gifts!'

> Yet you came, and were not turned away. You too found room before the manger. Your gifts were not needed, but they were accepted and put carefully by, for they were brought with love. In that new order of charity that had just come to life, there was room for you, too. You were not lower in the eyes of the Holy Family than the ox or the ass.
>
> 'You are my especial patrons', said Helena, 'and patrons of all late-comers, of all who have a tedious journey to make to the truth, of all who are confused with knowledge and speculation, of all who through politeness make themselves partners in guilt, of all who stand in danger by reason of their talents.'
>
> 'Dear cousins, pray for me', said Helena, 'and for my poor overloaded son. May he, too, before the end find kneeling-space in the straw. Pray for the great, lest they perish utterly . . . . For his sake who did not reject your curious gifts, pray always for all the learned, the oblique, the delicate. Let them not be quite forgotten at the throne of God when the simple come into their kingdom.'[3]

NOTES

Chapter one

1. Deirdre Bair, *Samuel Beckett* (Jonathan Cape 1978), p. 528.
2. Simone Weil, *Waiting on God* (Fontana 1959), p. 75.
3. Donald MacKinnon, *Borderlands of Theology* (Lutterworth 1968), p. 75.
4. Richard Swinburne, *The Coherence of Theism*. OUP 1977.
5. F.M. Dostoevsky, *The Brothers Karamazov* (Penguin 1976), vol. 1, p. 287.
6. Something needs to be said, and can be said, to counter Ivan Karamazov. I have tried to do this in 'Ivan Karamazov's Argument' (see Chapter 2).
7. Albert Camus, *The Rebel* (Penguin 1962), p. 51.
8. Bair, *Samuel Beckett*, p. 405.
9. Bair, *Samuel Beckett*, pp. 445–6.
10. Christopher Sykes, *Evelyn Waugh* (Penguin 1977), p. 363.
11. Albert Camus, 'The Growing Stone' in *Exile and the Kingdom* (Penguin 1974), p. 152.
12. Albert Camus, *The Plague* (Penguin 1960), p. 106.
13. Camus, *The Plague*, pp. 178–9.
14. Albert Camus, *Selected Essays and Notebooks* (Penguin 1970), p. 24.
15. Samuel Beckett, *For to End Yet Again and Other Fizzles*. J. Calder 1976.
16. Bair, *Samuel Beckett*, p. 640.
17. David Sylvester, *Interviews with Francis Bacon*. Thames & Hudson 1975.
18. Sylvester, *Interviews with Francis Bacon*, p. 83.
19. Sylvester, *Interviews with Francis Bacon*, p. 89.
20. Alec Vidler, *The Church in an Age of Revolution* (Penguin 1961), p. 113.

Chapter two

1. F.M. Dostoevsky, *The Brothers Karamazov* (Penguin 1976) vol. 1, p. 284.
2. Dostoevsky, *The Brothers Karamazov*, pp. 286–7.
3. John Hick, *Death and Eternal Life* (Collins 1976) p. 165.
4. Dostoevsky, *The Brothers Karamazov*, p. 287.
5. 'Ivan does not say that there is no truth. He says that if truth does exist it can only be unacceptable. Why? Because it is unjust. The struggle between truth and justice is brought into the open for the first time.' Albert Camus, *The Rebel* (Penguin 1962), p. 51.
6. See also John Hick, *Evil and the God of Love* (Fontana 1968), p. 385.
7. *Jesus Rediscovered* (Fontana 1969), p. 58.
8. *The Myth of Sisyphus* (Penguin 1975), p. 12.
9. Quoted in *The Observer* colour supplement 10 October 1976, p. 16.
10. Dostoevsky, *The Brothers Karamazov*, p. 287.
11. A. Flew and A. MacIntyre (ed.), *New Essays in Philosophical Theology* (SCM 1955), p. 96.
12. D. Z. Phillips, *The Concept of Prayer* (Routledge & Kegan Paul 1965), p. 94.

13. Phillips, *The Concept of Prayer*, p. 97.
14. Phillips, *The Concept of Prayer*.
15. 'Something about the facts, Freud feels, is brought out by saying not merely that often men do evil things but by saying too that "dark, unfeeling, and unloving powers determine human destiny." It's preposterous but we know what he means—not clearly but obscurely'. Professor Wisdom in 'The Logic of God' included in J. Hick (ed.), *The Existence of God* (Macmillan 1964), pp. 292–3.
16. Dorothee Soelle, *Suffering* (Darton, Longman & Todd 1975), p. 149.
17. Soelle, *Suffering*, p. 1976.
18. It is one of the merits of Brian Hebblethwaite, *Evil, Suffering and Religion* (Sheldon Press 1976), that Ivan Karamazov's question is kept in mind throughout the book. He also stresses the necessity of a transcendent goal to the creative process.

Chapter three

1 .Edwin Muir, 'One Foot in Eden' *Collected Poems*. Faber & Faber 1960.

Chapter five

1. Samuel Beckett, *Breath and other shorts*. Faber & Faber 1971.
2. Ruby Cohn, *Just Play: Beckett's Theater* (Princeton 1980), p. 4.
3. Samuel Beckett, *Waiting for Godot* (Faber & Faber 1965), p. 89.
4. Beckett, *Waiting for Godot*, p. 91.
5. Samuel Beckett, *Endgame* (Faber & Faber 1964) p. 12.
6. Beckett, *Endgame*, p. 49.
7. Beckett, *Waiting for Godot*, p. 63.
8. Samuel Beckett, *Happy Days* (Faber & Faber 1966), p. 20.
9. Beckett, *Happy Days*, p. 12.
10. Beckett, *Happy Days*, p. 42.
11. Beckett, *Happy Days*, p. 44.
12. Beckett, *Endgame*, p. 22.
13. Beckett, *Waiting for Godot*, p. 12.
14. Beckett, *Waiting for Godot*, p. 52.
15. Samuel Beckett, *Not I*. Faber & Faber 1973.
16. Samuel Beckett, *Play* (Faber & Faber 1968), p. 16.
17. Beckett, *Play*, p. 22.
18. Beckett, *Play*, p. 10.
19. Beckett, *Endgame*, p. 23.
20. Beckett, *Waiting for Godot*, p. 58.
21. Beckett, *Happy Days*.
22. Samuel Beckett, *Krapp's Last Tape* (Faber & Faber 1965), p. 16.
23. Deirdre Bair, *Samuel Beckett* (Jonathan Cape 1978), p. 405.
24. Beckett, *Endgame*, p. 19.
25. Beckett, *Krapp's Last Tape*, p. 13.
26. Cohn, *Just Play*.
27. Cohn, *Just Play*, p. 199.

28. Cohn, *Just Play*, p. 13.
29. Beckett, *Happy Days*, p. 40.
30. Beckett, *Endgame*, p. 18.
31. Bair, *Samuel Beckett*, p. 528.
32. Quoted by Cohn, *Just Play*, p. 131.

Chapter six

1. Robert Bernard Martin, *Gerard Manley Hopkins: A Very Private Life*. Harper-Collins 1991.
2. *Gerald Manley Hopkins, Selected Letters*, ed. Catherine Philips (OUP 1990), p. 212.
3. Martin, *Hopkins*, pp. 368 ff.
4. Martin, *Hopkins*, p. 373.
5. Martin, *Hopkins*, p. 398.
6. Hopkins, *Selected Letters*, p. 202.
7. Martin, *Hopkins*, p. 376.
8. *The Poetry of Gerard Manley Hopkins*, 4th edition, ed. W. H. Gardner and N. H. Mackenzie (OUP 1970) p. 101, cited as Hopkins, *Poetry*.
9. Hopkins, *Selected Letters*, p. 289.
10. Martin, *Hopkins*, p. 414.
11. Hopkins, *Selected Letters*, p. 212.
12. Hopkins, *Selected Letters*, p. 214.
13. Hopkins, *Poetry*, p. 99.
14. Paul Tillich, *The Courage to Be* (Fontana 1965), p. 171.
15. Hopkins, *Selected Letters*, p. 207.
16. Hopkins, *Poetry*, p. 106.
17. Hopkins, *Poetry*, p. 100.
18. Martin, *Hopkins*, p. 386.
19. Hopkins, *Poetry*, p. 101.
20. Martin, *Hopkins*, p. 385.
21. Hopkins, *Selected Letters*, p. 237.
22. Hopkins, *Poetry*, p. 101.
23. Hopkins, *Poetry*, p. 90.
24. 'Comments on the spiritual exercises of St Ignatius Loyola', *Gerard Manley Hopkins, Poems and Prose* (Penguin 1988) p. 145.
25. Hopkins, *Poetry*, p. 102.
26. 'Rules for the discernment of Spirits', VIII, Father Morris's edn, 1887, quoted in Norman H. Mackenzie, *A Reader's Guide to Gerard Manley Hopkins* (Thames & Hudson 1981), p. 185.
27. Hopkins, *Selected Letters*, p. 232.
28. Martin, *Hopkins* p. 396.
29. Hopkins, *Poetry*, p. 102.
30. Hopkins, *Poetry*, p. 106.
31. Hopkins, *Poetry*, p. 106.
32. Hopkins, *Selected Letters*, p. 215.
33. Martin, *Hopkins*, pp. 110, 395, 410.
34. Hopkins, *Poetry*, p. 31.

35. Hopkins, *Poetry*, p. 105.
36. Hopkins, *Poetry*, p. 194.
37. *Times Literary Supplement*, 12 April 1991. Other recent writing on Hopkins is open to the same criticism. As P. N. Furbank puts it in a review of Norman White's biography: 'As against Norman White and Robert Martin, then, I am inclined to respect Hopkins's decision in matters of religion.' *Times Literary Supplement*, 27 March 1992.
38. Hopkins, *Selected Letters*, p. 169.

Chapter seven

1. Iris Murdoch, *The Good Apprentice* (Chatto & Windus 1985), p. 147.
2. Iris Murdoch, *The Sovereignty of Good*. Routledge & Kegan Paul 1970.
3. As, for example, in W. Marxsen, *The Resurrection of Jesus of Nazareth*. SCM 1970.
4. Leo Tolstoy, *Resurrection* (F. R. Henderson 1900), p. 564.
5. F. M. Dostoevsky, *Crime and Punishment* (Penguin 1951), p. 559.
6. Dostoevsky, *Crime and Punishment*, pp. 341–2.
7. Patrick White, *Riders in the Chariot* (Penguin 1974), p. 484.
8. White, *Riders in the Chariot*, pp. 491–2.
9. White, *Riders in the Chariot*, pp. 426–7.
10. Philippians 3.8–11.
11. White, *Riders in the Chariot*, p. 423.
12. White, *Riders in the Chariot*, p. 453.
13. White, *Riders in the Chariot*, p. 492.
14. William Golding, *Darkness Visible* (Faber & Faber 1979), p. 19.
15. Golding, *Darkness Visible*, p. 43.
16. Golding, *Darkness Visible* p. 263.
17. D. H. Lawrence 'The Man who Died' in *Love among the Haystacks and other stories* (Penguin 1960), pp. 166–7.
18. Lawrence, 'The Man who Died', p. 170.
19. Edwin Muir, 'The Annunciation' *Collected Poems* (Faber & Faber 1960), p. 117.
20. R. C. Hutchinson, *Rising* (Michael Joseph 1976), pp. 212–30, 353.
21. Hutchinson, *Rising*, p. 359.
22. R. C. Hutchinson, *Johanna at Daybreak*. Michael Joseph 1969.
23. Among those concerned simply with the crucifixion or its re-enactment might be singled out *Christ Recrucified* and *The Last Temptation* by Nikos Kazantzakis, both published by Faber & Faber.
24. As, for example, in the Church of the Chora in Istanbul.

Chapter eight

1. Michael Howard, 'The Concept of Peace' (*Encounter*, December 1983, vol. LXI No. 4).
2. Howard, 'The Concept of Peace'.
3. J. F. Powers, the American writer of humorous short stories, describes in one of them life in a Roman Catholic rectory from the standpoint of

the cat. As the cat put it at one point: 'Unfortunately, it is naked power that counts in any rectory and as things stand now, I am safe so long as Father Malt retains it here.' J. F. Powers, 'Death of a Favorite' in *The Presence of Grace* (The Hogarth Press 1977), p. 152.

4. William Wordsworth, 'The Excursion' in *The Poems* (Penguin 1977) vol. 2, p. 152.
5. *The Cuddesdon Office Book* (OUP 1961), p. 179.
6. Eric Milner-White (ed.), *After the Third Collect*. Mowbray 1952.
7. Wilfred Owen, 'Insensibility' in Dominic Hibbert (ed.), *War Poems and Others* (Chatto & Windus 1975), p. 89.
8. Augustine, *The City of God* Book XIX, ch. 17. Augustine does not use Pax in the same sense that it is defined here.
9. Prayer adopted by the Corrymeela Community in Northern Ireland and originally published in Caryl Micklen (ed.), *Contemporary Prayers for Public Worship*. SCM 1967.

This lecture provided the basis for the first Chapter in the report *Peacemaking in a Nuclear Age* (Church House Publishing 1988). I am very grateful to the other members of the Working Party who helped to clarify and refine the concepts discussed here.

Chapter nine

1. R. Niebuhr, *Moral Man and Immoral Society* (Scribners, New York, 1932), p. 205.
2. Niebuhr, *Moral Man and Immoral Society*, p. 252.
3. Niebuhr, *Moral Man and Immoral Society*, p. 254.
4. R. Niebuhr, *Christianity and Power Politics* (Scribners, New York, 1940), p. 10.
5. Niebuhr, *Moral Man and Immoral Society*, p. 172.
6. Niebuhr, *Christianity and Power Politics*, p. 10.
7. He also maintained with Kant that 'only good will is intrinsically good' *Moral Man and Immoral Society*, p. 173.
8. Ronald Sider and Richard Taylor, *Nuclear Holocaust and Christian Hope* (Hodder & Stoughton 1983) p. 120 and note 60 on page 389. See also my 'Power, Coercion and Love' in Francis Bridger (ed.), *The Cross and the Bomb*. Mowbray 1983.
9. John 18.23.
10. Sider and Taylor, *Nuclear Holocaust and Christian Hope*, p. 130.
11. Willard Swartley and Alan Kreider in 'Pacifist Christianity: The Kingdom Way', *When Christians Disagree: Pacifism and War*, IVP 1984, argue along the same lines as Sider and Taylor. They allow the legitimacy of coercion—up to a point. The point at which they draw the line is 'permanent physical harm'. But in resisting a violent criminal there will always be the risk that this will occur.
12. James Childress in 'Reinhold Niebuhr's realistic critique of pacifism', an essay in his *Moral Responsibility in Conflict*, Louisiana State University Press 1982, argues that there is much more

significance than Niebuhr allows between direct force and indirect coercion. This is true but it is not in itself enough to justify pacifism. Childress, following Tolstoy says that if a child is about to be attacked: (a) We do not know for certain that the child will be harmed, and (b) We are not in a position to say that the life of the child is more valuable than that of the attacker. But, on the contrary, we may very well be in a position to know that the child will be harmed. Further, the attacker, in trying to harm the child forfeits his own right to protection. Finally, Christian love leads us to do all we can to save the child from hurt and this outweighs the risk we take that we might seriously harm the attacker.

13. G. H. C. Macgregor, *The Relevance of the Impossible*. Fellowship of Reconciliation 1941. A shortened version of th argument is contained in the same author's *The New Testament Basis of Pacifism* (Fellowship of Reconciliation, new and revised edn, 1953), pp. 99–105.
14. Niebuhr, *Christianity and Power Politics*, p. 2.
15. Macgregor, *The Relevance of the Impossible*, chap 3; Sider and Taylor, *Nuclear Holocaust and Christian Hope*, pp. 179–81; John Yoder, 'Reinhold Niebuhr and Christian Pacifism' (*Mennonite Quarterly Review* April 1955, vol. 29, pp. 101–117).
16. John Yoder, *Nevertheless* (Herald Press, San Fransico, 1971), pp. 123–28.
17. Yoder, *Nevertheless*, pp. 126–27.
18. Sider and Taylor, *Nuclear Holocaust and Christian Hope*, p. 26.
19. R. Niebuhr, *An Interpretation of Christian Ethics* (SCM, London, 1935), p. 67.
20. Niebuhr, *Christianity and Power Politics*, p. 11.
21. Macgregor, *The New Testament Basis of Pacifism*, p. 102.
22. Macgregor, *The New Testament Basis of Pacifism*, p. 104.
23. Sider and Taylor, *Nuclear Holocaust and Christian Hope*, p. 322.
24. Neibuhr, *Christianity and Power Politics*, p. 28.
25. Yoder, 'Reinhold Niebuhr and Christian Pacifism', p. 112.
26. R. Niebuhr, *Leaves from the Notebooks of a Tamed Cynic* (Meridian, New York, 1987), p. 68, *Christianity and Power Politics*, p. 31.

Chapter ten

1. Philip Toynbee, *Part of a Journey* (Collins 1981), p. 230.
2. Nadine Gordimer, *July's People*. Jonathan Cape 1981.
3. For an assessment of the continuing importance of Niebuhr see my re-review of *Moral Man and Immoral Society* (*Modern Churchman*, new series, vol. XXV, no. 1, 1982).
4. Max Weber, *The Theory of Social and Economic Organization* (Oxford 1947), p. 132.
5. W. H. Vanstone, *Love's Endeavour, Love's Expense*. Darton, Longman & Todd 1980.
6. Since law is 'grounded on the nature of things, and builds up acts that are for human happiness, it follows that its violation will incur contrary consequences, which will belong to the category of *malum*

poenae, deprivation in a condition of being, or, in legal terms, penalty. With natural law these consequences are inevitable unless they can be arrested by the intervention of a third factor, divine mercy and the repair of the breach; there is an interior connection between observance of the law and the good it will bring, between non-observance and the loss that will follow. Seek good and you will find it and all that goes with it, seek evil and you will find it and all that goes with it; the promise and the threat are implied in the very law, and are not arbitrarily attached to it by the ruling power.' Appendix 7, 'Coercion and Law' to volume 28 of the Blackfriars edition of the *Summa* of St Thomas Aquinas. Eyre & Spottiswoode 1966.

7. 'Law is laid down for a number of people, of which the majority have no high standard of morality. Therefore it does not forbid all the vices, from which upright men can keep away, but only those grave ones which the average man can avoid, and chiefly those which do harm to others and have to be stopped if human society is to be maintained, such as murder and theft and so forth.' St Thomas Aquinas, *Summa* 1a2ae. 96, 2. What is true of a nation is no less true in the international order.

8. 'The most conspicious theme in international history is not the growth of internationalism. It is the series of efforts, by one power after another, to gain mastery of the states-system—efforts have been defeated only by a coalition of the majority of other powers at the cost of an exhausting general war.' Martin Wight, *Power Politics* (Leicester University Press 1978), p. 30.

9. Andrew Pierre, *The Global Politics of Arms Sales*. Princeton 1982.

10. Wight distinguishes several senses of the phrase 'Balance of Power', see chapter 5 of *Power Politics*. It can indicate an even distribution of power, a state of affairs in which no power is so preponderant that it can endanger the others. From this meaning comes the principle that power ought to be evenly distributed i.e. it passes from a descriptive to a normative use. The normative use, based on this description, is being advocated here.

11. *The Church and the Bomb* (Church of England Board for Social Responsibility report, Hodder & Stoughton 1983) argued that both the use and the possession of nuclear weapons was immoral i.e. any coercion based on nuclear weapons would have to be ruled out on moral grounds. In my critique of the report in the Spring 1983 edition of *Christian* I argue that the possession, and use under some circumstances, of nuclear weapons does not violate the principles of discrimination and proportion in the absolute way suggested by *The Church and the Bomb*.

12. For this reason the recent motion by the General Synod of the Church of England condemning on moral grounds any first use of nuclear weapons and advocating on moral grounds a public declaration of no first use, can be criticized. If it is war itself, rather than simply nuclear war, which has to be avoided then a public declaration of no first use would be immoral for anyone who believed that this would make

war more likely. See my article in the April-June 1983 edition of *Crucible*.

13. For an elaboration of the points see my 'Conventional Killing or Nuclear Stalemate?' in D. Martin and P. Mullen (ed), *Unholy Warfare*. Blackwell 1983.

Chapter eleven

1. Ronald Dworkin, *Taking Rights Seriously* (Duckworth 1984) p. 198.
2. Romans 9. 20–21.
3. Reinhold Niebuhr, *Christianity and Power Politics* (Scribners, New York, 1940), p. 2.
4. Dworkin, *Taking Rights Seriously*, p. 198.
5. Dworkin, *Taking Rights Seriously*, p. xi.
6. Dworkin, *Taking Rights Seriously*, p. 269.
7. Jacques Maritain, *The Rights of Man and Natural Law* (Philadelphia, 1944), p. 37.
8. Martin Luther 'Against the robbing, murdering hordes of peasants', 1525 *Luther's Works* (St Louis, 1955), vol. 46.
9. Galatians 3.28.
10. Jose Miguez Bonino, 'Religious commitment and human rights: a Christian perspective', in Alan Falconer (ed.), *Understanding Human Rights: An Interdisciplinary and Integrated Study* (Irish School of Ecumenism, Dublin, 1980), p. 32.
11. Jurgen Moltmann, 'The original study paper: a theological basis of human rights and of the liberation of human beings', in Allen O. Miller (ed), *A Christian Declaration on Human Rights* (Eerdmans, Michigan, 1977), p. 32.
12. Michael Walsh and Brian Davies (ed), *Proclaiming Justice and Peace: Documents from John XXIII to John Paul*. Collins 1984.
13. H. L. A. Hart, 'Are there any natural rights?', in Jeremy Waldron (ed.), *Theories of Rights* (OUP 1984), p. 77.
14. Dworkin, *Taking Rights Seriously*, p. 12.
15. Dworkin, *Taking Rights Seriously*, p. 182.
16. Ronald Dworkin, 'Liberalism', in Stuart Hampshire (ed.), *Public and Private Morality*. CUP 1978.

Chapter twelve

1. Hamish McRae, *The Independent*, 12 May 1993.
2. Professor Anderson to The Royal Society of Physicians, London, reported in *The Independent*, 12 May 1992.
3. The *Far Eastern Economic Review*, 13 May 1993, p. 5.
4. W. Parker Mauldin and Steven Sinding from the Population Council Research Division Working Papers No. 50 (1993).
5. David Coleman, quoted by Bronwen Maddox in *The Independent*, 27 March 1993.
6. Steven W. Sinding, Director, Population Sciences, Rockefeller

Foundation, 'Getting to Replacement—Bridging the Gap between Individual rights and Democratic Goals'. From Senanayake and Kleinman (ed.), *Family Planning: Meeting Challenges: Promoting Choices.* IPPF 1992.

7. The Lambeth Conference Resolutions can be found in Rose Coleman (ed.), *Resolutions of the Twelve Lambeth Conferences 1867–1988.* Anglican Book Centre, Toronto 1992.

8. K. E. Kirk, *Conscience and its Problems*, (Longmans Green 1936), p. 292.

9. G. R. Dunstan, *The Artifice of Ethics* (SCM 1974), p. 48.

10. Janet E. Smith, *Humanae Vitae, a Generation Later.* Catholic University of America Press 1991.

11. Discussed by Smith, *Humanae Vitae*, p. 78.

12. Smith, *Humanae Vitae*, p. 100 and p. 88.

13. Smith, *Humanae Vitae*, p. 101.

14. Smith, *Humanae Vitae*, pp. 89 ff.

15. Dunstan, *The Artifice of Ethics*, p. 48.

16. John Mahoney, *The Making of Moral Theology* (Clarendon 1987), chapter 7.

Epilogue

1. Austin Farrer, *Saving Belief* (Hodder & Stoughton 1967), p. 25.

2. *The Tablet*, 13 October 1990.

3. Evelyn Waugh, *Helena* (Penguin 1978), p. 145.